Sustainability Beyond 2030

Sustainability Beyond 2030: Trajectories and Priorities for Our Sustainable Future is an indispensable guide to understanding our planet's sustainability past, present, and future. It is a tool for enlightenment, engagement, and empowerment towards shaping a sustainable world as we approach the milestone year of 2030.

Written by renowned sustainability experts Marco Tavanti and Alfredo Sfeir-Younis, who was a pioneer in the field and participated in the first 1972 United Nations Conference on the Human Environment, this book offers an in-depth analysis of critical environmental issues, human development challenges, and the economic complexities of fostering equitable and sustainable growth. In addition to evaluating various pivotal policies and events, by extracting patterns and trajectories that have shaped our present commitments to the 2030 SDGs and the 2050 climate goals, *Sustainability Beyond 2030* boldly projects into the future, identifying core priorities likely to guide the global agenda beyond our current commitments. This foresight is coupled with well-informed recommendations, essential for building resilience and fostering future opportunities.

This book is a call to action for current and future generations of sustainability leaders. It encourages readers, whether policymakers, academics, or engaged citizens, to participate in the collective responsibility of crafting a sustainable world for future generations.

Marco Tavanti is a Leadership and Sustainability Professor at the University of San Francisco's Masagung Graduate School of Management. He is a recognized scholar and global leader in cross-cultural relations, social innovation, and sustainability leadership.

Alfredo Sfeir-Younis worked for almost thirty years at the World Bank, becoming Director and Ambassador at the United Nations. As a Chilean economist and spiritual leader, he is a recognized authority in sustainable development, shared governance, and international relations.

The Principles for Responsible Management Education Series

Since the inception of the UN-supported Principles for Responsible Management Education (PRME) in 2007, there has been increased debate over how to adapt management education to best meet the demands of the 21st-century business environment. While consensus has been reached by the majority of globally focused management education institutions that sustainability must be incorporated into management education curricula, the relevant question is no longer why management education should change, but how.

Volumes within the Routledge/PRME book series aim to cultivate and inspire actively engaged participants by offering practical examples and case studies to support the implementation of the Six Principles of Responsible Management Education. Books in the series aim to enable participants to transition from a global learning community to an action community.

Transforming Business Education for a Sustainable Future
Stories from Pioneers
Edited by Linda Irwin, Isabel Rimanoczy, Morgane Fritz, and James Weichert

Organizational Corruption, Crime and COVID-19
Upholding Integrity and Transparency in Times of Crisis
Edited by Agata Stachowicz-Stanusch, Wolfgang Amann, Christian Hauser, Matthias Kleinhempel, and Shiv Tripathi

Sustainability Beyond 2030
Trajectories and Priorities for Our Sustainable Future
Marco Tavanti and Alfredo Sfeir-Younis

For more information about this series, please visit: www.routledge.com/The-Principles-for-Responsible-Management-Education-Series/book-series/PRME

Sustainability Beyond 2030

Trajectories and Priorities for Our Sustainable Future

Marco Tavanti and
Alfredo Sfeir-Younis

LONDON AND NEW YORK

Designed cover image: Getty Images

First published 2025
by Routledge
4 Park Square, Milton Park, Abingdon, Oxon, OX14 4RN

and by Routledge
605 Third Avenue, New York, NY 10158

Routledge is an imprint of the Taylor & Francis Group, an informa business

British Library Cataloguing-in-Publication Data
A catalogue record for this book is available from the British Library

ISBN: 978-1-032-79934-6 (hbk)
ISBN: 978-1-032-77928-7 (pbk)
ISBN: 978-1-003-49467-6 (ebk)

DOI: 10.4324/9781003494676

Typeset in Sabon
by codeMantra

To our ancestors

who guarded the past and cultivated resilience amidst adversity.

To the next generation of leaders

who kindle the flame of hope and transformation despite the many challenges.

May we all harness their lessons, values, and strength

to work effectively for our common good and interconnected future.

For a thriving world beyond 2030 and

for all generations to come.

Contents

Acronyms

10YFP	10-Year Framework of Programmes on Sustainable Consumption and Production Patterns
5Ps	People, Planet, Prosperity, Peace, and Partnership
B-Corp	Benefit Corporation Certification
BIPOC	Black, Indigenous, and People of Color
BOP	Base of the Pyramid
CBD	Convention on Biological Diversity
CBDR	Common but Differentiated Responsibilities
CBDR-RC	Common but Differentiated Responsibilities and Respective Capabilities
CBIT	Capacity-Building Initiative for Transparency
CCUS	Carbon Capture, Use, and Storage
CE	Circular Economy
CHS	Commission on Human Security
COP	Conference of the Parties
CSD	Commission on Sustainable Development
CSR	Corporate Social Responsibility
CSV	Creating Shared Values
ECOSOC	Economic and Social Council
EEG	German Renewable Energy Act
EGA	Environmental Goods Agreement
EITI	Extractive Industries Transparency Initiative
ESG	Environmental, Social, Governance
ESRS	European Sustainability Reporting Standards
FAO	Food and Agriculture Organization
G-20	Group of 20
GCF	Green Climate Fund
GDP	Gross Domestic Product
GHGs	Greenhouse Gasses
GNH	Gross National Happiness
GPPAC	Global Partnership for the Prevention of Armed Conflict

GRI	Global Reporting Initiative
GWP	Global Water Partnership
HDCA	Human Development and Capacity Approach
HDI	Human Development Index
IEP	Institute for Economics & Peace
IIRC	International Integrated Reporting Council
IMF	International Monetary Fund
IoT	Internet of Things
IPBES	Intergovernmental Science-Policy Platform on Biodiversity and Ecosystem Services
IPCC	Intergovernmental Panel on Climate Change
IPLCs	Indigenous Peoples and Local Communities
IUCN	International Union for Conservation of Nature
JPOI	Johannesburg Plan of Implementation
LDCs	Least Developed Countries
MDCs	More Developed Countries
MDGs	Millennium Development Goals
MRV	Monitoring, Reporting and Verification
MSPs	Multi-Stakeholder Partnerships
NDCs	Nationally Determined Contributions
NGO	Non-Governmental Organization
NLP	Natural Language Processing
OECD	Organization for Economic Co-operation and Development
PFAS	Per- and Polyfluoroalkyl Substances
PPP	Public–Private Partnership
R&D	Research and Development
REEEP	Renewable Energy and Energy Efficiency Partnership
ROI	Return on Investment
SASB	Sustainability Accounting Standards Board
SCP	Sustainable Consumption and Production
SDGs	Sustainable Development Goals
SMEs	Small and Medium Enterprises
SPI	Social Progress Index
SROI	Social Return on Investment
SSE	Social and Solidarity Economy
TRIPS	Agreement on Trade-Related Aspects of Intellectual Property Rights
UNCED	United Nations Conference on Environment and Development—Earth Summit 1992

UNDRIP Declaration on the Rights of Indigenous Peoples
UNEP United Nations Environmental Programme
UNESCO United Nations Educational, Scientific and Cultural Organization
UNFCCC United Nations Framework Convention on Climate Change
UNGA United Nations General Assembly
UNGC United Nations Global Compact
UNHRC United Nations Human Rights Council
UNIDO United Nations Industrial Development Organization
UNSG United Nations Secretary-General
VNRs Voluntary National Reviews
WBCSD World Business Council for Sustainable Development
WCS World Conservation Strategy
WEHAB Framework for Water, Energy, Health, Agriculture, and Biodiversity
WHO World Health Organization
WSSD World Summit on Sustainable Development—Johannesburg Summit 2002
WSUP Water and Sanitation for the Urban Poor
WTO World Trade Organization

Introduction

"You can't really know where you're going until you know where you have been." Maya Angelou's famous quote encapsulates the purpose of our book. It is very difficult to recognize priorities and articulate appropriate plans for a more resilient and sustainable future for all without considering previous sustainability trajectories. *Sustainability Beyond 2030* is written with this purpose in mind: to present an overview of the most important accomplishments and ongoing challenges that the next generation of sustainability leaders need to know.

This exploration is not just a historical recount of events and policies; it is an invitation to understand how our collective past has shaped our global sustainability agenda today. As we navigate the evolution and articulation of environmental, social, and economic challenges that have defined our journey thus far, we gain valuable insights into our current global commitments. Recognizing these trajectories is not merely an academic exercise—it's a crucial step in defining the priorities for our future and sustainable path forward. A sustainability mindset requires literacy in systems thinking, complex thinking, and future thinking, addressing short-term needs with long-term planning. We want to provide a "wider view" of knowledge and a "bird's-eye-view" perspective, urging all of us to reflect on past efforts as we move forward with greater purpose and clarity toward a more sustainable world.

First, we examine the most influential global environmental conferences and their outcome documents since the seminal 1972 Stockholm Conference on the Human Environment and later important subsequent United Nations conferences on the environment and sustainable development. Through these crucial dialogues, we witness the evolution of global thought and policy about environmental, social, and economic sustainability. We see how our understanding of these interlinked issues has

DOI: 10.4324/9781003494676-1

deepened, our commitment to tackling them has strengthened, and our challenges have evolved.

The method used to identify these trajectories includes a detailed analysis of the conferences and the documents they produced. We also review data about decisions, commitments, and actions implemented to uncover patterns and trends. Then, we identify key priorities and challenges that have persisted over the past several years and extrapolate how they might evolve.

Trajectory analysis in the context of environmental policies offers a systematic method of understanding how policies have evolved. This approach considers many factors, including discourse, ideologies, contexts, texts, and values, and the acknowledgment that policymaking is a complex process shaped by tangible and intangible influences. It recognizes that the dynamic interaction of knowledge, politics, culture, and social structures shapes our efforts to address environmental issues.

Discourse plays a significant role in shaping environmental policies. How we talk about and understand environmental issues—the narratives, metaphors, and terminologies we use—significantly influences our decisions. Discourse frames issues in a certain light and highlights particular aspects and directs attention toward specific solutions.

Underlying these discourses are ideologies that shape our fundamental understanding of environmental issues. Ideologies define what is valued, what is considered natural or unnatural, and what is deemed right or wrong. They influence the interpretation of facts and figures, the framing of problems and solutions, and the negotiation of interests and power.

Context is also crucial in trajectory analysis, as environmental policies do not exist in a vacuum. They are developed and implemented within specific political, socioeconomic, and cultural contexts. These contexts influence not only the policies themselves but also their reception, implementation, and impact.

Texts, in the form of legislation, regulations, treaties, and agreements, represent the tangible outcomes of the policymaking process. Analyzing these texts allows us to trace changes in policy over time, identify shifts in focus and priority, and examine the implementation and enforcement of policies.

Finally, values are at the heart of environmental policymaking. What we value in society—economic growth, biodiversity, human health, or social justice—shapes the policies we develop, our decisions, and our actions. Uncovering these values helps us understand policymakers' motivations and potential impacts.

By integrating these various elements, trajectory analysis provides a holistic understanding of the evolution of environmental policies. It allows us to trace the paths that have led us to our current state and to anticipate potential future trajectories. This understanding, in turn, can guide us in developing more effective, equitable, and sustainable policies for the future.

In exploring these trajectories, this book sheds light on the principles that have guided past and present decisions, our commitments, and the gaps we still need to address. We aim to provide an informed perspective on the future of sustainability, transcending the limitations of our current commitments and setting the stage for the grand challenges beyond 2030.

The 2030 Agenda for Sustainable Development, adopted by all United Nations member states in 2015, is an ambitious plan of action for people, planet, and prosperity. It proposes 17 Sustainable Development Goals (SDGs) and 169 targets that touch upon critical aspects of global development's social, economic, and environmental dimensions. As a bold manifesto for human development and ecological preservation, it merits appreciation for the breadth and depth of its vision.

However, despite these commendable attributes, a critical review of the 2030 Agenda reveals that it may need to address the difficulty and severity of the world's most pressing challenges. While undoubtedly significant and far-reaching, the agenda's goals may not be ambitious enough in light of the accelerated pace of climate change, biodiversity loss, rising inequities, and pollution's pervasive and persistent effects.

Furthermore, the agenda's reliance on existing socioeconomic paradigms raises questions about its capacity to drive the profound systemic change required to achieve true sustainability. Some of its goals could have been more transformational, challenging the structural drivers of global environmental change and social inequality.

In contrast, organizations such as the Club of Rome advocated for more radical shifts. Marking its 50th anniversary of the seminal report *The Limits to Growth*, the Club of Rome highlighted the need to embrace a more profound transformation that values the Earth and all its inhabitants. The Club's most recent report, *Earth for All*, presents alternate futures with more audacious solutions and radical shifts to sustainable pathways.[1]

Earth for All envisions scenarios that aim to alter the root causes of our current crises, proposing a fundamental transformation of our relationship with the planet. It emphasizes the need to move beyond the reductionist perspective that has dominated global policy for decades. Instead, it adopts a more holistic, system-oriented approach that aligns economic development with ecological health and social equity.

While the 2030 Agenda is a crucial step towards a more sustainable world, its goals must be more ambitious to grapple with the severity of the global environmental and social crises. Complementing it with more transformative visions like those proposed by the Club of Rome may be needed to address this call. A synthesis of these perspectives could provide a comprehensive and actionable framework for sustainable development, paving the way for a future where humanity lives in harmony with the planet.

Ultimately, this book is more than an academic exploration. It is a call to action, reminding us of our shared responsibility towards our planet and each other. It invites readers everywhere, regardless of their background or expertise, to engage with the issues defining our collective future.

Thinking about past and present challenges beyond 2030 with a more robust and effective sustainability agenda means inviting everyone to engage in this shared global responsibility. It is an invitation to recognize the historical "trajectories" that determined the evolution into the current goals. It is an exploration into some of the current priorities and future challenges that most likely will influence the identification and definition of the future agenda beyond 2030. Unfortunately, persisting challenges and delayed responses to current goals will most likely determine the continuation of numerous current priorities. Yet, the future is presenting new emerging challenges, from cybersecurity to migrant rights and from climate change mitigation to global health preparedness, just to mention a few.

Sustainability Beyond 2030 hopes to do more than raise academic knowledge and intellectual awareness. It hopes to provide a variety of tools where clear past trajectories are recognized and current "priorities" included into the new drawing of the Post-2030 Agenda.

These trajectories represent our shared wisdom and experiences. Such trajectories hold the solutions to the most pressing problems of our time, spanning numerous disciplines from the social to the technological. Like seeds in fertile soil, the solutions to these problems shall take root, grow, and bask in the sunlight of shared victories.

Sustainability Beyond 2030 extends an inclusive invitation for everyone to explore possibilities and understandings and engage proactively as knowledgeable stewards of our collective fate. Together, we can traverse the challenging currents of today while capitalizing on opportunities for change, steering towards a brighter and more secure future for all.

Note

1 Randers, J., Gaffney, O., Rockström, J., Ghosh, J., Dixson-Declève, S., & Stoknes, P.E. (2022). *Earth for All: A Survival Guide for Humanity*. Canada: New Society Publishers.

Part I

Trajectories

1 The Stockholm Trajectories

> We have made a global decision of immeasurable importance to which this meeting testifies [...]. Our purpose here is to reconcile man's legitimate, immediate ambitions with the rights of others, with respect for all life supporting systems, and with the rights of generations yet unborn. Our purpose is the enrichment of mankind in every sense, of that phrase. We wish to advance-not recklessly, ignorantly, selfishly, and perilously, as we have done in the past—but with greater understanding, wisdom and vision. We are anxious and rightly so, to eliminate poverty, hunger, disease, racial prejudice, and the glaring economic inequalities between human beings.
>
> (Opening Statement by UN Secretary-General Maurice Strong at the United Nations Conference on the Human Environment, 1972[1])

Overview

This chapter begins by exploring the pivotal moments of environmental policy, starting with the 1972 Stockholm Conference and Stockholm+50. We trace the evolution of global environmental priorities, from its emergence in the sociopolitical context of the 1972 Stockholm Conference and towards its 50th anniversary, Stockholm+50, in 2022.

We analyze critical outcomes from both conferences, highlighting how they have shaped global environmental discourse and policy. The influential Stockholm Declaration and Action Plan are dissected, along with the visions, principles, and recommendations that came out in 2022.

By exploring these landmark conferences, we can see how they have impacted the trajectory of environmental policy. It also allows us to reflect on our past experiences and actively look at what is possible to create a sustainable future.

DOI: 10.4324/9781003494676-3

1.1 The Stockholm Conference in 1972

The 1972 Stockholm Conference, officially called the United Nations Conference on the Human Environment, marked a historic turning point in our global understanding and approach to environmental issues. It was the first world conference to place the environment at the center of global concern, initiating an international environmental movement and setting the stage for future sustainability efforts.

The world was grappling with environmental, social, economic, and political challenges. Industrial development and the postwar economic boom had led to an unprecedented acceleration in environmental degradation. The increased use of fossil fuels, deforestation, and chemical pollution were causing significant harm to the Earth's ecosystems. Socially, there were concerns about the unequal distribution of resources and the environmental consequences of uncontrolled population growth. Economically, tensions were rising between the developed nations and the developing world overexploiting natural resources. Politically, the global community was beginning to understand the necessity of a coordinated, international response to address these issues.

The Stockholm Conference brought together representatives from various nations and sectors, from 113 countries, including developed and developing nations. These national delegations comprised government officials, environmental experts, and policymakers. Delegates from developed nations included countries like the United States, the United Kingdom, and many Western European countries, while the developing nations' representatives came from various regions, including Africa, Asia, and Latin America.

In addition to national delegations, representatives from numerous civil society organizations were also in attendance. The conference marked one of the first that involved NGOs in such discussions, reflecting the growing recognition of their role in addressing environmental challenges.

Representatives of United Nations agencies, including the United Nations Educational, Scientific and Cultural Organization (UNESCO), the United Nations Industrial Development Organization (UNIDO), the World Health Organization (WHO), and the Food and Agriculture Organization (FAO), were also present, underlining the cross-sectional nature of environmental issues.

Many scientific and technical experts attended the conference and contributed to discussions and decision-making processes. Their presence highlighted the need for scientific understanding to inform effective environmental policy.

The wide-ranging participation was also a testament to the growing recognition of environmental issues as a common concern that requires global cooperation. It set a precedent for the broad, inclusive participation characteristic of subsequent major environmental conferences.

The conference participants adopted a series of principles for the sound management of the environment, producing significant outputs, including the Stockholm Declaration and Action Plan for the Human Environment, along with several resolutions. The Stockholm Declaration outlined 26 environmental and development principles, providing a foundational framework for environmental policy at both the international and national levels. The Action Plan provided recommendations to address specific environmental issues such as marine pollution, air pollution, and the conservation of natural resources.

These outcomes highlighted the understanding that environmental protection was not just an isolated issue but intrinsically linked to social and economic development. This conference also laid the groundwork for subsequent ecological agreements and conventions. It paved the way for establishing the United Nations Environment Programme (UNEP), signaling a new era of global environmental governance. As such, the 1972 Stockholm Conference represents a pivotal moment in the history of international environmental politics. We will now consider, more specifically, its trajectories as pioneering contributions to environmental politics.

1.2 The Stockholm Principles

The Stockholm Declaration from the 1972 conference marked a significant shift in the global approach to environmental issues. Comprising 26 principles, the declaration crystallized an international consensus around protecting the environment and established a blueprint for future environmental policies.

The principles of the Stockholm Declaration were remarkable for their holistic and far-reaching view of the environment. They underscored that human rights must go hand in hand with the environment, emphasizing the fundamental right to freedom, equality, and adequate living conditions in an environment of quality that permits a life of dignity and well-being. This perspective was groundbreaking in recognizing the environment as a precondition for human well-being and vice versa.

Several principles outlined in the Stockholm Declaration had far-reaching implications and were instrumental in shaping future global environmental policy. Here are a few examples:

Principle 1: This principle establishes the essential link between humans and the environment, stating that "Man has the fundamental right to freedom, equality and adequate conditions of life, in an environment of a quality that permits a life of dignity and well-being." This groundbreaking principle established a fundamental connection between human rights and environmental quality.

Principle 2: It asserts that the natural resources of the Earth, including the air, water, land, flora, and fauna, especially representative samples of natural ecosystems, must be safeguarded for the benefit of present and future generations through careful planning or management, as appropriate.

Principle 4: This principle asserts the need to ensure that man does not escape from nature but remains within its bounds. It calls for safeguarding and improving the environment for the benefit of all people.

Principle 7: This principle declares that states should cooperate to develop international law regarding liability and compensation for pollution and other environmental damage victims.

Principle 10: It draws attention to the importance of environmental education and awareness. It states, "For the developing countries, stability of prices and adequate earnings for primary commodities and raw materials are essential to environmental management since economic factors, as well as ecological processes, must be considered."

Principle 21: This principle has been widely acknowledged and incorporated into international law. It establishes that states have the sovereign right to exploit their resources according to environmental policies. But they also have the responsibility to ensure that activities within their jurisdiction or control do not cause damage to the environment of other states or areas beyond the limits of national jurisdiction.

Principle 26: This principle focuses on the role of research, stating that "Scientific research and development in the context of environmental problems, both national and multinational, must be promoted."

These principles, along with others in the declaration, have helped shape our understanding of environmental policy and establish a trajectory for future discussions and agreements in environmental governance.

Notably, the Stockholm Principles also highlighted the critical need for international cooperation. The necessity of shared and common but differentiated responsibilities was recognized, paving the way for future environmental diplomacy. They acknowledged that ecological policy must consider different countries' economic development and technological capacities, emphasizing the unique role of developed countries in leading the effort to reduce pollution and environmental harm.

One of the significant political trajectories that emerged from the Stockholm Principles was recognizing the need for environmental governance at both the national and international levels. This resulted in establishing a dedicated body to coordinate environmental efforts across nations. Hence, the creation of UNEP.

The Stockholm Principles established a foundational framework for understanding and addressing environmental issues. The principles highlighted the intrinsic links between the environment, economic growth, and well-being and initiated a dialogue between industrialized and developing countries. The conference shifted global discourse and placed the environment and sustainability on the international political agenda.

1.3 The Stockholm Action Plans

The Action Plan adopted at the 1972 United Nations Conference on the Human Environment in Stockholm laid a roadmap for future environmental actions in three broad categories: a Global Environmental Assessment Programme, Environmental Management Activities, and International Measures.

1.3.1 Global Environmental Assessment Programme

The Global Environmental Assessment Programme, often called the "Watch Plan," is aimed at monitoring and evaluating the global environment. The Action Plan marked a significant shift in environmental governance, as it recognized the importance of science and data in informing policies. This trajectory emphasized the need for continuous surveillance of ecological changes and comprehensive research to understand these changes' implications. It marked the start of coordinated global efforts to collect, analyze, and share environmental data, enabling countries to act based on empirical evidence.

1.3.2 Environmental Management Activities

Environmental Management Activities underscored the necessity of active, ongoing efforts to maintain and improve the environment. These included practices such as conservation of natural resources, pollution control, and enhancement of environmental quality. The focus on management activities highlighted the role of human action in mitigating environmental degradation. It emphasized that environmental protection was not a one-time action but required sustained, long-term efforts. It established the trajectory toward long-term, integrated, and holistic approaches to environmental management.

1.3.3 International Measures

International Measures to support assessment and management activities emphasized the necessity of international cooperation and capacity-building. They highlighted the role of global governance structures and the need for developed countries to support developing nations in their environmental efforts. This category also recognized the value of technology transfer and financial support in helping countries implement ecological management activities, which have become standard elements of international environmental agreements.

The 109 recommendations the Action Plan provided detailed guidance for implementing these three broad categories: Global Environmental Assessment Programme, Environmental Management Activities, and International Measures. These recommendations have set trajectories for future environmental policies, emphasizing scientific research, management activities, and international cooperation. A few of them are now highlighted.

1.3.4 Global Environmental Assessment Programme (Watch Plan)

Recommendation 1: Establishment of an "Earth watch" program to coordinate and integrate the various international environmental monitoring activities.

Recommendation 6: Encouraging cooperation between nations to exchange meteorological data, particularly in monitoring how human activities influence weather patterns.

Recommendation 11: Conduct studies on the environmental implications of new energy sources and technologies.

1.3.5 Environmental Management Activities

Recommendation 35: The development of international principles to help states manage non-renewable resources, considering the needs of future generations.

Recommendation 50: Governments should integrate environmental concerns into urban planning and development.

Recommendation 53: Establishing marine parks and reserves and encouraging international cooperation in managing and conserving marine life.

Recommendation 75: Strengthening national institutions responsible for implementing environmental policies and increasing the competence of local authorities in environmental management.

Recommendation 96: Encouragement of educational programs that promote environmental awareness among all population sectors.

1.3.6 International Measures to Support Assessment and Management Activities

Recommendation 103: Creating an international fund to assist developing countries in implementing environmental policies and programs.

Recommendation 105: Technical assistance to developing countries for training personnel in the environmental field.

Recommendation 109: Establishment of a Governing Council and Secretariat within the UN system to follow the Stockholm Conference's recommendations.

These recommendations aimed to set a path for a coordinated global response to environmental challenges. They called for shared responsibilities, integrating environmental considerations into development planning, and supporting capacity-building in ecological management, especially in developing countries. These ideas have continued to shape the trajectory of ecological governance and policymaking. Thus, the Stockholm Action Plan provided a comprehensive framework that has supported subsequent environmental policies and established vital principles that continue to guide environmental governance until now.

1.4 Stockholm Critical Reviews

Many academic and policy studies have analyzed the conference. It is generally recognized as a significant turning point in environmental policy, setting the stage for decades of dialogue, research, and policymaking. Here are a few notable works that focus on the trajectories, political narratives, and environmental policy outcomes of the conference:

1. ***The Global Environment: Institutions, Law, and Policy*** by Regina S. Axelrod, Stacy D. VanDeveer, and David Leonard Downie.[2] This comprehensive work explores international environmental policy from a historical perspective, examining the key events, players, and outcomes. The authors dedicate significant attention to the Stockholm Conference, its impacts, and how it shaped the subsequent environmental governance structure.
2. ***The Earth Summit: The United Nations Conference on Environment and Development (UNCED)*** by Stanley P. Johnson.[3] Johnson's work analyzes the developments and outcomes of the Earth Summit in 1992 but also considers its roots in the 1972 Stockholm Conference, tracing the trajectory of environmental policies across these two decades.
3. ***Global Environmental Politics*** by Pamela S. Chasek, David L. Downie, and Janet Welsh Brown.[4] This book provides an overview of the key actors, structures, and processes that have shaped the evolution of global environmental politics, starting with the 1972 Stockholm Conference.
4. **"Making the Most of the Stockholm Conference"** by Johan Galtung, published in the *Bulletin of Peace Proposals*.[5]

This work from 1971, the year before the conference, anticipated key themes and issues explored and managed during the meeting. It makes a case for essential trajectories set forth for future environmental policies.

5. ***Environmental Policy in an International Perspective*** edited by L. Hens and Bhaskar Nath.[6] This edited volume contains several studies that analyze the outcomes of the Stockholm Conference and how it influenced the trajectory of environmental policies, particularly in an international context.

These studies offer a range of perspectives on the Stockholm Conference's impacts and legacies, shedding light on how it shaped environmental policy and setting the course for future discussions and agreements on environmental governance.

1.5 Stockholm at 50 in 2022

"Stockholm+50: A Healthy Planet for the Prosperity of All—Our Responsibility, Our Opportunity" was the name of the conference held in Stockholm, Sweden, in June 2022, marking the 50th anniversary of the inaugural 1972 conference. This gathering hoped to reflect on five decades of multilateral environmental action, foster urgency toward environmental health, and reignite robust measures to ensure a thriving planet.

"Securing a healthy and prosperous planet for all means embarking on a joint journey where our footprint of today does not hamper the well-being of current and future generations. Stockholm+50 presents an opportunity for co-creation and multistakeholder approach to accelerate implementation in the coming decade in areas fundamental to a sustainable future: the relationship between humans and nature, what we invest in, and how resources are used and shared."[7]

The conference strived to address the planet's three-fold crisis: climate change, biodiversity loss, and pollution. It sought to galvanize action on the UN Decade of Action to expedite the realization of the SDGs, the Paris Agreement on climate change, and the Post-2020 Global Biodiversity Framework. It also aimed to inspire the adoption of green recovery plans in the post-COVID-19 era, emphasizing the necessity of a sustainable, inclusive recovery.

Built on the principles of intergenerational responsibility, interconnectivity, and implementing opportunity, the conference aimed to renew relationships of trust, accelerate systemic actions, and bridge different environmental agendas. It also intended to revise conventional conceptions of progress and well-being to reflect a more sustainable paradigm.

Outcomes from Stockholm+50 centered on promoting the universal recognition of the human right to a clean, healthy, and sustainable environment. The event also explored the rights of nature, affirming the intrinsic value of the Earth's ecosystems. The conference called for mainstreaming alternative knowledge systems to complement traditional scientific methods in addressing environmental challenges. It highlighted the need for involving more youth, women, and Indigenous Peoples and Local Communities (IPLCs) in decision-making processes surrounding sustainability transitions.

This commemoration of the seminal 1972 conference strengthened its legacy, encapsulating five decades of environmental governance and aspiring for a future where prosperity does not compromise planetary health. Stockholm+50 served as a reflection on past achievements and a springboard for intensified, inclusive environmental action.[8]

The official report from the Stockholm+50 conference culminated in a robust list of recommendations to expedite sustainable development:

1. **Human Well-Being:** Centralize human well-being within a healthy planet and prosperity. The notion involves changing attitudes, habits, and behaviors to support our shared prosperity.
2. **Environmental Rights:** Implement the right to a clean, healthy, and sustainable environment, following the vision of Principle 1 of the 1972 Stockholm Declaration.
3. **Sustainability Economies:** Initiate a systemwide shift towards sustainability in the current economic system. This recommendation involves new measures of progress, investing in sustainable infrastructure, and phasing out fossil fuels.
4. **Evidence & Technology:** Enhance national legislation and frameworks to implement existing commitments for a healthy planet. This recommendation includes promoting

evidence-based policymaking and supporting environmentally sound technologies.

5. **Sustainability Investments:** Direct public and private financial flows towards environmental, climate, and sustainable development commitments. This recommendation involves reimagining subsidies, diversifying the economy, and using recovery measures and blended sources of capital.
6. **Systemic Change:** This recommendation implies accelerating systemic changes in high-impact sectors such as food, energy, water, building, manufacturing, and mobility through circularity, resource efficiency, and nature-based solutions.
7. **Cooperation & Capacity:** Restore trust for collaboration and solidarity. This recommendation involves developed countries taking the lead, supporting capacity-building and technology transfer for developing countries, and enabling all stakeholders to participate meaningfully in policy formulation and implementation.
8. **Multilateral Systems:** Revitalize the multilateral system to effectively support countries in delivering on their commitments. This recommendation involves strengthening the UNEP and promoting convergence and synergies within the UN system.
9. **Intergenerational Responsibility:** This recommendation recognizes intergenerational responsibility as a fundamental aspect of policymaking. It includes engaging with the Stockholm+50 Global Youth Task Force, promoting youth participation, and making funding more accessible for youth-led environmental action.
10. **Reinforcing Policy:** Carry forward the outcomes of Stockholm+50 by strengthening international processes, developing a new plastics convention, and engaging with relevant conferences, meetings, and summits.

These recommendations from Stockholm+50 provided a detailed roadmap for tackling our most pressing environmental, social, and economic challenges, emphasizing the urgency of accelerating our collective actions for a sustainable future.

Stockholm+50 marked a vital milestone in environmental policy, encapsulating 50 years of international efforts since the landmark 1972 conference. However, an examination of this historical trajectory through a critical lens, as featured in the book *Envisioning Our Environmental Future: Stockholm+50 and Beyond* (2022), reveals that despite the progress made, numerous challenges persist.[9]

This book reflects on the conference and underscores the importance of the questions posed half a century ago by Swedish Prime Minister Olof Palme and Indian Prime Minister Indira Gandhi. They emphasized the interconnected futures of people and nations and recognized development as a critical factor in improving the environment. In reiterating this perspective today, the Stockholm+50 conference underscores the urgency for a collective responsibility to address our shared environmental concerns.

However, the book also compels us to critically evaluate the journey, assessing what has gone awry in the trajectory. Despite the robust discourse and the broad vision of a healthy planet for all, the severity of ongoing environmental crises reveals that the scale and pace of action needs to be revised. These analyses invite readers to critically reassess the outcomes of Stockholm+50, illuminating paths that are yet to be explored comprehensively in global environmental policy.

As we conclude this chapter, the significance of Stockholm+50 becomes undeniably evident. Held five decades after the first major international environmental conference, it was a testament to the critical need for continued, collective action for a sustainable future. The vision underscored the inseparable link between a healthy planet and the prosperity of all its inhabitants, reinforcing the necessity of our responsibility and the opportunity for change.

The guiding principles—intergenerational responsibility, interconnectivity, and the implementation of opportunity—reaffirmed the values brought forth by the 1972 conference, adapting them to contemporary challenges and opportunities. The event highlighted the need to rebuild relationships of trust, accelerate sustainable recovery, and interconnect various agendas while rethinking conceptions of progress and well-being.

Significant opportunities were identified, such as supporting the universal recognition of the human right to a clean, healthy, and sustainable environment, exploring the rights of nature, and mainstreaming alternative knowledge systems. The event critically amplified the importance of youth, women, and IPLC's engagement in sustainability transitions. It also provided innovative solutions for using multilateral approaches to tackling climate, nature, and pollution crises, which emerged as a critical milestone in environmental policy. It symbolized both a reflection on past successes and failures and a renewed commitment to decisive, future-oriented action. As we look towards the journey beyond 2030, the echoes of Stockholm+50 will undoubtedly shape our pathways for a sustainable future.

Notes

1 Strong, Maurice F. (1972). *1972 Stockholm Conference: Opening Statement*. https://www.mauricestrong.net/index.php?option=com_content&view=article&id=154&Itemid=78
2 Axelrod, R.S., VanDeveer, S.D., & Downie, D.L. (2020). *The Global Environment: Institutions, Law, and Policy*. Rowman & Littlefield.
3 Johnson, S.P. (1993). *The Earth Summit: The United Nations Conference on Environment and Development (UNCED)*. Graham & Trotman/Martinus Nijhoff.
4 Chasek, P.S., Downie, D.L., & Brown, J. W. (2020). *Global Environmental Politics*. Routledge.
5 Galtung, J. (1971). Making the Most of the Stockholm Conference. *Bulletin of Peace Proposals*, 2(1), 21–39.
6 Hens, L., & Nath, B. (Eds.). (2003). *Environmental Policy in an International Perspective*. Springer Science & Business Media.
7 Stockholm+50—Overview: A Healthy Planet for the Prosperity of All—Our Responsibility, Our Opportunity. An international meeting hosted by Sweden and Kenya Stockholm, Sweden 2–3 June. (2022). https://wedocs.unep.org/bitstream/handle/20.500.11822/37743/SAP.pdf?sequence=3&isAllowed=y
8 Explore more on the 2022 Stockholm+50 conference at https://www.stockholm50.global/
9 Desai, B.H. (2022). *Envisioning Our Environmental Future: Stockholm+50 and Beyond*. Netherlands: IOS Press.

2 The Rio Trajectories

> The 27 principles of the "Rio Declaration", building on the Stockholm Declaration, clearly represent a major step forward in establishing the basic-principles that must govern the conduct of nations and peoples towards each other and the Earth to ensure a secure and sustainable future. [...] Agenda 21 is the product of an extensive process of preparation at the professional level and negotiation at the political level. It establishes, for the first time, a framework for the systemic, co-operative action required to affect the transition to sustainable development. And its 115 programme areas define the concrete actions required to carry out this transition. [...] The Earth Summit is not an end in itself, but a new beginning. The measures you agree on here will be but first steps on a new pathway to our common future. Thus, the results of this Conference will ultimately depend on the credibility and effectiveness of its follow-up. It is, therefore, of the highest importance that all Governments commit themselves to translate the decisions they take collectively here to national policies and practices required to give effect to them, particularly in the implementation of Agenda 21.
>
> (Statement by UN Secretary-General Maurice F. Strong at the 1992 Earth Summit Conference in Rio[1])

Overview

This chapter traces the trajectories of sustainable development policy set by two pivotal conferences: the 1992 Earth Summit and the Rio+20 in 2012. We explore the landmark Rio Declaration, UNFCCC, CBD, and Agenda 21 from the Earth Summit, each carving unique pathways for global environmental governance. These trajectories evolved over two decades, leading to the Rio+20 conference, culminating in the holistic and measurable approach of "The Future We Want." With new initiatives like the SDGs, a focus on the green economy, and reinforced

DOI: 10.4324/9781003494676-4

institutional frameworks, we can see how these Rio trajectories continue to shape our sustainable development pursuit.

2.1 The Earth Summit in 1992

The Earth Summit, officially known as the United Nations Conference on Environment and Development (UNCED), was held in Rio de Janeiro, Brazil, in June 1992 and marked a turning point in the global environmental discourse. With representation from 179 countries, including political leaders, scientists, media, and NGOs, the Earth Summit outlined a comprehensive blueprint for global action on environmental sustainability and socioeconomic development.

The conference was instrumental in acknowledging the interdependencies between socioeconomic and environmental factors, fostering an understanding that the progression of one sector is contingent upon synchronized action in others. The primary objective of the Earth Summit was to shape an international agenda that would direct development policy and global cooperation into the 21st century.

One of the transformative outcomes of the summit was recognizing sustainable development as an achievable global goal. The Earth Summit made a case for integrating economic, social, and environmental concerns at all levels—local, national, regional, and international—essential for sustaining human life on the planet. The conference emphasized that such integration necessitates a paradigm shift in production and consumption patterns, work-life balance, and decision-making processes.

The Rio Earth Summit led to several significant accomplishments, including formulating Agenda 21. This ambitious program of action advocated for novel strategies to ensure sustainable development in the 21st century, ranging from innovative educational methods to pioneering ways of preserving natural resources and participating in a sustainable economy.

The conference resulted in other landmark outcomes: the Rio Declaration with its 27 universal principles, the United Nations Framework Convention on Climate Change (UNFCCC), the Convention on Biological Diversity, and the Declaration on Forest Principles. It also facilitated the creation of the Commission on Sustainable Development, the first World Conference on the

Sustainable Development of Small Island Developing States in 1994, and negotiations for the Agreement on Straddling and Highly Migratory Fish Stocks.

The environmental and governance trajectories established at the Rio Earth Summit have profoundly impacted the development of environmental policies over the past decades. The conference fostered an unprecedented global commitment to environmental sustainability, setting the stage for future engagements and responsibilities in the environmental domain, which have continued to evolve in the face of changing global realities and emerging challenges.

2.2 The Evolution of Principles

The Rio Declaration in 1992 took significant strides from the founding principles established in the 1972 Stockholm Declaration. This subsequent declaration essentially served as a continuation and expansion of its predecessor[2] Several fundamental principles exemplify this evolution.

1. **Principle 1:** In the Stockholm Declaration, the first principle states, "Man has the fundamental right to freedom, equality, and adequate conditions of life in an environment of a quality that permits a life of dignity and well-being, and he bears a solemn responsibility to protect and improve the environment for present and future generations." In its first principle, the Rio Declaration expanded this by stating, "Human beings are at the center of concerns for sustainable development. They are entitled to a healthy and productive life in harmony with nature." The shift in focus to sustainable development and the explicit acknowledgment of living in harmony with nature show a growing understanding of the interconnectedness between human well-being and environmental sustainability.
2. **Principle 7:** The Stockholm Declaration addressed the responsibilities of states in Principle 21, stating, "States have, in accordance with the Charter of the United Nations and the principles of international law, the sovereign right to exploit their own resources pursuant to their own environmental policies." The Rio Declaration revisits this concept in Principle 7, adding a vital clause: "States have [...] the

responsibility to ensure that activities within their jurisdiction or control do not cause damage to the environment of other States or in areas beyond the limits of national jurisdiction." This principle reflects a growing awareness of transboundary environmental harm and the responsibility of states not just within but beyond their borders.

3. **Principle 10:** The Stockholm Declaration laid the groundwork for public participation in environmental matters in Principle 19, calling upon "Education in environmental matters, for the younger generation as well as adults [...] making them aware of the importance of environmental concerns." The Rio Declaration broadened this aspect in Principle 10: "Environmental issues are best handled with the participation of all concerned citizens, at the relevant level." It further advocated for public access to information, participation in decision-making processes, and access to judicial and administrative proceedings. This expanded principle shows a clear shift towards greater transparency, public involvement, and access to justice.
4. **Principle 27:** The Rio Declaration encapsulates a new principle, Principle 27, stating that "States and people shall cooperate in good faith and in a spirit of partnership in the fulfillment of the principles embodied in this Declaration." This principle was not present in the Stockholm Declaration, demonstrating an evolved understanding of the necessity of global cooperation and partnerships in achieving sustainable development.

These comparative examples show that the Rio Declaration has further developed and evolved from the principles formulated in Stockholm, reflecting the changing dynamics and deeper understanding of environmental issues and sustainable development over two decades.

2.3 The United Nations Framework Convention on Climate Change

The UNFCCC is the leading international treaty to combat climate change, established during the Rio Earth Summit in 1992. It aims to stabilize greenhouse gas concentrations in the atmosphere to prevent dangerous human-induced interference with the climate system. Specifically, the central objective of the UNFCCC is "to stabilize greenhouse gas concentrations in the atmosphere at a level that would prevent dangerous anthropogenic [human-induced] interference with the climate system."[3]

The UNFCCC operates on principles of equity and common good but differentiated responsibilities, recognizing that developed nations bear more responsibility due to their higher historic and per capita emissions.

Fundamental governance mechanisms of the UNFCCC include the annual Conference of the Parties (COP), two subsidiary bodies for scientific advice and implementation review, and a Secretariat that supports the process. Parties to the UNFCCC must regularly report their greenhouse gas emissions and efforts to implement the Convention. Financial mechanisms provide resources to developing countries for mitigation and adaptation efforts.

Two significant legally binding agreements, the Kyoto Protocol and the Paris Agreement, which we will review later, were adopted under the UNFCCC framework, establishing emission reduction targets for industrialized countries and universal commitments to combat climate change, respectively. The UNFCCC thus provides a platform for global cooperation to address climate change and drive towards a sustainable future.

The UNFCCC provides a forum for dialogue and decision-making to reduce the global carbon footprint, helping countries adapt to the inevitable impacts of climate change and steer the global economy towards a more sustainable path. It is a prime example of multilateral cooperation addressing a shared global challenge.

A confluence of political contexts, scientific insights, and urgent governance needs affected the trajectories leading to the establishment of the UNFCCC during the Rio Earth Summit in 1992. Here are a few of the factors:

1. **Scientific Understanding:** By the early 1990s, the scientific consensus around anthropogenic climate change had significantly solidified, primarily due to the work of the Intergovernmental Panel on Climate Change (IPCC), established in 1988. The IPCC's *First Assessment Report* in 1990 provided strong evidence that human activities were increasing the concentrations of greenhouse gases in the atmosphere,

leading to global warming. This increasing scientific clarity accelerated the need for an international framework to combat climate change.
2. **Global Cooperation:** The political trajectory was also set by the success of the Montreal Protocol in 1987, an international treaty designed to protect the ozone layer. This agreement demonstrated that global cooperation could address environmental challenges, paving the way for broader climate governance mechanisms.
3. **Emergence of Sustainable Development:** The concept of sustainable development, defined as development that meets the needs of the present without compromising the ability of future generations to meet their own needs, was gaining momentum. The Brundtland Commission's report in 1987, *Our Common Future*, had been instrumental in promoting this concept. At Rio, this resulted in integrating economic development, social equity, and environmental protection, underpinning the need for a convention like UNFCCC.
4. **Political Will and Public Awareness:** Growing public awareness and concern about environmental issues had begun to influence political agendas, generating the political will necessary for a global climate change treaty. Major environmental disasters in the preceding years have highlighted the vulnerability of our planet and the urgency of the climate issue.
5. **Diversity of Interests:** The Rio Summit acknowledged developed and developing nations' differing abilities and responsibilities in addressing climate change. This understanding, summed up in the principle of "common but differentiated responsibilities," was pivotal in shaping the UNFCCC.

These trajectories converged at the Rio Earth Summit, leading to the UNFCCC which aimed to "stabilize greenhouse gas concentrations in the atmosphere at a level that would prevent dangerous anthropogenic interference with the climate system." The UNFCCC was needed as the international community finally recognized the systemic nature of the challenge and the need for a comprehensive global response. This new organizational structure and treaty to support its mandate marked a significant milestone in global climate governance, setting the stage for subsequent agreements and negotiations.

2.4 The Convention on Biological Diversity

The Convention on Biological Diversity (CBD) was another critical establishment during the 1992 Rio Earth Summit. However, its roots trace back to earlier developments in global environmental governance and to other trajectories encompassing scientific, social, and political influences.

Scientific insight into the significance of biodiversity and the threats endangering it has been evolving since the 1960s with the advent of conservation biology as a distinct field of study. Numerous studies have highlighted the intricate connections among various species and ecosystems and their crucial roles in overall planetary health. This rising awareness of biodiversity culminated in the 1980 World Conservation Strategy (WCS) by the International Union for Conservation of Nature (IUCN), which emphasized the need to conserve biodiversity for the benefit of present and future generations.

Politically, the push came from the 1972 Stockholm Conference that marked the beginning of the international environmental agenda with the new and growing role of the UNEP. In the late 1980s, another push came from the Brundtland Report (*Our Common Future*) that introduced the concept of sustainable development, bridging the divide between development and environment and bringing the concept of biodiversity into sharper focus. Seminal books like Rachel Carson's *Silent Spring* also fueled growing public awareness and activism. NGOs, Indigenous groups, and grassroots movements were crucial in advocating for international action.

These trajectories converged at the Rio Earth Summit in 1992, where the global community recognized the value of biodiversity and the threats it faced. The result was the CBD, a comprehensive, legally binding agreement aimed at conserving biological diversity, the sustainable use of its components, and the fair and equitable sharing of benefits from using genetic resources.[4]

The CBD represented a significant shift in global environmental governance that still has impact today. Unlike previous agreements, it acknowledged that biodiversity conservation is a common concern of humankind and that the sovereign right of nations over their biological resources must be respected. CBD also contributed to the understanding that conservation is essential to sustainable development. The CBD has since been a significant platform for advancing global biodiversity goals and targets.

More specifically, the CBD consists of articles that outline obligations, procedures, and systems for maintaining biodiversity on a global scale. Here are a few key examples:

1. **Article 6—General Measures for Conservation and Sustainable Use:** This article obligates parties to develop national strategies, plans, or programs for the conservation and sustainable use of biological diversity. It represents an essential facet of biodiversity governance, pushing for national-level responsibility and action.
2. **Article 8—In-Situ Conservation:** It stresses the fundamental need for in-situ conservation, or the conservation of ecosystems and natural habitats, along with maintaining viable populations in their natural surroundings. It urges parties to establish protected areas, restore degraded ecosystems, and promote the recovery of threatened species, among other actions.
3. **Article 10—Sustainable Use of Components of Biological Diversity:** It advocates for integrating considerations of biodiversity conservation and sustainable use into national decisions, promoting practices that minimize adverse impacts, and encouraging cooperation between governments and the private sector in developing methods for sustainable use.
4. **Article 15—Access to Genetic Resources:** It affirms the sovereign rights of states over their natural resources and calls for access to genetic resources to be subject to national legislation. The aim is to facilitate access to genetic resources for environmentally sound uses by other Contracting Parties and to ensure fair and equitable sharing of the benefits arising from these genetic resources.
5. **Article 17—Exchange of Information:** Encourages the exchange of relevant information and calls for developing mechanisms to facilitate this. Transparency and information sharing are essential to biodiversity governance, as they enhance understanding, collaboration, and effective action.
6. **Article 26—Reports:** Mandates that parties report on measures taken to implement the CBD, which facilitates monitoring and offers insights into the effectiveness of actions taken under the CBD. This article advances an adaptive governance approach, continually evaluating and adjusting strategies and actions as necessary.

These and other CBD articles represent a comprehensive framework for biodiversity governance. They recognize the value of biodiversity, the need for conservation, and the importance of sustainable use and equitable benefit sharing, thereby setting a direction for national and international actions.

2.5 Agenda 21

Agenda 21 was another critical outcome of the 1992 Earth Summit in Rio de Janeiro. It represented a comprehensive action plan for sustainable development, covering social, economic, and environmental dimensions. Its name signifies the agenda for the 21st century. It consists of 40 chapters detailing actions to be taken globally, nationally, and locally by organizations of the United Nations, governments, and significant groups.[5]

Agenda 21 responded to our pressing and persisting challenges: increasing poverty, hunger, ill health, illiteracy, and the continuing deterioration of ecosystems. It reflected a conviction that humanity's ability to manage its relationship with the environment would determine future social and economic progress.

Among the many areas addressed by Agenda 21 were poverty, health, housing, unsustainable production and consumption patterns, conservation and management of resources, global and national-level governance, and the roles of various groups (e.g., women, youth, Indigenous peoples) in achieving sustainable development.

The trajectory of Agenda 21 has been substantial and enduring. Several initiatives and institutions emerged as a consequence of Agenda 21. National governments, for instance, were encouraged to create National Councils for Sustainable Development, and many did. On a global level, the Commission on Sustainable Development (CSD) was instituted to monitor progress in implementing Agenda 21.

In 2002, the Johannesburg World Summit on Sustainable Development reaffirmed Agenda 21 and adopted an implementation plan. Agenda 21 led to further advancements, including promoting Corporate Social Responsibility (CSR) and recognizing the global water crisis. In 2012, at the Rio+20 conference, countries agreed to launch a process to develop a set of Sustainable Development Goals built on Agenda 21 and the

Millennium Development Goals (MDGs). The 17 SDGs and 169 targets adopted in 2015 incorporated numerous Agenda 21 priorities.

Undoubtedly, Agenda 21 was and still is a comprehensive blueprint for global action in all areas where human activities impact the environment. Its principles and recommendations have significantly impacted international sustainable development initiatives. Here are a few examples demonstrating how future initiatives and commitments incorporated or drew influence from Agenda 21 principles:

1. **Sustainable Consumption and Production (Chapter 4):** Agenda 21 urged shifting towards more sustainable consumption and production patterns. The 2012 Rio+20 Conference adopted the 10-Year Framework of Programmes on Sustainable Consumption and Production Patterns, further promoting this principle.
2. **Combating Poverty (Chapter 3):** The principle of eradicating poverty as an indispensable requirement for sustainable development was a central tenet of Agenda 21. This chapter led directly to the formulation of the first Millennium Development Goal (MDG 1: Eradicate Extreme Poverty and Hunger), later becoming SDG 1 in the 2030 Agenda.
3. **Protection of the Oceans (Chapter 17):** Agenda 21 emphasized the critical importance of the oceans and seas and the need for sustainable management of marine resources. This chapter influenced the formulation of SDG 14 (Conserve and Sustainably Use the Oceans, Seas, and Marine Resources).
4. **Promotion of Sustainable Urban Development (Chapter 7):** The urban focus of Agenda 21 ultimately contributed to the development of SDG 11, aiming to make cities inclusive, safe, resilient, and sustainable. This chapter reflects some of the values and priorities of the New Urban Agenda adopted at Habitat III in 2016.
5. **Major Groups and Stakeholders (Section III):** Agenda 21 recognized nine groups as critical actors outside governmental institutions, including women, young people, Indigenous peoples, NGOs, workers, business and industry, farmers, scientists, and local authorities. The principle of broad stakeholder participation became deeply embedded in

subsequent global initiatives. For instance, the 2030 Agenda for Sustainable Development emphasizes the importance of the "whole of society" approach, reflecting this principle.

Agenda 21, as a comprehensive action plan for sustainable development, traced numerous trajectories carried forward in many ways. The roadmap it laid in Rio in 1992 has been at the core of the international community's approach to tackling the intertwined challenges of environmental degradation, socio-economic development, and inclusive governance.

Agenda 21 has had a role in shaping our global understanding of sustainability across various dimensions:

1. **Conceptual Trajectories:** Agenda 21 cemented the concept of sustainable development as a guiding principle for global development policy. It set forth a vision of development that respects the limits of the Earth's ecosystem and promotes social equity, thus establishing a trajectory for all future sustainable development discourse and action.
2. **Policy Trajectories:** Agenda 21 laid out a comprehensive framework for policy action that has informed national and international policymaking across a broad range of sectors, from agriculture and forestry to energy and industry. Its impact can be seen in many policy initiatives to align economic development with environmental preservation and social equity.
3. **Institutional Trajectories:** Agenda 21 set a precedent for participatory governance in sustainable development by emphasizing the importance of multi-stakeholder involvement. It strengthened civil society and increased public participation in decision-making processes at all levels, leading to a more inclusive governance model.
4. **Educational and Cultural Trajectories:** Agenda 21 recognized the essential role of education and cultural change in promoting sustainability. Its emphasis on public awareness, education, and training has paved the way for various initiatives to help integrate sustainability principles into educational systems and foster a culture of sustainability.
5. **Technological Trajectories:** Agenda 21 encouraged the development and diffusion of environmentally sound technologies, setting the course for technological innovation and cooperation in service of sustainable development.

The sustainable development landscape we see today, characterized by wide-ranging efforts to balance economic, social, and environmental considerations, can be traced back to the ambitious blueprint that was Agenda 21. By laying out a detailed action plan, Agenda 21 offered a tangible embodiment of the sustainable development paradigm and set us toward a more sustainable world.

2.3 The Rio+20 Conference

The Rio+20 conference held in 2012, officially named the United Nations Conference on Sustainable Development, served as an instrumental milestone in evolving global sustainability goals, embodying trajectories set forth from previous conferences and setting new paths for future commitments.[6]

Critical trajectories incorporated from previous summits included:

1. **Building on the MDGs:** Rio+20 took the achievement-oriented approach of the MDGs a step further, launching the process to develop the SDGs. This shift represented a significant advancement, as it sought to integrate the three dimensions of sustainable development—economic growth, social inclusion, and environmental sustainability—rather than treating them as separate, as the MDGs had mainly done.
2. **Embracing Agenda 21 Principles:** The conference continued to recognize the integral role of multi-stakeholder involvement, public participation, and the need for education in sustainable development, consistent with the principles in Agenda 21.

These initiatives made new strides in defining future commitments:

1. **Green Economy Guidelines:** The conference recognized the crucial role of a green economy as a vehicle for sustainable development. Innovative guidelines were adopted to support nations transitioning towards a green economy, marking a new trajectory towards economic models that value and invest in environmental sustainability.
2. **Sustainable Consumption and Production (SCP):** A significant outcome of Rio+20 was adopting a 10-year framework of programs on SCP patterns. This emphasized the need for

systemic changes to consumption and production to ensure sustainability, thereby starting a new action trajectory.

3. **Financing Sustainable Development:** Acknowledging the critical role of finance in achieving sustainable development, Rio+20 established a strategy for financing these goals, thereby initiating a new pathway of sustainable financial planning and resource mobilization.
4. **Thematic Decisions:** The conference also made forward-looking decisions in several thematic areas, including energy, food security, oceans, and cities, and set the stage for a third international conference on small island developing states in 2014.

The Rio+20 outcome document entitled *The Future We Want* reaffirmed the political commitments made in previous Rio documents but expanded upon them to encompass broader aspects of sustainable development, considering the changes in socioeconomic and environmental contexts since the original Earth Summit in 1992.

1. **Reaffirmation of Past Commitments:** *The Future We Want* recognizes and reasserts the Rio Principles, especially the principle of common but differentiated responsibilities, which underlines different nations' varying capacities and responsibilities in pursuing sustainable development.
2. **Moving beyond an Environmental Focus:** The original Rio documents, mainly Agenda 21, concentrated more on the environmental aspects of sustainable development. In contrast, *The Future We Want* illustrates a more holistic and integrated view of sustainability, encapsulating the three dimensions of sustainable development: economic, social, and environmental.
3. **Inclusive and Equitable Sustainable Development:** This document explicitly includes social inclusivity and economic equality within its discourse, a progression from the mainly environmentally focused previous Rio documents. It acknowledges the need to eradicate poverty, improve human welfare, and promote social equity and gender equality as integral parts of the sustainability agenda.
4. **The Green Economy:** The concept of the green economy is given significant emphasis in *The Future We Want*. It became an essential tool for achieving sustainable development and

poverty eradication, a focus not as developed in the original Rio documents.

5. **Sustainable Development Goals:** The document set the stage for the development of what later was defined as the SDGs, representing a clear shift towards a more measurable, outcome-oriented approach to sustainability, whereas previous documents mainly focused on establishing broad principles and norms. The document solicited that goals be institutionally supported at all levels and follow the principles of effectiveness, transparency, accountability, and democracy.
6. **Institutional Frameworks:** *The Future We Want* outlined the need for more robust institutional frameworks for sustainable development at all levels, advocating for strengthening the UNEP and creating the United Nations High-Level Political Forum on Sustainable Development.
7. **Emphasis on Partnerships:** The document further emphasizes the role of multiple stakeholders, including civil society, the private sector, and international institutions, reflecting a growing recognition of the importance of collaborative efforts in achieving sustainable development.

While some critics viewed *The Future We Want* as less ambitious due to its lack of concrete commitments, it is crucial to understand that this document serves a different function than previous Rio documents. As an outcome document of a major UN conference, it aimed to create a general framework and vision for a future sustainable development agenda. This effort paved the way for more detailed and focused initiatives such as the SDGs. It reflected the consensus and compromises of the international community at that time and served as a stepping stone towards further progress in global sustainability efforts.[7]

Notes

1 Strong, Maurice F. (1992). *Opening Statement to the Rio Summit.* United Nations Conference on Environment and Development, Rio de Janeiro, Brazil, 3 June 1992. https://www.mauricestrong.net/index.php?option=com_content&view=article&id=36:rio2&catid=13&Itemid=59

2 Atapattu, S. (2007). *Emerging Principles of International Environmental Law.* Netherlands: Brill.

3 UNFCCC (2020). The UNFCCC secretariat (UN Climate Change). https://unfccc.int/
4 CBD Secretariat (2014). *Handbook of the Convention on Biological Diversity*. United Kingdom: Taylor & Francis.
5 United Nations (2013). *Agenda 21: Earth Summit: The United Nations Programme of Action from Rio*. United States: CreateSpace Independent Publishing Platform.
6 Doods, F. (2019). *The Way Forward: Beyond Agenda 21*. United Kingdom: Taylor & Francis.
7 Thompson, L., Dodds, F., & Laguna-Celis, J. (2014). *From Rio+20 to a New Development Agenda: Building a Bridge to a Sustainable Future*. United Kingdom: Taylor & Francis.

3 The Johannesburg Trajectories

> Not far from this conference room, in Lesotho, Malawi, Mozambique, Swaziland, Zambia and Zimbabwe, 13 million people are threatened with famine. If any reminder were needed of what happens when we fail to plan for and protect the long-term future of our planet, it can be heard in the cries for help from those 13 million souls. And if there is one word that should be on everyone's lips at this summit, one concept that embodies everything we hope to achieve here in Johannesburg, it is responsibility. Responsibility for each other—but especially the poor, the vulnerable, and the oppressed—as fellow members of a single human family. Responsibility for our planet, whose bounty is the very basis for human well-being and progress. And most of all, responsibility for the future—for our children, and their children. Over the past decade, at conferences and summit meetings such as this one, the world has drawn up a far-reaching blueprint for a stable, prosperous twenty-first century. This summit, like its landmark predecessors in Stockholm and Rio de Janeiro, focuses on a key component of that blueprint: the relationship between human beings and the natural environment.
>
> (Statement by UN Secretary-General Kofi Annan to the World Summit on Sustainable Development in Johannesburg, September 2, 2002[1])

Overview

This chapter explores the dynamics and impact of the 2002 Johannesburg Summit, officially known as the World Summit on Sustainable Development (WSSD). It addresses the interplay of political, social, and economic factors that led to the adoption of various initiatives and the creation of a framework for sustainable development. Despite significant global challenges such as 9/11 and a shifting political focus on terrorism, the summit underlined the vital need for global partnerships, private sector engagement, and inclusive governance for sustainability.

DOI: 10.4324/9781003494676-5

This chapter critically evaluates the strengths and weaknesses of the Johannesburg Summit, its continuity with prior summits, and its role in influencing future agendas, particularly its linkage with the United Nations Global Compact (UNGC) and the emergence of sustainable business strategies in the Global South. This chapter highlights missed opportunities, such as giving more attention to climate change and integrating the MDGs. It concludes with a reflection on the significance of the MDGs as a benchmark for multilateral commitment to development, providing lessons for future trajectories.

3.1 The World Summit on Sustainable Development

The 2002 Johannesburg Summit is essential in the trajectory of global sustainability efforts. Ten years after the transformative 1992 Earth Summit, it drew together over a hundred world leaders and numerous representatives from governments and non-governmental organizations. The summit aimed to advance global sustainability objectives by refining and expanding upon the initial trajectories set in motion in Rio.

The summit's outputs—the Political Declaration and Implementation Plan—encapsulated an ambitious agenda covering diverse areas such as water, energy, health, agriculture, and biodiversity. These were not merely disparate goals; they represented interconnected trajectories aimed at achieving sustainable development in an integrated manner.

Water management became a priority with a push for public-private partnerships under government regulation. The energy trajectory veered towards diversification and the inclusion of renewable sources. Health commitments reaffirmed the fight against HIV/AIDS, stressing universal medication access under WTO intellectual property rights rules.

Agricultural trajectories embraced negotiations on the WTO Agreement on Agriculture, focusing on market access and reduced export subsidies. Regarding biodiversity, the summit called for a fair and equitable international regime governing the use of genetic resources.

The summit also pressed forward in the fight against climate change, emphasizing implementing the Kyoto Protocol's targets for reducing greenhouse gas emissions. It marked a significant step forward in the climate change trajectory initiated in 1992, urging states still needed to ratify the protocol to do so.

The summit sought to tackle poverty by creating a Global Solidarity Fund. It also launched decade-long programs to support sustainable production and consumption, indicative of a trajectory designed to foster sustainable socioeconomic systems at national and regional levels.

In summary, the 2002 Summit built upon and expanded the trajectories set in motion during the Earth Summit in Rio, simultaneously forging new paths toward a sustainable future. It was a pivotal moment in global sustainability governance, emphasizing integrated and cooperative action to address sustainable development's complex, interrelated challenges.

3.2 The Summit's Global Landscape Challenges

The 2002 Johannesburg Summit occurred amidst a unique global landscape marked by deep-seated political complexities, impacting sustainability agendas' pace and direction. Studies that have analyzed the key areas of focus and primary outcomes of the summit have concluded that, despite some progress in advancing the sustainable development agenda, it also missed some opportunities due to political and global challenges.[2]

One significant obstacle was the marked shift in international priorities following the terrorist attacks on September 11, 2001. The subsequent War on Terror initiated by the United States and its allies redirected political focus, resources, and public attention away from sustainability objectives toward security issues. It led to a dilution of commitment to environmental concerns at the highest political levels, especially in nations deeply involved in the security response.

The geopolitical tension created by the War on Terror also disrupted the collaborative spirit needed to make substantial progress on sustainability objectives. Deepening divides, particularly between the Global North and South, created an atmosphere of mistrust and defensiveness. These dynamics affected international negotiations, making fostering consensus on the multifaceted issues of sustainable development more challenging.

Another obstacle was the need for more agreement on fundamental principles of sustainable development. Industrialized nations often prioritized economic growth and technological solutions, while developing nations stressed the importance of poverty alleviation and socioeconomic development as prerequisites for environmental sustainability. This divergence led to protracted debates and delays in implementing sustainable solutions.

Additionally, there was an ongoing debate over the concept of "sustainable development." Critics argued that proponents were using it to promote a neoliberal economic agenda under the guise of environmentalism, thereby exacerbating social inequalities.

Lastly, the summit faced criticism for an alleged lack of substantial progress and accountability. While the summit produced ambitious goals and action plans, critics argued that there needed to be more mechanisms to ensure their implementation, contributing to skepticism about the summit's long-term impact.

Overall, the 2002 Johannesburg Summit occurred at a challenging time in global history that impeded some possible outcomes. It faced substantial obstacles, not least the global political reshuffling following 9/11, differences in national priorities, ideological disagreements, and criticism over its perceived effectiveness. These factors collectively shaped its outcomes and the trajectories it set in motion.

3.3 Stockholm-Rio-Johannesburg Trajectories

Despite the myriad of challenges that the Johannesburg Summit encountered, it marked a significant milestone in the progression of global sustainable development efforts, expanding on the efforts made in Stockholm and Rio.

Firstly, the summit was remarkable for recognizing the critical linkages between poverty eradication, changing consumption and production patterns, and protecting the natural resource base. This holistic perspective was evident in the Johannesburg Plan of Implementation (JPOI), which outlined comprehensive actions across key thematic areas such as water, energy, health, and agriculture.

For example, regarding water and sanitation, the summit set a goal of halving, by 2015, the proportion of people without access to clean drinking water and sanitation. In the energy sector, stakeholders emphasized improving energy efficiency, increasing the global share of renewable energy sources, and facilitating energy access in developing countries.

Secondly, the summit was crucial in establishing a global framework for corporate sustainability, further developing Principle

10 of the Rio Declaration, which emphasizes public participation in environmental decision-making. WSSD promoted the notion of CSR and Private Sector Voluntary Initiatives, thus enhancing the role of the private sector in achieving sustainable development.

Thirdly, the summit successfully integrated the three dimensions of sustainable development—social, economic, and environmental—into a comprehensive plan, advancing the core concept that had first emerged in Rio. For instance, the JPOI linked the commitment to fight against HIV/AIDS to the provisions of the Agreement on Trade-Related Aspects of Intellectual Property Rights (TRIPS), highlighting the intersection of health (social), access to medicines (economic), and IP rights (legal).

Lastly, the summit made a significant contribution by calling for the development of a 10-year framework of programs on sustainable consumption and production patterns. This call paved the way for establishing the Marrakech Process in 2003 and eventually for the adoption of the 10-Year Framework of Programmes on Sustainable Consumption and Production Patterns (10YFP) at Rio+20.

In conclusion, despite the political and ideological hurdles, the Johannesburg Summit forged a significant continuation of the trajectories that emerged in Stockholm and Rio. It consolidated the sustainable development agenda by advancing a comprehensive, integrative approach that combined social, economic, and environmental considerations.

3.4 The Political Leadership Trajectory

The political leadership of key figures such as Kofi Annan, then Secretary-General of the United Nations, and Nelson Mandela, former president of South Africa, was instrumental in advancing the sustainable development agenda at the 2002 summit in Johannesburg.

Kofi Annan receives credit for his critical role in steering the summit's focus toward a more integrated approach to sustainable development. His "Water, Energy, Health, Agriculture, and Biodiversity" (WEHAB) framework presented before the summit helped to crystallize discussions around these five key areas, prompting participants to view them not in isolation but as interconnected pieces of the giant sustainable development puzzle.

Furthermore, Annan's call for a "Global Compact," enlisting the participation of businesses, labor groups, and government bodies, marked a critical step towards acknowledging the necessity of multi-stakeholder participation in addressing global challenges.

Nelson Mandela's presence at the summit brought a moral authority, and his calls for social equality, poverty eradication, and sustainable development resonated deeply. His advocacy for the rights of the poor and the marginalized also played a crucial role in ensuring that issues of social equity and justice were central to the discussions. Mandela's vision of a more equitable and sustainable world powerfully underscored the moral imperatives of the sustainable development agenda.

Moreover, under their leadership, the summit stressed the importance of inclusive global governance. It brought together a wide array of actors, including government representatives, NGOs, businesses, and Indigenous groups, acknowledging the value of diverse perspectives and the importance of cooperation in addressing complex, global challenges. This commitment to multilateralism and multi-stakeholder participation has become fundamental in subsequent sustainable development negotiations.[3]

Indeed, the leadership of figures such as Kofi Annan and Nelson Mandela, coupled with the emphasis on inclusive global governance, played a critical role in shaping the summit's outcomes and advancing the broader sustainable development agenda. Their contributions resonate in today's efforts to achieve a more sustainable and equitable world.

3.5 The Sustainable Business Trajectory

The announcement of the initiative to grow a sustainable business in the world's poorest countries at the Johannesburg Summit was a significant milestone for the UNGC. This principle-based framework encourages businesses worldwide to adopt sustainable and socially responsible policies. This initiative was explicitly aimed at promoting sustainable business strategies in developing countries, profoundly influencing future sustainable business strategies in the Global South.

This initiative was pioneering as it emphasized the role of private sector companies in driving sustainable development in low-income countries. It acknowledged that corporations could play a vital role in contributing to economic development, poverty alleviation, and environmental conservation. This focus led to a significant shift in business operations, driving many to incorporate social and environmental considerations into their strategies.

In the years following the summit, many companies operating in developing countries have integrated these principles into their operations, contributing to sustainable development on multiple fronts. For example, companies like Unilever and Nestlé, operating in Africa, have initiated programs that work with local farmers to improve their agricultural practices, enhance yields, and increase income, all while minimizing environmental impact.

In another example, mobile network operators in Kenya and Bangladesh have helped bridge the digital divide by offering affordable services, thus enabling greater access to information, education, and financial services.

Additionally, the initiative has spurred the growth of social enterprises in the Global South—businesses that aim to solve social problems while being financially sustainable. For instance, Grameen Bank in Bangladesh, a microfinance organization and community development bank, provides credit to the poorest of the poor in rural Bangladesh without requiring collateral, addressing poverty and promoting financial inclusion.

These examples illustrate the trajectory that the UNGC initiative has influenced, highlighting the critical role that sustainable business strategies play in tackling development challenges in the Global South. They also underscore the potential of multi-stakeholder partnerships in promoting sustainable development and the value of integrating social and environmental considerations into business strategy.

This initiative, aiming to expand sustainable business in the world's poorest countries, is a precursor to the concept of the "Base of the Pyramid" (BOP) model. The BOP model, popularized by C.K. Prahalad, states that businesses can be profitable while contributing to poverty alleviation by serving the 4 billion people in the lowermost part of the economic pyramid.

This approach reframes the world's poorest people as resilient and creative entrepreneurs and conscious consumers. Therefore, rather than seeing them as passive beneficiaries of philanthropy, the BOP model encourages businesses to actively engage with them in the marketplace by developing affordable, quality products and services that meet their specific needs and aspirations.

Applying the BOP model in the Global South has led to many innovative and successful business strategies. For instance, as previously mentioned, mobile telecommunications companies have managed to penetrate markets in the most remote areas of developing countries. Their services' affordability and broad reach have opened new opportunities for low-income people in mobile banking, agricultural information dissemination, and telemedicine, enhancing livelihoods and achieving business growth.

Another example is affordable, small packaged consumer goods, such as shampoo sachets or single-use packets of washing powder. These cater to the budget constraints of low-income people but have also turned out to be successful marketing strategies, enabling companies to expand their market reach.

Furthermore, in the agricultural sector, companies like Jain Irrigation Systems in India provide small-scale farmers with affordable micro-irrigation systems, improving crop yields while conserving water resources. In doing so, they serve a previously untapped market, contributing to food security and water conservation while building a profitable business.

These sustainable business strategies derived from the BOP model demonstrate the potential of the private sector to contribute positively to economic and social development in the Global South. By recognizing and tapping into the untapped potential at the BOP, businesses can drive innovation, economic growth, and social progress. This approach complements and extends the trajectory initiated by the UNGC at the Johannesburg Summit, further contributing to the evolution of sustainable business practices.

3.6 The Multi-Stakeholder Partnership Trajectory

The partnership initiatives announced at the Johannesburg Summit were crucial in recognizing the importance of collaboration between diverse sectors and stakeholders in achieving sustainable development. These partnerships, often involving a mix of governments, international organizations, private businesses, and civil society groups, are known as Public–Private Partnerships (PPPs) or Multi-Stakeholder Partnerships (MSPs).

These PPPs and MSPs offer new approaches to addressing complex global environmental issues by utilizing the strengths and resources of different sectors. They operate on the principle that, although governments are responsible for setting policy frameworks, the successful implementation of SDGs demands involvement and expertise from both the private sector and civil society. It included the expertise of numerous scientists who contributed during the conference and throughout these partnership initiatives to make the sustainable development agenda more grounded in science and technology.[4]

For example, the Renewable Energy and Energy Efficiency Partnership (REEEP) launched at the summit aimed to accelerate and expand the market for renewable energy and energy efficiency technologies. It included participants from governments, businesses, and NGOs, with each partner contributing resources and expertise towards a shared goal.

Similarly, the Water and Sanitation for the Urban Poor (WSUP) initiative is a multisector partnership that includes water utilities, businesses, and NGOs. It seeks to address the problem of inadequate water supply and sanitation in many urban areas in the developing world.

The Global Water Partnership (GWP), announced at the Johannesburg Summit, is another example of a successful MSP. The GWP aims to promote integrated water resources management. Its partners include government agencies, private companies, and NGOs, each bringing different skills, resources, and perspectives.

These partnerships represent a significant shift in international environmental governance. They reflect a growing understanding that sustainable development is a shared responsibility that requires the engagement of all sectors of society. Moreover, they offer an innovative model for pooling resources, sharing risks, and harnessing the different skills and capabilities of a broad range of actors. This model has been increasingly adopted in subsequent years, further embedding the partnership approach in the global sustainable development agenda.

3.7 Missed Opportunities and Trajectories

The Johannesburg Summit marked an important milestone in the international sustainable development agenda, but it also faced substantial criticism for what some observers saw as missed opportunities. One of the significant criticisms was that the summit did not adequately address the urgent issue of climate change despite the mounting evidence of its impacts worldwide.

At the time of the summit in 2002, the world was already experiencing the effects of climate change with increased frequency and intensity of extreme weather events such as flooding and droughts. These events had significant socio-economic implications, particularly for vulnerable communities in developing countries. Despite the evident and immediate need for action, climate change was off the formal agenda. It was a significant oversight given the cross-cutting nature of climate change, which affects virtually all aspects of sustainable development.

The absence of any substantial measure to combat climate change, such as a carbon tax or other market mechanisms, was another missed opportunity. Such measures could have provided a powerful tool to reduce greenhouse gas emissions and mitigate the impacts of climate change. A carbon tax could have incentivized industries to transition towards more sustainable practices by making polluting more expensive.

Despite experts calling for advancing mechanisms to enforce environmental laws, the Johannesburg Summit missed the chance to address this and the following topics:[5]

1. **Absence of Climate Change on the Formal Agenda:** Perhaps one of the most glaring missed opportunities was the absence of climate change as a vital issue on the formal agenda of the summit. Despite the ever-increasing recognition of climate change as a global crisis and the commitment made in Kyoto five years earlier to reduce global greenhouse gas (GHG) emissions, this critical issue did not find prominent space in the discussions and the outcome document.
2. **Lack of Specific Targets:** While the summit's action plan mentioned climate change, it did not set clear or binding targets for GHG emissions reduction. The absence of firm commitments made monitoring progress and holding countries accountable for their contributions to global emissions difficult.
3. **No Concrete Mechanisms for Kyoto Protocol Enforcement:** The Kyoto Protocol was a groundbreaking treaty that binds signatory countries to specific emissions reduction targets.

However, the enforcement mechanisms for these obligations could have been more straightforward and effective. The summit could have been a critical platform to establish and strengthen such mechanisms, but it failed to do so.

4. **Failure to Encourage Ratification:** The summit could have been crucial in encouraging countries to ratify the Kyoto Protocol. Many significant emitting countries, including the United States and Australia, had yet to ratify the treaty by the time of the summit. While the summit did call on countries to ratify the protocol, it needed to provide more substantial incentives or pressure to encourage this crucial step.
5. **Insufficient Support for Adaptation Measures:** The effects of climate change, such as increased frequency and intensity of extreme weather events, disproportionately affect developing countries. The summit missed the opportunity to emphasize and bolster financial and technological support for these countries to adapt to these changes.

Indeed, the trajectory from the Kyoto Protocol and the UNFCCC towards the Johannesburg Summit in 2002 represented a critical period in global climate governance. However, the summit should have capitalized on the momentum and the established frameworks, not doing so resulted in a significant gap in global climate action.

Moreover, the lack of substantial commitments towards renewable energy and a low-carbon economy was another missed opportunity. As the urgency of transitioning to a more sustainable energy model was already well-recognized, the summit could have been a platform to accelerate progress in this area. Instead, the issue was primarily sidelined.

These missed opportunities highlighted a broader challenge in the international sustainable development agenda. While the summit made strides in certain areas, the failure to address the critical issue of climate change suggested a lack of political will. It highlighted the challenges in consensus on complex and politically sensitive issues. This absence underscored the need for a more ambitious and inclusive approach to addressing climate change and supporting sustainable development in subsequent years.

3.8 The Missed MDGs Connections

The 2002 Johannesburg Summit missed opportunities to garner more commitments to the recently launched MDGs. The MDGs, set by the UN from 2000 to 2015, represented a pivotal moment in global development. They encouraged unprecedented multilateralism, providing the first global, quantifiable targets addressing various aspects of extreme poverty. The MDGs fostered a global commitment to development, offering clear, measurable goals that improved accountability for states and international organizations. They emphasized the need for inclusive, human-centered strategies, focusing on marginalized and disadvantaged populations.

Furthermore, the MDGs mobilized international aid and guided national policymaking. Despite some criticisms, the lessons learned from the MDGs heavily influenced their successor, the SDGs, adopted in 2015. Some of the criticism has been the missed opportunity to make the linkage between the 2002 Johannesburg Summit and the 2000 Millennium Declaration that launched the MDGs. In short, the missed Summit-MDGs connection neglected the opportunity for action, commitment, and resolution for addressing the root causes of violence, inequalities, discrimination, and unsustainable development. Specifically, not making these linkages more prominent resulted in additional missed opportunities and largely ignored trajectories. For example:

1. **Lack of Alignment and Integration:** One of the most significant missed opportunities was the need for alignment between the summit's agenda and the MDGs. While both shared common goals, such as environmental sustainability and poverty eradication, there needed to be more effort made to integrate the MDGs into the summit's discussions and outcomes. This lack of integration reduced the effectiveness of global efforts towards sustainable development.
2. **Insufficient Emphasis on Goal 7:** The MDGs include a specific goal (Goal 7) dedicated to ensuring environmental sustainability. However, although the summit focused on sustainable development, organizers should have emphasized this goal more during the program. The lack of focus on Goal 7, directly related to the summit's core objective of promoting sustainable development, represents a significant missed opportunity.

3. **Lack of Clear Strategies for MDGs Achievement:** While the UN had already established the MDGs in 2002, the summit needed to articulate clear strategies or action plans for achieving these goals, representing a missed opportunity to leverage the summit's momentum to accelerate progress toward the MDGs.
4. **Inadequate Focus on Implementation:** Both the MDGs and the outcomes of the summit suffered from a lack of focus on implementation. There needed to be more attention on the "how"—the mechanisms, resources, and partnerships required to achieve these goals.
5. **No Recognition of Linkages:** Finally, another significant missed opportunity was to recognize the linkages between the MDGs and the objectives of the summit. The sustainable development agenda is inherently interconnected—improvements in one area often depend on or lead to improvements in others. Recognizing and leveraging these interconnections could have led to more integrated and more effective approaches to achieving the MDGs and the summit's objectives.

In summary, while the 2002 Johannesburg Summit made progress in promoting the sustainable development agenda, its limited engagement with the MDGs represents a missed opportunity to create a more aligned and integrated approach to addressing the world's most pressing challenges.[6]

In conclusion, in the analysis of the Johannesburg trajectories, we must also consider how, despite the missed opportunities, the new MDGs were brought to the forefront as a remarkable shift in multilateral commitment to development. Established at the turn of the millennium, the MDGs provided a set of clear, quantifiable, and time-bound objectives that unified the global community in a commitment to addressing pressing issues such as poverty, education, health, and environmental sustainability.

These eight MDGs were instrumental in shaping global policies, mobilizing resources, and inspiring collaborations between governments, international organizations, and civil society. Parallel to the substantial progress, the Johannesburg Summit revealed gaps and shortcomings in achieving these goals, particularly in climate action and environmental sustainability.

Looking back, we can learn several important lessons for future trajectories. First, the MDGs highlighted the power of a shared vision, reminding us that setting universal and specific targets can galvanize international action and collaboration. Second, they underscored the interdependence of social, economic, and environmental sustainability, prompting a need for integrated solutions that reflect this interconnectedness.

Moreover, the challenges encountered during the Johannesburg Summit and in the MDG era underscored the importance of inclusive governance and the active participation of all stakeholders, including governments, the private sector, and civil society, in pursuing sustainable development. In many ways, this realization informed the spirit and design of the succeeding SDGs, which strongly emphasized the universality, interconnectedness, and inclusivity of sustainable development efforts.

In sum, the Johannesburg Summit and the MDGs have influenced global sustainable development discourses and actions, providing valuable insights and understandings that continue to guide our collective quest for a more sustainable and equitable world.[7]

Notes

1 Annan, K. (2021). *Secretary-General Kofi Annan to the World Summit on Sustainable Development in Johannesburg, 2 September*. United Nations. https://www.un.org/sg/en/content/sg/speeches/2002–09-03/secretary-general-kofi-annan-world-summit-sustainable-development

2 Oberthür, S., & Ott, H. E. (2003). *The Kyoto Protocol: International Climate Policy for the 21st Century.* Springer Science & Business Media.

3 Churie-Kallhauge, A., Corell, E., & Sjöstedt, G. (2017). *Global Challenges: Furthering the Multilateral Process for Sustainable Development*. United Kingdom: Taylor & Francis.

4 Svedin, U., & Aniansson, B. (2003). From Rio to Johannesburg: Reflections on the Role of Science in the Transition Towards Sustainability. *Environmental Science & Policy*, 6(3), 219–227.

5 Lye, L.H., & Manguiat, M.S.Z. (2003). *Towards a "Second Generation" in Environmental Laws in the Asian and Pacific Region: Select Trends*. Switzerland: IUCN.

6 Hens, L. & Nath, B. (2005). *The World Summit on Sustainable Development: The Johannesburg Conference.* Germany: Springer Netherlands.

7 Poku, N., & Whitman, J. (2017). *The Millennium Development Goals: Challenges, Prospects and Opportunities*. Taylor & Francis.

4 The Brundtland Trajectories

> "A global agenda for change"—this was what the World Commission on Environment and Development was asked to formulate. It was an urgent call by the General Assembly of the United Nations: to propose long-term environmental strategies for achieving sustainable development by the year 2000 and beyond; to recommend ways concern for the environment may be translated into greater co-operation among developing countries and between countries at different stages of economic and social development and lead to the achievement of common and mutually supportive objectives that take account of the interrelationships between people, resources, environment, and development; to consider ways and means by which the international community can deal more effectively with environmental concerns; and to help define shared perceptions of long-term environmental issues and the appropriate efforts needed to deal successfully with the problems of protecting and enhancing the environment, a long term agenda for action during the coming decades, and aspirational goals for the world community.
>
> (Gro Harlem Brundtland, Chairman of the World Commission on Environment and Development, in the Foreword to *Our Common Future*, Oslo, March 20, 1987[1])

Overview

This chapter critically explores the profound impact of the Brundtland Commission on the sustainable development trajectory. Established amidst conflicting ideological landscapes and increasing global environmental challenges, the Commission was instrumental in integrating economic growth, environmental protection, and social equality into the definition of sustainable development. The innovative approach of the Commission broadened the concept of sustainability, marking a paradigm

DOI: 10.4324/9781003494676-6

shift in global policy discussions. This chapter investigates the principles articulated by the Commission and their influence on subsequent international policies and SDGs. The lasting legacy of the Commission's work is evident in the ongoing global shift towards sustainability, illustrating the foundational role of the Brundtland Commission in shaping sustainable development discourse and practice.

4.1 The Brundtland Commission

The Brundtland Commission, formally known as the World Commission on Environment and Development (WCED), holds a significant place in the history of sustainable development. In 1983 UN Secretary-General Javier Pérez de Cuéllar urged the Commission to build international cooperation and synergy towards sustainable development efforts. They chose the former prime minister of Norway, Gro Harlem Brundtland, to chair the commission due to her expertise in the sciences and public health.

The Brundtland Commission, in its relatively brief existence, had an enormous impact on global environmental and development discourse. Its most enduring contribution is arguably the popularization of the term "sustainable development." This was first used in the Commission's 1987 report entitled *Our Common Future*, also known as the Brundtland Report. This report defined sustainable development as "development that meets the needs of the present without compromising the ability of future generations to meet their own needs."

The Brundtland Report was not just influential in terms of its definition of sustainable development; it also provided a compelling vision for achieving sustainability at all levels, from the local to the global. It presented a broad framework for integrating economic growth, social equity, and environmental protection, and outlined the necessity of balancing these three pillars of sustainable development in policymaking and practice.

Despite the dissolution of the Brundtland Commission in 1987, its legacy continues to shape the sustainable development landscape. The Center for Our Common Future was established in 1988 to carry forward the work initiated by the Commission. Over three decades later, the principles outlined in the Brundtland Report continue to guide international negotiations on sustainable development, and the concept of sustainable development remains at the heart of global efforts to create a more equitable and sustainable world.

In this chapter, we will delve deeper into the trajectory created by the Brundtland Commission, tracing its influence on subsequent international environmental agreements, and explore how the concept of sustainable development has evolved and operationalized over time.

4.2 Principles for New Development Trajectories

The Brundtland Commission's report, *Our Common Future*, proposed a framework of sustainable development built on three interconnected pillars: economic growth, environmental protection, and social equality.[2] These principles are derived from the Commission's definition of sustainable development as "development that meets the needs of the present without compromising the ability of future generations to meet their own needs."

1. **Economic Growth:** This aspect of sustainable development recognizes the importance of economic activities for improving people's living standards. However, the Commission emphasized that economic growth should not come at the expense of environmental degradation and should contribute to social equality.
2. **Environmental Protection:** The Commission underlined the need for development that respects and conserves the environment. It stressed that environmental protection is not a barrier to economic growth but is, in fact, essential for long-term, sustainable economic development.
3. **Social Equality:** The Commission argued that social equity and justice are integral parts of sustainable development. It underscored the need for policies that ensure fair distribution of the benefits of economic growth and environmental protection.

The three-pillar concept of sustainable development is a significant legacy of the Brundtland Commission. It has influenced various international policies and agreements, including the UNFCCC, the MDGs, and the SDGs. These principles continue to guide international efforts toward achieving a sustainable world.

In addition, the Brundtland Commission crystallized the idea of sustainable development in the global consciousness. It reinforced previously introduced fundamental principles and introduced new ones that have since guided international efforts towards sustainability. Some of these principles are as follows:

1. **Inter-Generational Equity:** The idea that the present generation should ensure that its actions will enable future generations to enjoy the same level of resources and opportunities is central to the Commission's definition of sustainable development.
2. **Integration of Environment and Development:** The Commission emphasized that economic development and environmental conservation are not mutually exclusive but can and should be pursued simultaneously. This principle led to the understanding that environmental considerations should be integrated into all areas of economic policy.
3. **Focus on the Quality of Growth:** The Commission stressed that it's not just the quantity of economic growth but also the quality of growth that matters. This includes equitable distribution of resources and benefits and growth that does not harm the environment.
4. **Common but Differentiated Responsibilities (CBDR):** Although this term was later formalized in the 1992 Rio Summit, the Brundtland Report set the stage for it by recognizing that while all nations should cooperate to achieve sustainable development, developed nations, with their greater historical and current contributions to global environmental issues, have the greater responsibility to take the lead.
5. **Participation:** The Commission highlighted the importance of public participation in decision-making processes related to the environment and development. This principle later influenced the inclusion of significant groups and stakeholders in the UN's sustainable development processes.
6. **Peace, Security, and Mutual Respect among Nations:** The Commission recognized the interconnection between peace, development, and environmental protection, noting that sustainable development cannot be achieved without peace and security, and vice versa.

The Brundtland Commission built on the accomplishments of the 1972 Stockholm Conference by reiterating the necessity of a balanced and integrated approach to environment and development. However, it proposed a new development pathway—sustainable development—that has since been embedded into international policy through significant events like the Rio Earth Summit in 1992, the Johannesburg World Summit on Sustainable Development in 2002, and the adoption of the MDGs and SDGs. In this sense, the trajectories initiated by the Brundtland Commission continue to shape the global sustainable development agenda to this day.

4.3 The Contested Ideological Landscapes

The decade following the 1972 United Nations Conference on the Human Environment was marked by an increasingly palpable tension between economic growth and environmental sustainability. A host of unresolved environmental challenges—including pollution, acid rain, deforestation, desertification, and ozone depletion—underscored the urgency of reconciling economic development with environmental protection. However, achieving this delicate balance proved to be an enormously complex task, fraught with ideological contestations and practical difficulties.

On one hand, the neoliberal ideology, and the doctrine of economic globalization, championed by figures such as Ronald Reagan and Margaret Thatcher, held sway in the world's leading trading nations. On the other hand, institutions like the International Monetary Fund (IMF) and the World Bank exerted considerable influence over developing countries' economic and social policies, particularly in the aftermath of the 1945 Bretton Woods Conference. Amid these contrasting ideological landscapes, the quest for sustainable development was, in many ways, a search for a middle ground.

At the heart of these debates was a series of contentious questions. Were local environmental problems the offshoots of local development processes, or were they the fallout of a global economic system that essentially coerced developing countries into exploiting their natural resources? Were environmental burdens the byproducts of unrestrained economic growth, or did they stem from insufficient economic development? Could technological advancements offer a way to reconcile economic and environmental objectives, or would this reconciliation necessitate deeper social, political, and structural changes? [3]

While various attempts were made to tackle these questions, a definitive answer remained elusive. For instance, the 1980 *World Conservation Strategy* by the International Union for Conservation of Nature contained a brief chapter on "sustainable development," advocating for global structural changes. However, its reach was limited.[4]

4.4 Ideologies in Corporate Responsibilities

These contested ideological landscapes also shaped the evolution of theories around corporate responsibility.

In the 1970s and 1980s, the neoliberal ideology gave rise to the shareholder-only theory of corporate responsibility, predominantly championed by Milton Friedman, who asserted that a corporation's exclusive social responsibility was to enhance profits for its shareholders. This viewpoint, anchored in a narrow, finance-centric conception of corporate duty, was in sync with the prevailing ethos of free-market capitalism of that era, but it began facing heightened scrutiny amidst growing awareness of the environmental and social repercussions of unchecked economic expansion. Concurrently, in 1986, the United Nations unveiled the "Declaration on the Right to Development at 25" as a framework for socially responsible organizations, emphasizing the universal right of individuals to partake in, contribute to, and benefit from economic, social, and cultural development while being acutely aware of environmental impacts. This holistic approach to development found further refinement in 1997 when John Elkington, in his seminal book *Cannibals with Forks: Triple Bottom Line of 21st Century Business*, expanded on the metrics for organizational success, thereby preparing for the Triple Bottom Line (TBL) concept. The TBL framework advocated for corporations to concurrently pursue economic viability, social equity, and environmental sustainability, offering a broader, more integrative perspective on corporate responsibility compared to the limited, profit-focused approach advanced by predecessors like Friedman.

However, Elkington himself has acknowledged the limitations of the TBL approach, noting that its original intent—to drive a radical shift in business practices towards greater sustainability and responsibility—has been diluted over time. Critics have pointed out that TBL, while groundbreaking, was perhaps too simplistic and did not fully encapsulate the intricate dynamics between corporations, society, and the environment. Furthermore, it has been argued that companies could superficially align with TBL principles as a form of "corporate greenwashing" without implementing meaningful changes in their operations. Reflecting on these concerns, Elkington has called for a "recall" of the TBL concept, urging businesses to either genuinely commit to sustainable practices or make way for entities that will. In this light, while TBL was a progressive step beyond the shareholder-only theory, it requires revisiting and refining to effectively address the complexities of corporate responsibility in today's context.[5]

The Brundtland Report and the TBL concept share a foundational commitment to balanced and equitable progress across economic development, social equity, and environmental protection. Defined by the Brundtland Report, sustainable development is portrayed as a paradigm meeting current generational needs without undermining the capacity of future generations to satisfy theirs. This definition not only underlines intergenerational fairness but also calls for the harmonious integration of economic and environmental factors in planning and policy.

Initially conceived in 1994, Elkington's TBL also mirrors this commitment but extends its application specifically to the corporate sphere. It presents a tripartite framework of "people, planet, profit" advocating that businesses should be assessed on their financial profitability and held accountable for their societal and environmental footprints. However, as discussed earlier, while TBL represented a significant step towards a more comprehensive understanding of corporate responsibility, its original intent and application have somewhat diverged over time, necessitating a critical reevaluation and refinement of the concept to ensure it drives corporations toward sustainability and responsibility.

However, there are also limitations and areas of tension between the two concepts:

1. **Vagueness and Interpretation:** The Brundtland Report and TBL definitions are criticized for being somewhat vague. The Brundtland definition needs specific metrics or indicators, leading to varied interpretations of sustainable development. Similarly, the TBL framework is often criticized for needing

more standardization in its metrics, leading to inconsistent applications and reporting.

2. **Integration vs. Balance:** The Brundtland definition emphasizes integrating economic development with environmental sustainability. In contrast, TBL often leads to a balancing act, where companies attempt to offset adverse impacts in one area with positive impacts in another. This can sometimes lead to tradeoffs that are outside the principles of sustainable development.
3. **Focus on Business vs Society:** The TBL concept primarily aims at businesses, encouraging them to adopt sustainable practices. The Brundtland definition, however, is broader and encompasses sustainable development at the societal level, involving governments, communities, and other stakeholders.
4. **Short-term vs. Long-Term Focus:** TBL, when implemented by corporations, may still be influenced by market pressures and short-term profit motives, which can sometimes undermine long-term sustainability objectives. The Brundtland definition emphasizes long-term thinking, particularly in terms of intergenerational equity.

In summary, while both TBL and the Brundtland definition of sustainable development emphasize the need to consider economic, social, and environmental factors, TBL is more business-centric and can sometimes be applied in ways that do not fully align with the holistic and long-term perspective of sustainable development as envisioned by the Brundtland Report.

4.5 The Brundtland Definition and its Trajectories

The Brundtland definition of sustainable development has been widely praised for its integrative perspective and its emphasis on intergenerational equity. However, it has also been critiqued for its vagueness and potential contradictions. Let's analyze these elements in relation to economic growth, social needs, environmental protection, and multilateral political agreements:

1. **Economic Growth and Development:** The Brundtland definition reconciles economic development with environmental sustainability. It acknowledges that economic growth is necessary, especially for less developed countries,

but emphasizes that such growth must not occur at the expense of future generations. While this is a valuable perspective, critics argue that it fails to challenge the prevailing growth-centric paradigm, which is often associated with overconsumption and environmental degradation.
2. **Social Needs and Equity:** The definition recognizes the social dimension of sustainable development and implicitly calls for social equity, both within and between generations. It underscores the need to meet the essential needs of the world's poor, which is a priority. However, it does not explicitly address the issues of inequality, social justice, and human rights, which have since become integral to discussions on sustainable development.
3. **Environmental Protection and Conservation:** By emphasizing the need to preserve the ability of future generations to meet their needs, the Brundtland definition highlights the importance of environmental conservation. However, the report has been criticized for its anthropocentric focus, framing environmental protection largely in terms of human needs and interests. Furthermore, it does not provide specific guidance on how to balance immediate human needs with long-term environmental preservation.
4. **Multilateral Political Agreements and Governance:** The Brundtland definition and the report it originated from have been instrumental in shaping global sustainability discourse and influencing multilateral agreements. The principles articulated in the report informed the discussions at the Earth Summit in 1992, which led to the creation of key environmental conventions. However, the definition's broadness and flexibility have also allowed for varied interpretations, which can lead to diluted commitments and diverging priorities among nations.

Overall, the Brundtland definition of sustainable development offers a valuable framing of the concept, emphasizing the integration of economic, social, and environmental concerns and the principle of intergenerational equity. However, its broad and flexible nature, while enabling widespread adoption, has also led to critiques regarding its inability to challenge the growth-centric paradigm, its limited treatment of social equity issues, its anthropocentric perspective, and the difficulties in translating it into actionable and consistent global commitments.

In addition, the Brundtland Report broadened the scope of sustainable development, previously grounded in the context of sustainable yield in forestry and fisheries, and integrated economic and ecological considerations into a cohesive framework.

In the tumultuous context of the late 20th century, marked by economic shocks such as the oil crises, severe environmental challenges including droughts in Africa and widespread deforestation, and critical global concerns such as the depletion of the ozone layer, the report's holistic approach to these interconnected problems resonated deeply.[6]

Through its comprehensive analysis, the Brundtland Report made it clear that environmental issues were not isolated incidents but were intrinsically linked to economic and social conditions. The report helped to illuminate the intricate relationship between economic development and environmental protection, challenging the prevailing idea that these areas could be considered in isolation. By emphasizing that economic and environmental policies were fundamentally interdependent, the report brought a new level of nuance and complexity to these discussions.

One of the lasting impacts of the Brundtland Report is that it permanently changed the discourse around environmental and economic policy. The notion of separate compartments for these policies has been discarded in favor of a more integrated, holistic perspective. The report advanced the idea that sustainable development necessitates a balanced integration of economic, social, and environmental considerations.

This shift in perspective encouraged future initiatives and policies that approach economic development and environmental sustainability as two sides of the same coin. The Brundtland Report has, therefore, played a pivotal role in shaping our contemporary understanding of sustainable development. It has underscored the necessity for harmonizing economic growth and environmental protection, and in doing so, has influenced a generation of policymakers and environmental advocates.

4.6 Misplaced Optimism

The Brundtland Commissioners discussed the future and estimated that humanity would complete the global shift into sustainability by the year 2000. Their optimism might seem misplaced in retrospect, given that the global shift towards sustainability has been slower and more complex than the commissioners initially anticipated. However, it's worth noting that the report was a product of its time, reflecting the hope and ambition of an era that was beginning to recognize the environmental challenges and was eager to address them.

Considering today's context, the SDGs reflect a renewed commitment to the vision put forth by the Brundtland Commission, albeit with a more realistic timeframe but perhaps still optimistic for the year 2030. The SDGs are arguably more comprehensive and detailed than the broad objectives outlined in the Brundtland Report, reflecting the complexity and interconnectedness of our global challenges. The 2030 Agenda acknowledges the lessons learned since the time of the Brundtland Commission, emphasizing the need for all countries to work together in a spirit of global partnership.

While we are indeed 30 years behind the original schedule proposed by the Brundtland Commission, the legacy of the report lives on in the SDGs. The SDGs embody the same vision of sustainable development that balances economic growth, social inclusion, and environmental protection, and they stand as a testament to the enduring relevance of the Brundtland Commission's pioneering work.

Notes

1 Brundtland, G.H. (1987). *Report of the World Commission on Environment and Development: Our Common Future* (p. 41). United Nations. https://sustainabledevelopment.un.org/content/documents/5987our-common-future.pdf
2 Brundtland, G.H. (1987). *Report of the World Commission on Environment and Development: Our Common Future*. United Nations. Available at https://sustainabledevelopment.un.org/content/documents/5987our-common-future.pdf
3 Borowy, I. (2014). *Defining Sustainable Development: the World Commission on Environment and Development (Brundtland Commission)*. Milton Park: Earthscan/Routledge.
4 International Union for Conservation of Nature and Natural Resources (IUCN), United Nations Environment Programme (UNEP), World Wildlife Fund (WWF) (1980). *World Conservation Strategy: Living Resource Conservation for Sustainable Development*. Available at https://portals.iucn.org/library/efiles/documents/wcs-004.pdf

5 Gerasimova, K. (2017). *The Brundtland Report: Our Common Future*. United Kingdom: Macat Library.
6 See: Karliner, J. (1997). *The Corporate Planet: Ecology and Politics in the Age of Globalization*. Sierra Club Books. See also: Borowy, I. (2013). *Defining Sustainable Development for Our Common Future: A History of the World Commission on Environment and Development (Brundtland Commission)*. Routledge.

5 The Paris Trajectories

> This agreement is ambitious, with every nation setting and committing to their own specific targets, even as we take into account differences among nations. We'll have a strong system of transparency, including periodic reviews and independent assessments, to help hold every country accountable for meeting its commitments. As technology advances, this agreement allows progress to pave the way for even more ambitious targets over time. And we have secured a broader commitment to support the most vulnerable countries as they pursue cleaner economic growth. In short, this agreement will mean less of the carbon pollution that threatens our planet, and more of the jobs and economic growth driven by low-carbon investment. Full implementation of this agreement will help delay or avoid some of the worst consequences of climate change, and will pave the way for even more progress, in successive stages, over the coming years.
>
> (Statement by US President Barack Obama on the signing of the Paris Climate Agreement, December 12, 2015[1])

Overview

This chapter delves into the complexities and nuances of the 2015 Paris Agreement, a landmark in global efforts to combat climate change. We trace the agreement's origins, specifically in relation to the Kyoto Protocol, mapping the evolution of principles and protocols for limiting carbon emissions. We examine the political resistance faced by both agreements and assesses the implications of such resistance on national-level climate commitments. This chapter also assesses the lessons gleaned from these experiences and their significance for shaping the trajectory of global environmental governance. We evaluate the impact of the Paris Agreement, juxtaposing the urgency of the IPCC's climate action warnings against the mitigations agreed upon. The chapter concludes by exploring

DOI: 10.4324/9781003494676-7

the challenges and opportunities associated with transforming the Paris Agreement's principles into actionable and enforceable mechanisms, particularly regarding the contentious issue of "loss and damage." We underscore the need for bridging governance gaps and enhancing the practical implementation of the agreement.

5.1 The Paris Agreement

In the long-standing discourse of sustainable development, the Paris Conference on Climate Change in 2015, also known as COP21, stands out as a turning point. The conference culminated in the signing of the Paris Agreement, an international treaty that fundamentally reshaped the trajectory of global climate policy. This landmark agreement has been signed and ratified by an impressive 187 countries, signifying broad international commitment to combatting climate change.

This chapter explores the Paris trajectories, detailing the evolution of global climate governance around the COP 21 conference's outcome—the Paris Agreement—that marked a promising shift from prior international climate agreements. Notably, it is the first-ever universally ratified agreement on climate change, mandating all nations to undertake efforts to combat climate change and adapt to its effects.

At the heart of the Paris Agreement is the ambitious target of limiting global warming to well below 2 degrees Celsius, compared to pre-industrial levels, and pursuing efforts to limit the temperature increase even further to 1.5 degrees Celsius. Such a goal is to prevent dangerous anthropogenic interference with the climate system.

The trajectory that COP21 set into motion continues to have far-reaching implications for global climate governance, environmental policy, and sustainable development. It represents a global consensus on the urgency of the climate crisis and a shared responsibility in addressing it. By exploring the Paris trajectories, we delve into the strategies, mechanisms, and challenges of implementing the Paris Agreement and working towards a more sustainable future.

In this chapter, we examine the significant aspects of the Paris Agreement and its implementation, the role of national and international actors in driving its objectives, and the interplay of the Paris Agreement with other sustainable development agendas.

Furthermore, we will evaluate the progress made since COP21 and the persistent challenges to achieving the agreement's ambitious targets. Finally, we will project the Paris trajectories into the future, examining potential paths and obstacles ahead in the global quest to stabilize the Earth's climate and achieve sustainable development.

5.2 From the Kyoto Protocol to the Paris Agreement

The precursors to the Paris Agreement provide a rich backdrop of initiatives and treaties that aim to address climate change at the international level. Central among these was the Kyoto Protocol, which came into force in 2005 and marked the first significant step towards binding nations into a commitment to reduce greenhouse gas emissions.

The Kyoto Protocol was established under the UNFCCC and helped set up international collaboration on tackling climate change. It mandated legally binding emission reduction targets for developed countries, known as Annex I countries, based on the principle of "common but differentiated responsibilities."

This approach recognized that developed nations, being largely responsible for past and current greenhouse gas emissions, should take the lead in combating climate change. However, the Kyoto Protocol was critiqued for excluding major emitters amongst developing countries (such as China and India) from its emission reduction targets.

Following the Kyoto Protocol, a series of annual COP meetings under the UNFCCC sought to build upon this foundational agreement. Notably, the Copenhagen Accord (COP15 in 2009) aimed to establish a more inclusive, albeit non-legally binding, framework that also involved developing nations in mitigation efforts. However, disagreements on the binding nature of the Accord and differentiation of responsibilities led to mixed outcomes.

The Doha Amendment to the Kyoto Protocol (2012) and the Cancun Agreements (2010) further progressed the international climate discourse, focusing on financing climate action in developing countries, deforestation issues, and technological support. But these instruments failed to spark global climate action at the scale required to prevent dangerous climate change impacts.[2]

The trajectory of these developments led to the landmark Paris Agreement in 2015. Unlike its predecessors, the Paris Agreement introduced Nationally Determined Contributions (NDCs), allowing countries to set their own emission reduction targets in accordance with their capacities and national circumstances. This made the agreement more inclusive and universally applicable. It was a breakthrough moment in the history of international climate governance, signaling a collective commitment to limiting global warming and adapting to the unavoidable impacts of climate change.

The Paris Agreement represents a significant evolution from its precursors. It maintains the principle of "common but differentiated responsibilities" but brings all nations into a common framework for action. Combining both bottom-up (through NDCs) and top-down (through a global temperature goal and regular review cycles) elements provide a more flexible and dynamic approach to addressing climate change. This reflects the recognition of the complex and interconnected nature of the climate crisis that needs different levels of commitment and participation from different countries, all towards a collective goal.[3]

5.3 The Evolution of Principles and Protocols

The evolution of principles and protocol dynamics from Kyoto to Paris represents a significant shift in international climate diplomacy. This transition has been shaped by changing political, economic, and environmental realities, which led to a broadened understanding of how to tackle climate change effectively and equitably.

1. **Binding Commitments to Voluntary Pledges:** The Kyoto Protocol imposed legally binding emissions reduction targets on developed countries. However, this approach met resistance due to perceived inequities and the absence of binding commitments for rapidly developing economies. Conversely, the Paris Agreement ushered in the NDCs system in which each country determines its targets, plans, and actions according to its capabilities and national circumstances.
2. **Differentiation:** Both the Kyoto Protocol and the Paris Agreement recognize the principle of "common but differentiated responsibilities and respective capabilities" (CBDR-RC),

acknowledging that different countries have contributed differently to the current state of the environment and have varying abilities to address these issues. However, the way this principle is operationalized in each agreement varies significantly. Under Kyoto, differentiation was starker, with emission reduction obligations imposed only on developed nations. Paris took a more nuanced approach, applying differentiation across various agreement elements (mitigation, adaptation, finance, etc.) and expecting all parties to enhance their efforts over time.

3. **Flexibility:** The Paris Agreement introduced a more flexible framework for international climate action. It combines bottom-up elements (NDCs) and top-down elements (global temperature goal, transparency, and review mechanisms) to create a dynamic system that can adapt to changing circumstances and progressively increase ambition.
4. **Transparency and Accountability:** While the Kyoto Protocol had mechanisms for transparency and accountability, these were significantly strengthened and expanded under the Paris Agreement. The Enhanced Transparency Framework under Paris is a more robust system for tracking and reporting countries' emissions and efforts, contributing to greater accountability and trust among nations.
5. **Scope of Action:** The Kyoto Protocol primarily focused on mitigation (reducing or preventing greenhouse gas emissions). The Paris Agreement, recognizing the interconnected nature of climate change impacts, significantly broadened this scope to include adaptation measures, loss and damage, finance, technology development and transfer, and capacity-building. It also placed greater emphasis on sustainable development and efforts to eradicate poverty.
6. **Long-Term Goals:** Both agreements aim to prevent dangerous anthropogenic interference with the climate system but articulate this objective differently. Kyoto imposed quantified emission limitation and reduction objectives on developed countries. On the other hand, the Paris Agreement set a more explicit long-term temperature goal, aiming to hold the global average temperature increase to well below 2 degrees Celsius above pre-industrial levels and pursuing efforts to limit the temperature increase to 1.5 degrees Celsius.

In summary, the evolution from Kyoto to Paris reflects an iterative learning process in international climate policy. While the Kyoto Protocol was the first effort to move in this direction, the Paris Agreement represents a more comprehensive, flexible, and inclusive framework for global climate action, responding to the lessons learned from previous efforts.[4]

5.4 The Resistance to Change and Its Lessons

The hesitancy to accept the Kyoto and Paris protocols emerged from various sources. Key among them were the question of equity, the mandatory nature of commitments, the economic costs associated with carbon reduction, the roles of developed and developing nations, and concerns over national sovereignty.

1. **Equity and Differentiation:** Both protocols faced criticism regarding their handling of differentiation between developed and developing countries. Some developed nations criticized the Kyoto Protocol for not imposing emission reduction obligations on major developing economies. While implementing a more flexible structure, the Paris Agreement faced pushback from developing nations who felt the agreement needed to sufficiently distinguish between the historical responsibilities of developed nations and the developmental needs of poorer nations.
2. **Mandatory vs. Voluntary Commitments:** The Kyoto Protocol was based on binding, top-down targets, which led to resistance from countries concerned about the potential economic impacts and the constraints on their national policy choices. The US, for instance, never ratified the Kyoto Protocol. In contrast, the Paris Agreement adopted a voluntary, bottom-up approach. While this has led to broad participation, it has also been criticized for potentially needing to be more effective as there are no enforcement mechanisms for the Nationally Determined Contributions.
3. **Economic Costs:** Reducing carbon emissions often implies a shift away from fossil fuels, which has significant economic implications, especially for countries heavily reliant on fossil fuel production and consumption. This has led to resistance as economies grapple with balancing economic growth and sustainable development.

4. **Changing Political Landscapes:** Changes in political administrations have played a significant role. The most notable example is the US—it did not ratify the Kyoto Protocol under the Bush administration, played a key role in shaping the Paris Agreement under President Obama, withdrew from it under President Trump, and re-joined under President Biden.
5. **National Sovereignty:** Some critics argue that international environmental agreements like Kyoto and Paris impinge on national sovereignty. This perspective views the restrictions or commitments as an intrusion on a country's freedom to manage its own resources and economic development.

The lessons from these resistances form valuable trajectories for global environmental governance:

1. **Embrace Differentiation:** Future protocols need to recognize a country's different capacities and responsibilities. Striking a balance between fairness and ambition is vital to achieving wide participation and substantial impact.
2. **Foster Flexibility:** The shift from mandatory to voluntary commitments has shown that flexibility can increase participation. However, the challenge is in ensuring that this flexibility doesn't lead to a lack of ambition or action.
3. **Enhance Transparency:** Transparency mechanisms must be strong to ensure that nations can hold each other accountable, building trust and facilitating collective action.
4. **Facilitate Finance and Technology Transfer:** Addressing climate change requires considerable resources. Assisting developing nations by providing finance and facilitating technology transfer is crucial for global efforts.
5. **Engage Diverse Stakeholders:** Going beyond nation-states to include cities, businesses, NGOs, and civil society can complement national actions and provide innovative solutions.

Drawing from the lessons of Kyoto and Paris, the evolution of global environmental governance may take on several trajectories:

1. **Emergence of Networked Governance:** As global environmental issues become more complex and interrelated, governance will likely shift from traditional nation-state

negotiations to a more networked approach. This involves diverse stakeholders, including non-state actors such as cities, businesses, NGOs, and civil society. These actors have shown significant promise in initiating actions on the ground. For instance, the Global Covenant of Mayors for Climate and Energy comprises thousands of cities voluntarily committing to ambitious climate action.

2. **Strengthening of Multilevel Governance:** This trajectory suggests strengthening coordination among different levels of governance—global, national, and subnational. Such a model can promote coherence between international commitments and national and local actions. It allows for a more flexible and context-specific approach, while still maintaining a global outlook.
3. **Evolution of Financing Mechanisms:** Financial support for developing nations is crucial for global efforts. This trajectory points towards the evolution of more innovative, diverse, and larger-scale financing mechanisms. These could include green bonds, climate funds, carbon pricing mechanisms, and public-private partnerships.
4. **Emphasis on Just Transition:** Future environmental governance will need to emphasize a "just transition"—that is, a shift towards a low-carbon economy that is fair and equitable. This means considering the social implications of climate policies, providing support for communities dependent on fossil fuel industries, and ensuring access to green jobs and sustainable development opportunities.
5. **Enhanced Use of Technology and Data:** Future trajectories may involve greater use of technology and data for monitoring, reporting and verification (MRV) of climate actions. This would enhance transparency and trust among nations. Additionally, technology can play a vital role in climate mitigation and adaptation actions, ranging from renewable energy to climate-smart agriculture.
6. **Resilience and Adaptation:** While mitigation remains crucial, the increased severity of climate impacts highlights the importance of resilience and adaptation. This suggests a trajectory where policies and actions are designed not only to reduce emissions but also to enhance the capacity of communities to adapt to changing climatic conditions.

These trajectories paint a picture of a more inclusive, comprehensive, flexible, and transparent global environmental governance system. They hint at the possibility of a paradigm shift from "governments" to "governance," where various stakeholders work in a synergistic manner to address environmental challenges.[5]

5.5 The Impact and Criticism of the Paris Agreement

The Paris Agreement, which emerged from the COP21 meeting in 2015, marked a significant shift in the global approach to climate change. Here are some of its impacts:

1. **Global Momentum and Multilateralism:** The Paris Agreement brought almost all nations into a common cause. As of September 2021, 190 out of 197 Parties to the UNFCCC have ratified the agreement. This show of multilateralism underscored a shared recognition of the climate crisis and built momentum for action.
2. **Framework for Action:** The agreement established a framework for limiting global warming to well below 2 degrees Celsius above pre-industrial levels, and pursuing efforts to limit it to 1.5 degrees Celsius. It provided each country the flexibility to set its own emission reduction targets, known as Nationally Determined Contributions, and a mechanism to ratchet up ambition over time.
3. **Enhancing Transparency:** The agreement introduced a transparency framework to track countries' progress in meeting their NDCs, promoting accountability and facilitating the sharing of best practices.
4. **Financing for Climate Action:** The Paris Agreement reaffirmed the commitment of developed countries to mobilize $100 billion a year in climate finance for developing countries by 2020, and to continue that level of support through 2025.

However, despite these advances, the Paris Agreement has faced criticism:

1. **Insufficient Ambition:** Current NDCs are insufficient to reach the goal of limiting global warming to 1.5 degrees Celsius. According to the UN Environment Programme, even if

all current NDCs are implemented, global temperatures are projected to rise by around 3 degrees Celsius by the end of the century.

2. **Slow Implementation:** The gap between commitment and action remains a concern. While most countries have ratified the agreement, the progress of implementation has been slow and uneven across countries.
3. **Inadequate Support for Vulnerable Countries:** There is ongoing concern that financial and technological support for adaptation and mitigation in developing and least developed countries is insufficient.

The question of "is it too little, too late?" can be debated. On the one hand, the Paris Agreement alone cannot solve the climate crisis, particularly given current levels of commitment and action. On the other hand, the Paris Agreement has set a critical framework for international cooperation and could serve as a foundation for more ambitious action in the future.[6]

The imperative for prompt and profound climate action has never been more explicit. As the IPCC's reports in 2021, 2022, and 2023 warn, urgent and sweeping reductions in greenhouse gas emissions are indispensable to staving off the direst impacts of climate change. The 2022 IPCC report delves deeper into the interplay between climate, ecosystems and biodiversity, and human societies, reflecting on non-climatic global trends unfolding in parallel, including unsustainable natural resource consumption, land and ecosystem degradation, rapid urbanization, demographic shifts, and socioeconomic disparities, all amidst a global pandemic.

Further escalating the urgency, the 2023 IPCC report confirms the looming reality that, despite numerous mitigation strategies stemming from the Paris Agreement, global warming is projected to surpass 1.5 degrees Celsius in the 21st century, making it increasingly challenging to cap warming below 2 degrees Celsius. It identifies a discrepancy between projected emissions from implemented policies and those outlined in the Nationally Determined Contributions. Additionally, it flags that finance flows are currently inadequate to meet climate goals across various sectors and regions.

Given these trends and the assessed data, it remains uncertain whether the Paris Agreement can effectively instigate the degree of action required to address this crisis. A significant challenge of the Paris Agreement, much like with other global climate-related treaties, lies in turning promises and principles into tangible actions, underpinned by robust enforcement mechanisms. The issue of "loss and damage," enshrined in Article 8 of the Paris Agreement, exemplifies the complex negotiations and unanswered questions that persist in the climate change discourse.

The inclusion of loss and damage within the Paris Agreement marked a key departure, but the distinction between it and adaptation remains blurred. Understanding this difference has legal and practical implications for the treaty's implementation. The legal repercussions of including loss and damage as an article in a legal treaty are still being explored.[7]

The question of how to best channel financial assistance and compensation to those affected by climate change loss and damage remains a point of contention. It is further complicated by gaps in the governance system around loss and damage. These gaps can result in inadequate policy responses and uneven distribution of resources.

Notes

1 Obama, B. (2015, December 12). *Statement by the President on the Paris Climate Agreement.* The White House. https://obamawhitehouse.archives.gov/the-press-office/2015/12/12/statement-president-paris-climate-agreement#:~:text=Today%2C%20thanks%20to%20strong%2C%20principled,Thanks
2 Mayer, B. (2018). *The International Law on Climate Change.* Cambridge University Press.
3 Klein, D. et al. (2017). The Paris Agreement on Climate Change: Analysis and Commentary. United Kingdom: OUP Oxford.
4 Johnson, J. (2017). *From Kyoto to Paris: Global Climate Accords.* United States: Cavendish Square Publishing.
5 Popovski, V. (2018). The Implementation of the Paris Agreement on Climate Change. United Kingdom: Taylor & Francis.
6 Van Calster, G., & Reins, L. (2021). *The Paris Agreement on Climate Change: A Commentary.* United Kingdom: Edward Elgar Publishing Limited.
7 Romera, B.M. and Broberg, M. (2021). *The Third Pillar of International Climate Change Policy: On 'Loss and Damage' After the Paris Agreement.* United Kingdom: Taylor & Francis.

6 The SDG Trajectories

> This Agenda is a plan of action for people, planet and prosperity. It also seeks to strengthen universal peace in larger freedom. We recognise that eradicating poverty in all its forms and dimensions, including extreme poverty, is the greatest global challenge and an indispensable requirement for sustainable development. All countries and all stakeholders, acting in collaborative partnership, will implement this plan. We are resolved to free the human race from the tyranny of poverty and want and to heal and secure our planet. We are determined to take the bold and transformative steps which are urgently needed to shift the world onto a sustainable and resilient path. As we embark on this collective journey, we pledge that no one will be left behind. The 17 Sustainable Development Goals and 169 targets which we are announcing today demonstrate the scale and ambition of this new universal Agenda. They seek to build on the Millennium Development Goals and complete what these did not achieve. They seek to realize the human rights of all and to achieve gender equality and the empowerment of all women and girls. They are integrated and indivisible and balance the three dimensions of sustainable development: the economic, social and environmental. The Goals and targets will stimulate action over the next fifteen years in areas of critical importance for humanity and the planet.
>
> (Preamble to *Transforming our World: the 2030 Agenda for Sustainable Development*, resolution adopted by the UN General Assembly on September 25, 2015[1])

Overview

This chapter reviews the genesis, implications, and challenges of the SDGs and the 2030 Agenda. It chronicles the journey from the MDGs to the SDGs, focusing on the transformative political trajectories that led to this new, holistic development agenda.

DOI: 10.4324/9781003494676-8

The chapter delves into the unique facets of the SDGs, including their universality, integration of sustainability domains, and the ambition of leaving no one behind. It also evaluates progress made, future projections, and systemic issues yet to be effectively addressed.

Moreover, the chapter explores resistance to the SDGs, addressing conflicts with national priorities, economic concerns, and policy compatibility. It highlights the need for global cooperation to realize the SDGs' transformative vision. This chapter provides valuable insights into the SDGs as significant political trajectories toward a sustainable, inclusive world.

6.1 The Post-2015 Trajectories

The post-2015 process was crucial for critically evaluating the achievements and limitations of the MDGs. Subsequently, it paved the way for the establishment of the SDGs. This process was critical in global development policies and commitments, marking a shift towards more holistic, integrated, and ambitious targets.

The journey to the SDGs began with a broad recognition that while the MDGs had spurred significant progress in certain areas, they fell short in others. Criticisms included their top-down nature, lack of attention to environmental sustainability, absence of precise mechanisms for accountability, and the reductionist view of poverty.

A robust and inclusive consultation process was initiated to shape the new agenda in response to these shortcomings. The initial stages of the process included the establishment of a UN System Task Team, a High-Level Panel of Eminent Persons, and broad consultations on regional, national, and global levels, which includes civil society, academia, businesses, and other stakeholders.

One of the key outputs of this process was the *Panel on the Post-2015 Development Agenda Report*, which underscored the need for a shift from traditional aid models to a more holistic approach to development. This marked the first significant step in the conceptualization of the SDGs.

Following these consultations, in 2014, the Open Working Group on SDGs proposed a set of 17 goals with 169 targets, which, after a year of intergovernmental negotiations, were formally adopted by the UN General Assembly in September 2015 as part of the 2030 Agenda for Sustainable Development.

Unlike the MDGs, the SDGs' development was characterized by a more inclusive and transparent process, reflecting diverse voices and perspectives. The new framework marked a significant step forward in addressing the integrated nature of sustainable development and aligning this with the needs of people, the planet, prosperity, peace, and partnerships.

This chapter further analyzes the specific merits of this process, the goals themselves, and their ongoing implementation and challenges as we continue to navigate the trajectories toward global sustainable development.

Between 2005 and 2015, other important conferences and events were instrumental in reviewing the progress of the MDGs and preparing for the next iteration of the goals. These pivotal moments include the 2005 World Summit (MDG+5), the High-Level Meeting on the MDGs in 2008, the MDG Summit in 2010, and the President of the General Assembly's Special Event towards achieving the MDGs in 2013.

6.1.1 The 2005 World Summit

The 2005 World Summit was the major follow-up summit meeting after the United Nations' 2000 Millennium Summit with its Millennium Declaration and the establishment of the MDGs. The 2005 Summit was pivotal point in the trajectory of international development, providing a critical opportunity to review the progress on the MDGs, which were then at the five-year mark, and helped set up the next phase of the global development agenda.

The event brought together an unprecedented number of world leaders, reflecting the scale and importance of the challenges under discussion. The summit's agenda was structured around Secretary-General Kofi Annan's *In Larger Freedom Report* which proposed comprehensive reforms to address the interconnected challenges of development, security, and human rights.

The report was far-reaching in its scope and ambition, pushing for a more robust global partnership for development. It called for a renewed commitment to meeting the MDGs, more efficient use of resources, robust accountability mechanisms, and a more coherent and integrated approach to peace and security.

Notably, the report underscored the importance of integrating environmental sustainability into development strategies, marking a significant shift in global discourse and helping prepare everyone for the subsequent inclusion of sustainability in the SDGs.

The outcomes of the 2005 Summit, as outlined in the *Summit Outcome Document*, highlighted the achievements and shortcomings of the MDG agenda. While it noted significant progress in some areas, it also underscored the uneven progress across goals and regions and the persistent resource gaps, including the need to address new and emerging challenges.

The summit also produced several significant agreements, including the responsibility to protect populations from genocide, war crimes, ethnic cleansing, and crimes against humanity, and the creation of the Peacebuilding Commission and the United Nations Human Rights Council (UNHRC). It also committed to achieving universal access to treatment for HIV/AIDS.

Overall, the 2005 World Summit represented a critical juncture, sparking debates and discussions that ultimately helped shape the post-2015 development agenda. These debates emphasized the interconnectedness of development, peace, security, and human rights, the importance of sustainability, and the need for global partnerships—themes that would later be at the heart of the SDGs. The summit marked an important milestone in the trajectory of global development, acknowledging the successes and limitations of the MDGs and preparing for the broader and more ambitious SDG framework.

6.1.2 The 2008 Halftime Review

The High-Level Meeting on Achieving the MDGs in 2008 marked another significant milestone in the trajectory of achieving the MDGs and the broader development agenda. It brought together international leaders to take stock of progress, identify gaps, and pledge to redouble efforts to achieve the MDGs by the 2015 deadline.

At the midpoint in the timeline towards 2015, it was evident that while some progress had been made, it needed to be more balanced and sufficient to meet the MDGs across all regions and sectors. Specific goals, such as those related to maternal health and environmental sustainability, needed to be revised.

The meeting was a clear call to action, emphasizing the need to step up efforts, mobilize resources, and implement effective strategies to accelerate progress.

A notable feature of the High-Level Meeting was the call for leaders to announce specific plans and proposals for achieving the MDGs. This served two essential functions. First, it highlighted the responsibility of individual countries in driving progress towards the MDGs, encouraging accountability at the national level. Second, it facilitated sharing best practices, enabling countries to learn from each other's successes and challenges.

The meeting also highlighted the importance of partnerships in achieving the MDGs. It recognized that progress required the concerted efforts of all stakeholders—governments, international organizations, civil society, and the private sector—and encouraged greater collaboration and coordination among these different actors.

Overall, the High-Level Meeting in 2008 helped to reinvigorate the global commitment to the MDGs and created momentum for their implementation. It reinforced the MDGs as a central reference point for international development, setting the stage for the development of the SDGs and continuing the trajectory towards a more inclusive, sustainable, and resilient future.

6.1.3 The 2010 MDG Summit

The Global Strategy for Women's and Children's Health, launched during the Millennium Development Goals Summit in 2010, was a pivotal event that brought women's and children's health issues to the forefront of the global development agenda. The strategy aimed at accelerating progress towards achieving the health-related MDGs, particularly MDG 5, which focused on reducing maternal mortality.

The strategy was born from the realization that, despite some progress, the world was significantly off track in meeting MDG 5. High maternal mortality rates remained a stark indicator of health inequities, and an alarmingly large number of women continued to die from preventable causes related to pregnancy and childbirth. Furthermore, a lack of progress on women's and children's health had ripple effects on all other MDGs, highlighting the interconnected nature of the goals.

Adopting the Global Strategy for Women's and Children's Health clearly demonstrated renewed political will and commitment to address these challenges. Over $40 billion in aid was pledged at the summit, with contributions from various stakeholders, including heads of state and government, private sector entities, foundations, international organizations, civil society, and research institutions.

This marked a significant shift in the trajectory towards achieving the MDGs, particularly in the field of women's and children's health. The strategy signaled a new level of global consensus on the importance of investing in women's and children's health as a fundamental driver of socioeconomic development. This development included specific goals for women's and children's health in the subsequent SDGs.

In conclusion, the Global Strategy for Women's and Children's Health was a landmark event in the trajectory of the global development agenda. It helped intensify progress in the area of women's and children's health, leading to increased commitment, coordination, and investment, thereby setting a path towards the more ambitious targets of the SDGs.

6.1.4 The 2013 Special Event

The President of the United Nations General Assembly (UNGA)'s Special Event towards Achieving the MDGs, held on September 25, 2013, was indeed a significant juncture in the transition from the MDGs to the SDGs. This event set the realization that while significant strides had been made under the MDGs, there was still a vast amount of work to be done, especially considering the emerging and future challenges of the time.

Member states used this occasion to reaffirm their commitment to achieving the MDGs by 2015 and, importantly, agreed to convene a High-Level Summit in September 2015 to adopt a new set of goals. This pivotal decision acknowledged the necessity of a post-2015 development agenda that would address the unfinished business of the MDGs and confront new challenges.

The envisaged goals were to strike a balance among three critical dimensions of sustainable development: economic transformation, social justice, and environmental protection. This holistic view shifted from the MDGs' focus primarily on social issues. The new trajectory acknowledged that economic growth was a necessary (but not sufficient) condition for poverty alleviation, social justice was integral to creating equitable societies, and environmental protection was non-negotiable in a time of increasing ecological fragility.

In summary, the 2013 Special Event played a crucial role in shaping the trajectory of the SDGs. By considering the strengths and weaknesses of the MDGs and recognizing the need for a more balanced, holistic approach to global development, this event established the formulation and subsequent adoption of the SDGs in 2015.[2]

6.2 The Trajectories of the 2030 Agenda

The 2015 event, namely the United Nations Sustainable Development Summit held in September 2015, marked the official transition from the MDGs to the SDGs. In this historical moment, 193 countries unanimously adopted the 2030 Agenda for Sustainable Development, outlining a roadmap to achieving a set of 17 SDGs, encompassing 169 targets. This transition represented a shift in global developmental trajectories, with lessons learned from the MDGs informing the creation of the SDGs.

Firstly, the SDGs expanded the thematic scope of the MDGs. While the MDGs primarily focused on social development issues in developing countries, the SDGs have a more universal focus, applicable to all countries regardless of their development status. The SDGs cover many themes: inequality, infrastructure, industrialization, urbanization, peace, and justice. This acknowledges that sustainability challenges are interconnected, cross-border issues that demand comprehensive solutions.

Secondly, the process of formulating the SDGs was far more inclusive than that of the MDGs. The creation of the MDGs was criticized for being a top-down process, primarily driven by technocrats and experts. In contrast, the SDGs were formulated through an extensive multi-stakeholder process that included national governments, civil society, the private sector, and the academic community. This inclusive process signified a shift towards a more participatory global governance approach.

Thirdly, the SDGs introduced an integrated vision of development, recognizing the interlinkages between social, economic, and environmental dimensions of sustainability. This was encapsulated in the five guiding principles of the 2030 Agenda:

People, Planet, Prosperity, Peace, and Partnership (the 5Ps). This trajectory indicates an evolution in understanding the complexity and interconnectedness of sustainability challenges.

Lastly, the SDGs aim to leave no one behind, explicitly focusing on reaching the most vulnerable first. This is a critical trajectory that highlights the commitment to addressing inequality and promoting inclusivity, thereby ensuring that development benefits are equitably distributed.

Ultimately, the trajectories emerging from the 2015 event and the formulation of the 2030 Agenda signify a broadening in scope, a commitment to inclusivity and participation, an integrated vision of sustainability, and a focused drive to address inequality. These trajectories guide the global development agenda towards a more sustainable, equitable, and inclusive future.

6.3 The SDG Trajectories

The 17 SDGs and the 169 targets underpinning them were designed to encapsulate the most critical areas that need addressing to achieve a sustainable and equitable future for all. These goals and targets embody the five key principles or the 5Ps—People, Planet, Prosperity, Peace, and Partnerships—reflecting a holistic and integrated approach to sustainable development.

1. **People:** The goals related to "people" aim to end poverty and hunger in all forms and ensure dignity and equality for all. This is reflected in goals such as No Poverty (SDG 1), Zero Hunger (SDG 2), Good Health and Well-being (SDG 3), Quality Education (SDG 4), Gender Equality (SDG 5), and Reduced Inequalities (SDG 10). These goals were prioritized in recognition of the fact that human well-being forms the basis of any developmental effort.
2. **Planet:** Recognizing the ecological boundaries of our planet, several goals aim to protect our ecosystems for future generations. These include Clean Water and Sanitation (SDG 6), Affordable and Clean Energy (SDG 7), Responsible Consumption and Production (SDG 12), Climate Action (SDG 13), Life below Water (SDG 14), and Life on Land (SDG 15). These goals emerged from an increasing awareness of environmental degradation and the need for sustainable resource use.

3. **Prosperity:** Prosperity goals aim to ensure that all people enjoy prosperous and fulfilling lives but do so in harmony with nature. These include Decent Work and Economic Growth (SDG 8), Industry, Innovation, and Infrastructure (SDG 9), and Sustainable Cities and Communities (SDG 11). The focus here is on creating conditions for sustainable economic growth, acknowledging the need for employment, innovation, and infrastructure.
4. **Peace:** SDG 16 is solely devoted to Peace, Justice, and Strong Institutions, highlighting the necessity of peace, stability, human rights, and effective governance for achieving sustainable development. This goal acknowledges the role of peaceful societies and accountable institutions in underpinning development progress.
5. **Partnerships:** Lastly, SDG 17, Partnerships for the Goals, underlines the importance of cooperation and partnerships in achieving the SDGs. This goal recognizes that global challenges require collective action and that no country can achieve these ambitious targets alone.

Why were these goals chosen and not others? The SDGs resulted from a comprehensive and inclusive process involving member states, civil society, the private sector, and academia. This broad-based participation enabled a wide range of perspectives to be incorporated, ensuring that the goals cover all critical aspects of sustainable development. Also, lessons learned from the MDGs played a significant role in articulating the SDGs, specifically the need for an integrated approach, the importance of addressing inequality, and the necessity of environmental sustainability. Finally, these goals aligned with the aspirations outlined in the UN Charter and the Universal Declaration of Human Rights, aiming to "free the human race from the tyranny of poverty and want and to heal and secure our planet."[3]

6.4 The SDG Principles

The 2030 Agenda for Sustainable Development represents a substantial evolution in the discourse for sustainable development, marking a shift from the MDGs, which were more targeted at developing countries. The SDGs, in contrast, are universal and apply to all countries, recognizing the interconnectedness of our world. Here are the fundamental principles that underpin the SDGs:

1. **Universality:** Unlike the MDGs, the SDGs apply to every nation, not just developing countries. The challenges addressed by the SDGs are global in nature and require the commitment of all countries for their resolution.
2. **Integration:** The SDGs recognize that social, economic, and environmental issues are deeply intertwined and cannot be addressed in isolation. This is a significant advancement over the MDGs which treated various areas of development as distinct.
3. **Inclusivity:** The SDGs aim to "leave no one behind." This represents an increased focus on reaching the most vulnerable and marginalized populations, ensuring that progress is evenly distributed.
4. **Human Rights and Gender Equality:** The SDGs put a stronger emphasis on human rights and gender equality than the MDGs, recognizing these as essential elements of sustainable development.
5. **Participation and Partnerships:** The SDGs encourage the active participation of all stakeholders—governments, civil society, the private sector, and citizens—in the process of achieving sustainable development. This multi-stakeholder approach acknowledges the need for collective action.
6. **Accountability and Transparency:** The SDGs have a comprehensive framework for follow-up and review, ensuring that countries are held accountable for their commitments.

These principles signal an evolution in the discourse for sustainable development in several ways. Firstly, they acknowledge the complexity and interrelatedness of sustainable development challenges, moving away from the siloed approach of the MDGs. Secondly, they emphasize the necessity of including all stakeholders in the development process, recognizing that top-down approaches are insufficient. Thirdly, they prioritize social inclusion and equality, recognizing that sustainable development cannot be achieved unless its benefits reach all sections of society. Finally, by applying to all countries, the SDGs acknowledge that issues like poverty, inequality, and environmental degradation are not confined to the developing world but are global challenges that require a global response.[4]

6.5 The Progress and Projections for 2030

Assessing progress toward the SDGs and projections for 2030 is a complex task due to the wide range of goals, targets, and indicators involved, as well as differing national and regional contexts. The United Nations provides regular updates on the progress towards the SDGs in its annual *Sustainable Development Goals Report*. At the time of this writing, about six years before 2030, progress is being made in many places, but, overall, action to meet the goals is not yet advancing at the speed or scale required.

In general, prior to the COVID-19 pandemic, progress was observed in several areas, including a decrease in global poverty rates, improvements in health in some regions, and increased access to electricity. However, progress was uneven across regions and even within countries, and many targets needed to be on track. For example, progress in reducing hunger and combating climate change needed to be improved, and in some cases, progress was reversing. The impact of the COVID-19 pandemic has also exacerbated existing inequalities and reversed progress in several areas.

In addition, the persistence and escalation of conflict devastates societal structures and disrupts various natural cycles and ecosystem services. Prior to the onset of the Russian-Ukrainian conflict in 2022, nearly half of the natural gas and a third of the oil consumed by European Union nations was sourced from Russia. The Russian act of aggression, followed by consequential sanctions imposed on Russia, led to an energy price surge of a magnitude unseen since the 1970s. This war further unsettled global trade, which was in the process of recuperating from the effects of the pandemic. Such crises undermine the progress toward the 2030 Agenda and the achievements of SDG goals and targets by 2030 and 2050.

In terms of projections for 2030, the outlook depends heavily on how quickly the world recovers from the COVID-19 pandemic, how peaceful solutions to conflicts will emerge, and how effectively countries implement strategies for sustainable development. Likely, some goals related to poverty reduction, education, and health will only be fully met by some countries, given the current pace of progress.

Many challenges remain in achieving the SDGs. Significant barriers to achieving the goals are systemic issues such as socioeconomic inequality, inadequate policy integration, weak institutional capacity, insufficient financing, and data gaps.

Intersecting topics like refugees, disability, and mental health are recognized within the SDGs but could benefit from more explicit attention and action. For instance, Goal 10 aims to reduce inequality within countries and implicitly includes refugees. A separate target on refugees would encourage more focused action. Similarly, Goal 3 aims to ensure health and well-being for all. Mental health could be more comprehensively addressed with a separate target of its own.

Addressing these complex issues requires transformative change that considers the interconnected nature of the SDGs, including changes in governance, economic structures, and societal norms. Moreover, it requires global solidarity and the recognition that these are shared problems that need cooperative solutions. It is critical to emphasize that the SDGs are not separate goals to be achieved independently but are deeply interconnected. Achieving one goal can significantly impact the achievement of others.

The Sustainable Development Goals Report 2020 provides a snapshot of the progress on the SDGs prior to the outbreak of the COVID-19 pandemic while also highlighting the initial devastating impacts of the virus on specific goals and targets. This report, an outcome of collaboration between the United Nations Department of Economic and Social Affairs and over 200 experts from 40+ international agencies, relied on the most recent data and estimates.

Before the pandemic hit, the report acknowledges that strides had been made in a few areas, including maternal and child health enhancement, expanded electricity access, and increased female representation in government. However, setbacks such as rising food insecurity, environmental degradation, and persistent inequalities overshadowed these improvements.

The COVID-19 crisis, being a novel and unparalleled event, brought about further disruptions to SDG progress, with the worst impacts being felt by the poorest and the most vulnerable, including children, the elderly, persons with disabilities, migrants, refugees, and women.

Key findings of the report include:

1. The pandemic threatens to push an estimated 71 million people back into extreme poverty in 2020, marking the first rise in global poverty since 1998. The loss of income, inadequate social protection, and inflation might render even those previously secure vulnerable to poverty and hunger.

2. Due to the crisis, around 1.6 billion workers in the informal economy, accounting for half of the global workforce, face significant impacts. These already vulnerable workers are likely to see their incomes fall by 60% in the initial month of the crisis.
3. Over one billion people living in slums worldwide are extremely vulnerable to COVID-19 due to inadequate housing, shared sanitation facilities, overcrowded public transport, and limited access to healthcare services.
4. The pandemic disproportionately affects women and children. Disruptions to health and vaccination services may lead to additional deaths among children under 5 and mothers. Many countries reported an increase in domestic violence incidents against women and children.
5. School closures have impacted 90% of students globally, causing over 370 million children to miss out on school meals. Remote learning is inaccessible to many due to the lack of computers and internet connectivity at home.
6. The plummet of families into extreme poverty increases the risk of child labor, child marriage, and child trafficking, reversing global gains in reducing child labor for the first time in 20 years.
7. The report also warns that climate change is progressing at a pace faster than anticipated. With 2019 being the second warmest year on record, land degradation, species extinction, and unsustainable consumption and production patterns continue unabated.

In essence, the report underscores the multifaceted challenges posed by the pandemic and re-emphasizes the need for a robust and coordinated global response to meet the SDGs. [5]

6.6 The SDG Limits and Innovations

The political trajectories represented by the SDGs and the 2030 Agenda reflect a global shift towards a more integrated, inclusive, and sustainable development paradigm. Here are the main trajectories:

1. **Integrated Approach:** The SDGs recognize the interconnectedness of economic, social, and environmental issues. This contrasts with past approaches that often dealt with issues

such as poverty, environment, and human rights separately. The SDGs encompass a broad range of issues from poverty reduction to climate change, gender equality, and responsible consumption, reflecting a holistic approach.

2. **Global Inclusivity and Partnership:** The SDGs apply to all countries, not just developing ones. This universal application is significant as it acknowledges that challenges such as climate change and inequality are global. The SDGs also emphasize the importance of partnerships (Goal 17) among governments, the private sector, and civil society.
3. **Leave No One Behind:** One of the critical principles of the SDGs is to ensure that development reaches the most marginalized and vulnerable populations. This is a commitment to ensure that development benefits are shared equitably.
4. **Accountability and Monitoring:** The 2030 Agenda strongly emphasizes data's role in monitoring progress and ensuring accountability. The SDGs come with a set of targets and indicators that are meant to provide concrete metrics for tracking progress.
5. **Sustainability:** The 2030 Agenda strongly emphasizes sustainability, ensuring that development today does not compromise the ability of future generations to meet their own needs. This is reflected not only in the goals directly related to the environment but also in goals related to economic and social issues.

Despite these positive trajectories, there has been resistance from some quarters for various reasons:

1. **National Sovereignty:** Some governments see the SDGs as an imposition on their national sovereignty and are wary of external influence over their development policies.
2. **Resource Constraints and Prioritization:** Implementing the SDGs requires significant resources. Some countries are concerned about how to finance these efforts and may prioritize short-term economic gains over long-term sustainable development.
3. **Incompatibility with Existing Policies or Interests:** Certain goals may conflict with the interests of powerful groups within countries. For example, goals related to reducing inequality or combating climate change may be perceived as threats by economic elites or industries like fossil fuels.

4. **Complexity and Scope:** The sheer number of goals and targets can be overwhelming for some governments, especially in developing countries with limited capacities to address such a wide array of challenges.

What is innovative about the SDGs:

1. **Universality:** Unlike the MDGs, which focused primarily on development in poorer nations, the SDGs apply to all countries. This recognizes that challenges like inequality and environmental sustainability are global issues.
2. **Integration:** The SDGs' integrated approach recognizes the connections between the social, economic, and environmental issues and seeks to address them holistically.
3. **Inclusivity and Stakeholder Engagement:** The SDG framework was developed through an inclusive process that sought input from governments, civil society, the private sector, and other stakeholders. This broad-based engagement was itself an innovative method to collect feedback.
4. **Detailed Targets and Indicators:** The SDGs' specific targets and indicators aim to create accountability and enable the measurement of progress more rigorously than past frameworks.

Overall, the SDGs represent an ambitious and innovative agenda for global sustainable development. However, the success of this agenda will depend on the collective efforts of all stakeholders and the willingness of countries to make the necessary commitments and compromises.[6]

6.7 The Summit of the Future: *Our Common Agenda*

The Secretary-General's vision, captured within *Our Common Agenda* report, emphasizes re-evaluating our SDG approach as we edge closer to 2030. This call to action is rooted in the belief that a new form of multilateralism, one that is inclusive, networked, and effective, can be our guiding light. Such an approach can ensure that global cooperation is maintained and enhanced to address existing and emergent challenges, delivering tangible benefits for everyone and the planet.

6.7.1 Impact of Global Challenges on SDG Progress

Unforeseen global challenges have dramatically altered the trajectory towards achieving the SDGs. The devastating effects of the COVID-19 pandemic have reversed years of progress in diverse areas, ranging from health and economic growth to education and the fight against inequalities. As health infrastructures were stretched to their limits, the cascading consequences disrupted global supply chains and crippled economies, causing rising unemployment and deepening poverty. Adding to these complications, the war in Ukraine intensified human suffering and strained international ties, diverting crucial resources and attention from sustainable development initiatives. The culmination of the triple planetary crisis, characterized by climate change, biodiversity loss, and escalating pollution, further underlines the world's multifaceted challenges.

6.7.2 A Renewed Global Commitment: The Summit of the Future

The looming challenges underscore the primary objective of *Our Common Agenda*—to convene a Summit of the Future in 2024. This summit aspires to be more than just a discussion platform. It represents a moment of global recalibration, an opportunity to redefine the essence of cooperation, to mend structural and governance shortcomings, and to solidify robust, actionable pathways to achieve the SDGs. Drawing from insights gathered during the 2023 SDG Summit, this pivotal event in 2024 aims to reassess and recalibrate priorities in light of recent setbacks, reaffirm global commitments, spark deeper international collaboration, and innovate governance structures for more responsive and adaptable multilateralism.

6.7.3 Commitments for *Our Common Agenda*

The 2021 *Our Common Agenda* report by UN Secretary-General António Guterres outlines a vision of collaboration, foresight, and adaptive governance. This vision encompasses six central objectives that emphasize important trajectories emerging at the halfway mark to the 2030 Agenda. It also suggests some urgent priorities to be considered by policymakers and the international community for the future agenda:[7]

1. **Global Solidarity and the Common Good:** The report emphasizes the need for renewed global solidarity, focusing especially on immediate requirements like a worldwide vaccination plan against COVID-19. Addressing the tripartite planetary crisis of climate change crisis, biodiversity loss, and pollution is central to this objective, aiming to preserve the planet for present and future generations.
2. **Renewing the Social Contract:** Mr. Guterres calls for a refreshed social contract that reinforces trust between governments and their citizens. This entails acknowledging comprehensive human rights, ensuring the active participation of women and girls, and prioritizing public welfare through improved governance. There's a push for universal access to health, education, decent work, housing, and the internet as a fundamental right by 2030. Inclusive national consultations are proposed, allowing citizens to shape their country's future.
3. **Combatting Misinformation—The "Infodemic":** The report identifies the urgency of battling the misinformation pandemic, advocating for a unified, fact-based worldview. Mr. Guterres emphasizes the importance of science and expertise in policy and budgetary decisions and proposes a global code of conduct for public information integrity.
4. **Re-Evaluating Economic Metrics:** The report critically examines the limited perspective offered by traditional economic metrics like GDP, which may overlook the environmental or social costs associated with certain business activities. Mr. Guterres suggests the development of complementary metrics to provide a more holistic understanding of economic impacts on people and the environment.
5. **Prioritizing the Future and Younger Generations:** The emphasis here is on forward-thinking, catering to the youths' and future generations' needs. Proposals include repurposing the Trusteeship Council, establishing a Futures Lab, and creating roles such as a Special Envoy for Future Generations. These initiatives intend to ensure that policies consider long-term consequences. Furthermore, there's a call for enhanced readiness to anticipate and tackle global risks,

suggested via instruments like a regular Strategic Foresight and Global Risk Report and a potential Emergency Platform for global crises.

6. **Strengthening and Networking Multilateral Systems:** Mr. Guterres envisions a robust, networked, and inclusive multilateral system rooted in the United Nations. Suggestions include a new peace agenda, multi-stakeholder dialogues on outer space, a Global Digital Compact, and increased engagement between global entities like the Group of 20 (G-20) and the Economic and Social Council (ECOSOC). The aim is to enhance the adaptability of the UN and involve various stakeholders, including local and regional governments, in global decision-making processes.

6.7.4 The Critical Juncture of *Our Common Agenda*

The release of the *Our Common Agenda* report by the UN Secretary-General came at a pivotal time. The world grappled with challenges like the COVID-19 pandemic and the existential threat of climate change, while also navigating the complex terrains of effective peacebuilding processes, and fast technological advancements. Concurrently, progress toward achieving the SDGs seemed to stagnate. The report emphasized our intensified global interconnectedness and articulated an urgent need to rejuvenate the multilateral system.

6.7.5 Solidarity and Renewed Multilateralism

At the heart of *Our Common Agenda* were two interconnected ideas. The first centered on fostering a renewed sense of solidarity—bridging divides between people, nations, and generations. The second underscored the necessity for a revitalized multilateral system, ensuring that existing global commitments are accelerated and that new emerging gaps in global governance, identified since 2015, are effectively addressed.

6.7.6 The Summit of the Future: A Landmark Event

The "Summit of the Future" was proposed to capture these aspirations. Envisioned as a transformative event, it aims to set a fresh course for global cooperation. Following the foundation set by the SDG Summit in 2023, the Summit of the Future in September 2024 is anticipated to culminate in an "action-oriented Pact for the Future." This pact is organized into five distinct yet interrelated chapters:

1. **Sustainable Development and Financing:** The planned Summit of the Future focuses on the practical aspects of achieving the SDGs, particularly emphasizing the financial mechanisms that will drive these initiatives.
2. **Peace and Security:** Delving into global peace and trust-building measures, this summit aims to underscore the importance of cooperative strategies for international security.
3. **Technological Advancement:** Recognizing the swift technological changes afoot, this summit aims to emphasize harnessing these for collective good while mitigating potential risks or divisions.
4. **Engaging the Youth:** This summit aims to accentuate the importance of the youth, advocating for their active participation and ensuring their aspirations are central to shaping future policies.
5. **Global Governance Reimagined:** This summit aims to critically evaluate the existing global governance structures, proposing reforms to make them more inclusive, adaptive, and effective.

The United Nations Secretary-General (UNSG) provided 11 in-depth Policy Briefs to support the preparation for this transformative summit. These documents offer an expansive view of specific proposals from *Our Common Agenda*, ensuring member states have a robust foundation to make informed decisions. Both *Our Common Agenda* and the forthcoming Summit of the Future represent a global commitment to chart a path of unity, innovation, and shared responsibility. Together, they aim to craft a vision for a future that's not only sustainable but also equitable for all. These trajectories reflect the priorities that emerged in the UN75 Declaration *The Future We Want; The United Nations We Need* (September 2020). This was a process of global consultations with people worldwide on their hopes and fears for the future. Twelve key insights emerged from these dialogues that culminated in the UN75 Declaration adopted by world leaders in September 2020. These insights were expressed as commitments and as collective aspirations of the member states in various critical areas, ranging from environmental protection to gender equality, digital cooperation, peace and security, and more.[8]

1. **We Will Leave No One Behind:** This commitment emphasizes the importance of inclusive growth, equality, and social protection for all.
2. **We Will Protect Our Planet:** Reflects the urgency of addressing environmental challenges, notably climate change, biodiversity loss, and pollution.
3. **We Will Promote Peace and Prevent Conflict:** This underscores the UN's foundational goal of maintaining international peace and security.
4. **We Will Abide by International Law and Ensure Justice:** Reinforces the importance of the international legal framework and the peaceful resolution of disputes.
5. **We Will Place Women and Girls at the Center:** A commitment to gender equality, recognizing the central role of women in development, peace, and security.
6. **We Will Build Trust:** This speaks to the need for improving transparency, accountability, and effectiveness in global governance.
7. **We Will Improve Digital Cooperation:** Recognizes the growing significance of the digital realm in every facet of life and the need for better global cooperation in this arena.
8. **We Will Upgrade the United Nations:** Focuses on making the UN more transparent, accountable, and efficient.
9. **We Will Ensure Sustainable Financing:** Emphasizes the importance of having the necessary resources to address global challenges.
10. **We Will Boost Partnerships:** Reflects the understanding that complex global challenges require the concerted effort of various stakeholders, including the private sector, civil society, and international organizations.
11. **We Will Listen to And Work with Youth:** Recognizes the importance of involving the younger generation in decision-making processes, as they will be the ones most affected by today's decisions in the future.

12. **We Will Be Prepared:** Highlights the need for readiness in facing emerging and future challenges, be they health crises like pandemics, environmental disasters, or other unforeseen events.

6.7.7 SDG Summit High-Impact Initiatives

The 2023 SDG Summit was a crucial event that underscored the commitment of the international community to accelerate progress towards achieving the SDGs by 2030. The summit highlighted the urgency of action given the approaching deadline and the world's various challenges. It focused on 12 high-impact initiatives.[9]

1. **Energy Compacts:** Focuses on amplifying global efforts to achieve SDG7, ensuring access to affordable, reliable, sustainable, and modern energy for all.
2. **Nature Driving Economic Transformation:** Highlights the vital role biodiversity and nature play in driving equitable economic progress and sustainable development.
3. **Food Systems Transformation:** Emphasizes the need to revolutionize our food systems to eradicate hunger, improve nutrition, and promote sustainable agriculture.
4. **Transforming Education:** Recognizes that quality education is the foundation for a better future, emphasizing inclusivity and lifelong learning.
5. **Global Accelerator:** Addresses the need for jobs and robust social protection systems, ensuring that the transition to a sustainable economy is just and equitable.
6. **Digital Public Infrastructure:** Promotes the importance of creating inclusive and open digital ecosystems to facilitate the achievement of the SDGs.
7. **The SDG Stimulus:** Focuses on channeling long-term financing that's both accessible and affordable for the realization of the SDGs.
8. **Transforming4Trade:** Seeks a shift in trade paradigms to boost economic development and ensure that trade benefits all.
9. **Local2030 Coalition:** Emphasizes the importance of local action and strategies in achieving the SDGs by the 2030 deadline.

10. **FutureGov:** Aims to build the capacities of public sectors, ensuring they're equipped to meet future challenges.
11. **Power of Data:** Highlights the transformative potential of data in tracking, evaluating, and achieving the SDGs.
12. **Spotlight Initiative:** A crucial initiative dedicated to eradicating violence against women and girls, recognizing gender equality as a core pillar of sustainable development.

Drawing from past trajectories, how previous actions and decisions have shaped our present state becomes evident. As we reflect on these historical patterns and anticipate the future, we stand on the cusp of several upcoming summits that will set the stage for the new agenda post-2030. Moreover, special sessions on gender equality, digitalization, and development in complex settings serve not only as deep dives into critical components of SDG success but also as bridges between our past experiences and future ambitions. These topics are imperative, encompassing the essential themes of inclusivity, modernization, and the nuanced challenges observed in varied contexts.

The 2023 SDG Summit, while rooted in the lessons of the past, presents a forward-looking vision and showcases the unwavering commitment of the global community to forge a brighter future. With enhanced clarity on these initiatives and fortified commitments from world leaders, the summit is poised to collaboratively address challenges, inspiring renewed enthusiasm, momentum, and unified action as we journey towards the 2030 milestones and beyond.

Notes

1 United Nations (2015). *Transforming Our World: The 2030 Agenda for Sustainable Development | Department of Economic and Social Affairs*. https://sdgs.un.org/2030agenda#:~:text=We%20resolve%2C%20between%20now%20and,protection%20of%20the%20planet%20and

2 Dodds, F., Donoghue, A.D., & Leiva Roesch, J. (2016). *Negotiating the Sustainable Development Goals: A Transformational Agenda for an Insecure World*. United Kingdom: Taylor & Francis.

3 Hanson, K.T., Puplampu, K.P., & Shaw, T.M. (2017). *From Millennium Development Goals to Sustainable Development Goals: Rethinking African Development*. United Kingdom: Taylor & Francis.

4 van Tulder, R., & van Mil, E. (2022). *Principles of Sustainable Business: Frameworks for Corporate Action on the SDGs*. United Kingdom: Taylor & Francis.
5 Kroll, C., Fuller, G., Lafortune, G., Sachs, J., Schmidt-Traub, G., & Woelm, F. (2021). *Sustainable Development Report 2020: The Sustainable Development Goals and Covid*. Cambridge University Press.
6 Braumann, H., & Hujo, K. (2016). *Policy Innovations for Transformative Change: Implementing the 2030 Agenda for Sustainable Development*. Switzerland: United Nations Research Institute for Social Development.
7 United Nations (2021). *Our Common Agenda: Report of the Secretary-General*. https://www.un.org/en/content/common-agenda-report/assets/pdf/Common_Agenda_Report_English.pdf
8 Unites Nations (2020). *UN75 Report: The Future We Want, The UN We Need*. United Nations. https://www.un.org/en/un75/presskit
9 United Nations (2023). *SDG Summit 2023*. United Nations. https://www.un.org/en/conferences/SDGSummit2023

Part II

Priorities

7 Social Well-Being Priorities

> In some parts of the world, divides based on identity are becoming more pronounced. Meanwhile, gaps in newer areas, such as access to online and mobile technologies, are emerging. Unless progress accelerates, the core promise of the 2030 Agenda for Sustainable Development—to leave no one behind—will remain a still distant goal by 2030. The inequality challenge is global, and intimately connected to other pressing issues of our times: not only rapid technological change, but also the climate crisis, urbanization and migration. In many places, the growing tide of inequality could further swell under the force of these megatrends. [...] The future course of these complex challenges is not irreversible. Technological change, migration, urbanization and even the climate crisis can be harnessed for a more equitable and sustainable world, or they can be left to further divide us.
>
> (Statement by UN Secretary-General António Guterres in the Foreword to the *World Social Report 2020*[1])

Overview

This chapter delves into the multifaceted nature of social well-being as a crucial component of sustainable development. It critically reviews the notion of development as growth and introduces key multidimensional indicators for well-being beyond economic-only measurements. It considers different levels and dimensions of well-being from physical to mental and spiritual. It examines key priorities such as health, education, equity, social inclusion, and cultural diversity, detailing how they intersect and influence broader sustainability trajectories.

7.1 Development as Well-Being

The concept of development has undergone significant evolution over the decades, shifting in accordance with societal values, technological advances, and our growing understanding of the

DOI: 10.4324/9781003494676-10

Earth's environmental limits. The definitions of development can be broadly segmented into three eras: development as growth, development as freedom, and development as well-being.

1. **Development as Growth:** In the earlier stages of our understanding of development, the focus was primarily on economic growth and modernization. This perspective, often labeled as "development as growth," considered development a linear economic expansion process, typically measured by Gross Domestic Product (GDP). The aim was to transform "traditional" societies into "modern" ones, using industrialization and urbanization as the primary engines of growth. However, this perspective often disregards social inequality, environmental degradation, and cultural erosion as negative externalities of the process [2]
2. **Development as Freedom:** Building on the criticism of the growth-centered view, the "development as freedom" perspective, most famously articulated by economist Amartya Sen, emerged. This view recognized development as a process of expanding human freedoms and capabilities. It emphasized the importance of political freedoms, social opportunities, transparency guarantees, and protective security in development. This marked a shift from purely economic parameters towards a more holistic and human-centered approach, considering elements such as education, health, and resource access.[3]
3. **Development as Well-Being:** The current "development as well-being" era expands the concept even further. This perspective aligns closely with the principles of the sustainable development agenda. It integrates economic prosperity, social equity, and environmental sustainability, aiming for a balanced and inclusive development model that respects planetary boundaries. The focus is on enhancing overall societal well-being, encompassing elements like mental health, happiness, social relations, and the preservation of cultural and natural heritage.[4]

The Post-2030 Agenda is likely to be centered around the notion of development as well-being for the following factors:

1. **Greater Awareness of Mental Health:** As societies progress, there's an increasing acknowledgment of the importance of mental health. A nation's progress cannot just be about

increasing wealth if its people are increasingly stressed, anxious, or unhappy.
2. **Environmental Concerns:** The climate crisis and environmental degradation have demonstrated that relentless economic growth without concern for the environment is not sustainable. The well-being paradigm considers environmental health as integral to human well-being.
3. **Interconnected Global Challenges:** Critical events such as pandemics have shown that global challenges are inherently interconnected. One health crisis can lead to multiple economic, social, and psychological crises. The well-being model accepts this interconnectedness and aims for holistic solutions.
4. **Limitations of Previous Models:** The limitations of measuring development solely in terms of GDP growth are becoming more evident. For example, a country might have a high GDP but also have high inequality, environmental degradation, or low life satisfaction among its citizens.
5. **Shift Towards Sustainable Development:** The SDGs already shift towards a more holistic view of development that aligns closely with the well-being paradigm.
6. **Public Demand:** As people around the world become more aware and educated, there's a growing demand for a life that's not just free and prosperous but also meaningful, happy, and sustainable.

As we move beyond 2030, the development as well-being paradigm will likely gain more traction as societies globally recognize the need for a more holistic, inclusive, and sustainable approach to development. Therefore, it is our collective responsibility to understand the multifaceted dimensions, appropriate measurements, and policy implications of human and societal integrated well-being.

7.2 The Multifaceted Dimensions of Well-Being

Well-being is a multifaceted concept that integrates different aspects of the human experience. When we talk about well-being about social development and sustainable development, we must consider several key dimensions:

1. **Physical Well-Being:** This includes the individual's health, encompassing aspects like nutrition, exercise, access to

healthcare, and the absence of diseases or infirmities. In a sustainable development context, this involves ensuring everyone has access to these aspects, regardless of their socio-economic status, hence improving overall population health.
2. **Mental and Emotional Well-Being:** This dimension focuses on mental health, emotional stability, and overall psychological wellness. It is increasingly recognized as crucial for overall well-being and is highly interconnected with other dimensions. Factors such as stress levels, self-esteem, and the prevalence of mental health disorders fall into this category. Promoting mental health and providing adequate services are vital for sustainable development.
3. **Social Well-Being:** This involves the quality and depth of interpersonal relationships, a sense of belonging in one's community, and the availability of social support networks. It also includes issues of equity and social justice, which are central to SDGs.
4. **Economic Well-Being:** This includes financial security, decent work, and the ability to meet basic needs. Economic well-being is closely tied to issues of poverty reduction, income equality, and sustainable economic growth.
5. **Environmental Well-Being:** This relates to living in a healthy and sustainable environment. It involves aspects like access to clean water and air, exposure to nature, and living in a sustainable and resilient community. Environmental well-being is a core pillar of sustainable development, linked to both individual health and the health of the planet.
6. **Cultural and Spiritual Well-being:** This involves respect for cultural diversity, preservation and promotion of cultural heritage, and opportunities for spiritual expression. This dimension recognizes the diversity of human experience and the importance of cultural and spiritual aspects in overall well-being.

These dimensions of well-being are deeply interconnected, and improvements in one area often can lead to improvements in others. At the same time, these dimensions provide a comprehensive framework for understanding and measuring social development. The holistic approach to well-being in sustainable development aims to balance these different facets, recognizing that they all contribute to the overall quality of human life.

7.3 Multidimensional Measurements of Well-Being

Over the years, several multidimensional measurements of well-being have been developed to overcome the limitations of traditional economic indicators, such as GDP. Here are four main alternative multidimensional measurements to GDP that demonstrate a more comprehensive and inclusive approach.

1. **Gross National Happiness (GNH):** The concept of GNH was developed in Bhutan as an alternative to GDP. GNH measures societal progress in nine domains: psychological well-being, health, education, culture, governance, community vitality, time use, ecological diversity and resilience, and living standards. This holistic approach recognizes the interconnections between these areas and prioritizes happiness and well-being over economic growth.[5]
2. **Social Progress Index (SPI):** The SPI assesses a society's capacity to meet its citizens' basic human needs, establish the building blocks for individuals to improve their lives, and create the conditions for individuals and communities to meet their full potential. This index includes dimensions such as basic human needs, foundations of well-being (e.g., access to basic knowledge, health and wellness, and environmental quality), and opportunity (e.g., personal rights, personal freedom and choice, and inclusiveness).[6]
3. **Human Development Index (HDI):** Developed by the United Nations, the HDI combines indicators of life expectancy, educational attainment, and income into a composite measure. It goes beyond GDP to provide a broader picture of human well-being and capabilities. More recently, it has added more accurate measurements such as the Inequality-adjusted Human Development Index (IHDI), the Gender Development Index (GDI), and the Gender Inequality Index (GII) used to measure gender disparities.[7]
4. **Sustainable Development Goals (SDGs):** The SDGs in themselves are an alternative measurement with its 5Ps and the 17 goals that include 169 targets and 232 indicators. They cover a broad range of dimensions of sustainable development, including poverty, hunger, health, education, gender equality, clean water and sanitation, affordable and clean energy, decent work and economic growth, industry and infrastructure, reduced inequalities, sustainable cities and

communities, responsible consumption and production, climate action, life below water, life on land, peace, justice and strong institutions, and partnership.[8]

Contrasting with GDP, which only measures the market value of all final goods and services produced in a country in a given period, these multidimensional measurements capture a much more holistic and nuanced picture of societal progress and well-being. GDP, for instance, does not account for income inequality, environmental degradation, or social factors like education and health.

Future measurements should continue refining and expanding these multidimensional indicators, seeking to integrate better subjective well-being experiences and cultural variation in well-being definitions. We should also strive to improve data collection in currently undermeasured areas, such as mental health, social connections, and the quality of employment. Including these factors in future measurements will provide a more comprehensive understanding of progress toward well-being goals.

7.3.1 Measuring Well-Being and Progress

The Organization for Economic Co-operation and Development's (OECD) initiative to measure well-being and progress significantly contributes to the evolving field of well-being research, which strives to construct a holistic understanding of societal progress that extends beyond the limited purview of traditional economic indicators like the GDP.

The fundamental recognition behind this initiative is that societal progress is intrinsically linked to the well-being of people and households. In this light, it becomes imperative to not only evaluate the performance of the economy but also to consider the diverse experiences and living conditions of individuals.

The OECD Framework for Measuring Well-Being and Progress encapsulates this broader approach, integrating recommendations from the 2009 Commission on the Measurement of Economic Performance and Social Progress, as well as insights from earlier OECD work and various national initiatives. This framework is structured around three critical components:

1. **Current Well-Being:** Assesses people's quality of life based on various factors such as income, jobs, housing, health, work-life balance, education, social connections, civic engagement and governance, environmental quality, personal security, and subjective well-being.
2. **Inequalities in Well-Being Outcomes:** Acknowledges the disparities within societies, stating that averages can often be misleading when there is a significant divide in the population's experiences. It's essential to consider different dimensions of inequalities, including income, education, health, and life satisfaction, and how these are distributed among different societal groups.
3. **Resources for Future Well-Being:** Recognizes that present well-being should not compromise the ability of future generations to enjoy a similar or better standard of living. This section thus encompasses aspects such as natural, economic, human, and social capital.

The OECD's ongoing work in measuring well-being and progress represents an ambitious move towards a more comprehensive understanding of societal development. The inherent emphasis on a multidimensional approach ensures that the resulting measurements will accurately represent individual and societal well-being, ultimately leading to more informed and effective public policies. This is critical for bolstering the credibility and accountability of public policies and sustaining the democratic process itself.[9]

7.4 The Haunting Crisis Scenario Post-2030

Investing in social development and sustainable well-being is crucial for navigating potential crises in the post-2030 era for several key reasons:

1. **Human-Centric Approach:** A sustainable well-being approach puts people and their quality of life at the center of development strategies. It focuses on material wealth and health, education, human rights, social relations, security, cultural identity, and natural and built environments. Such an approach acknowledges that true progress involves more than just economic growth.

2. **Mitigating Inequality:** Social development investments work to reduce inequalities that can fuel social tension, conflict, and instability. These investments help to ensure that the benefits of development are shared more equally across society, improving social cohesion, and promoting peace.
3. **Climate Change and Environmental Degradation:** Investment in sustainable well-being is also critical for addressing environmental crises. By considering social and environmental factors together, sustainable well-being approaches promote the kind of integrated decision-making needed to tackle complex, interconnected challenges like climate change, biodiversity loss, and pollution.
4. **Resilience:** Investments in social and sustainable development can strengthen community resilience to future shocks. This includes not only environmental shocks like extreme weather events and pandemics, but also social and economic shocks like recessions or conflicts.
5. **Future Generations:** Investing in sustainable well-being today will help to safeguard the interests of future generations. This is particularly important given the long-term nature of many sustainability challenges, from education and health to climate change and biodiversity conservation.
6. **Sustainable Economic Growth:** Well-being-focused policies can stimulate sustainable economic growth. By promoting green technologies, for instance, these policies can spur innovation, open new markets, and create jobs.

In essence, investing in sustainable well-being and social development isn't just about just addressing immediate issues; it's about putting society on a long-term sustainable path. It's about recognizing and responding to the interconnected nature of our social, economic, and environmental challenges and opportunities. And ultimately, it's about creating a world that can sustain us not just now, but for generations to come.

7.5 The Social Factors for a New Earth Summit

Given the high possibility of a major social/environmental crisis in the near future, it is essential to consider whether a New Earth Summit could facilitate the cooperation needed to address imminent environmental and social crises. Such a summit, built on shared, fundamental values, could provide the foundation for a new form of planetary livelihood and help to instill the values necessary for creating a new planetary well-being.

Critical factors may include:

1. **The Livelihood Factor:** The summit would need to focus on sustainable livelihoods, ensuring that the planet's resources are used wisely and equitably, and promoting ways of living that align with the Earth's ecological limits and capacities.
2. **The Education Factor:** The summit must highlight the need for broad-based education focused on sustainability, respect for nature, and the responsibilities of everyone towards our planet. This education is crucial in fostering a collective understanding of the pressing environmental issues we face and how to tackle them.
3. **The Enforcement Factor:** For the summit's decisions to be effective, they must be embedded in law and regulation at national and international levels. Civil society, parliamentarians, and justices should be included organically to ensure widespread acceptance and enforcement of these laws. Moreover, the support of domestic and international courts is needed to ensure accountability and implementation.

Should a New Earth Summit be convened, it must be a platform for genuine global cooperation. It should serve as a conduit for the sharing of scientific knowledge, innovative ideas, and best practices. Like the Rio+20 Conference, to be truly inclusive and representative, a New Earth Summit must involve all stakeholders—from global leaders, scientists, business and industry leaders to civil society representatives, youth, and Indigenous communities.[10]

A New Earth Summit can serve as a powerful catalyst for the formulation of a new set of global goals and priorities focused on social and environmental well-being. The summit could provide an inclusive and democratic platform for diverse stakeholders, where new goals can be co-created based on collective values and shared visions for a sustainable future. Here are some key dimensions that should be considered:

1. **Interconnectedness:** Acknowledging that social and environmental well-being are interdependent and addressing these two facets in an integrated manner would be a fundamental

shift. Our goals should reflect this interconnectedness and look at challenges through a holistic lens.

2. **Inclusiveness:** The goals should consider the needs and rights of all people, regardless of their age, gender, ethnicity, socio-economic status, or geographical location. Special attention should be paid to historically marginalized or vulnerable populations.
3. **Future-Orientation:** The summit should recognize the need to consider the interests of future generations. Therefore, the goals should embody a long-term vision that balances the needs of the present with the needs of the future.
4. **Sustainability:** Goals should promote a circular economy, sustainable consumption and production, and the protection and restoration of biodiversity and ecosystems.
5. **Equity:** The goals should address systemic injustices and aim for equitable access to resources, opportunities, and benefits. They should also aim to reduce disparities within and among countries.
6. **Resilience:** The goals should promote adaptive capacities to respond to shocks and stresses, including those related to climate change, public health crises, and economic volatility.
7. **Human Rights:** The summit should stress the need to anchor goals in the framework of human rights, recognizing that social and environmental well-being are inextricably linked to the realization of these rights.
8. **Transparency and Accountability:** The goals should be accompanied by clear, measurable indicators and an effective monitoring and evaluation framework to ensure transparency and accountability.

The New Earth Summit would not only set the stage for the creation of these new goals but would also provide momentum for their implementation. The summit's diverse representation can create buy-in and foster a sense of shared responsibility, thereby driving collective action towards achieving these goals.

By fostering collective values and a shared vision for a sustainable future, the New Earth Summit could ignite the global action needed to face the environmental and social challenges of the post-2030 world.

7.6 Social Priorities for Post-2030 Agenda

To develop a comprehensive social/environmental well-being agenda post-2030, several key priorities need to be established in the areas of health, education, equity, social inclusion, cultural diversity, and governance participation. Acknowledging the intersections of these dimensions will guide the creation of an integrated and transformative agenda that can influence sustainability trajectories.

1. **Health:** Priorities in health should extend beyond traditional healthcare and disease management to include the promotion of mental health, preventative care, and overall well-being. Recognizing the link between environmental health and human health is key, and actions should be taken to reduce pollution, enhance air quality, and ensure access to clean water and sanitation facilities. Public health systems need to be robust and resilient to manage future pandemics and health crises.
2. **Education:** Priorities should include global citizenship education and sustainable development education, which can empower learners to make informed decisions and take responsible actions for environmental integrity, economic viability, and a just society. Lifelong learning opportunities should be made available to all, and education systems should be adaptable to evolving societal needs and technological advancements.
3. **Equity:** A primary focus should be on addressing systemic inequities, both social and economic. This includes income and wealth distribution, resource access, opportunities, and services. The goal should be to ensure that everyone, irrespective of their socioeconomic status, has a fair chance at leading a fulfilling life.
4. **Social Inclusion:** Priorities should aim to create inclusive societies where all individuals, including marginalized and vulnerable groups, participate actively in decision-making processes. Social protection systems need to be strengthened, and efforts should be made to eliminate all forms of discrimination.
5. **Cultural Diversity:** The agenda should celebrate cultural diversity and promote intercultural understanding. This includes protecting the rights of Indigenous peoples and

local communities, preserving cultural heritage, and promoting the diversity of cultural expressions.

6. **Governance Participation:** This entails the active engagement and representation of all societal factions in governance processes, ensuring that decision-making is transparent, inclusive, and responsive to the needs of all stakeholders. Strengthening mechanisms for public consultations, feedback, and collaborative policymaking should be at the forefront.

The intersectionality of these dimensions means that interventions in one area can have profound impacts on the others. For instance, education is not only critical for individual development but can also contribute to improved health, reduced inequality, and enhanced social inclusion. Similarly, social inclusion can facilitate improved health and education outcomes and contribute to cultural diversity. The acknowledgment and understanding of these intersections will be instrumental in the creation of an integrated and holistic post-2030 social/environmental well-being agenda.

7.7 Social Policy Recommendations

Clearly, numerous priorities must be considered to formulate adequate, inclusive, and sustainable policies. The following list synthesizes the ten most urgent priorities for social sustainability and well-being when considering global urgencies and their potential impacts on broad populations. While these priorities have urgencies and policy implications specific to social aspects, they are interconnected to other environmental, economic, governance, peace, and technology dimensions of sustainability. The lessons learned from the SDGs suggest the importance of working together and including all stakeholders and nations along with focusing on the interlinkages of the goals and the intersectionality of the goals (like gender with age and disability for example).[11] Crafting policy-specific recommendations for these priorities requires having a mindset that recognizes these interlinkages and intersectional identities through a forward-thinking and multidimensional approach. The following are ten of the most urgent needs and recommendations that can translate these priorities into action and help shape the creation of a new sustainability agenda beyond 2030:

1. **Equity and Social Justice**
   - **Urgency:** Disparities in economic opportunities and social privileges fuel global challenges, from heightened crime rates to political upheavals and potential human rights breaches. Societies that prioritize equality are more resilient, cohesive, and likely to thrive sustainably.
   - **Policy Recommendation:** Advocate for progressive taxation structures, establish firm guidelines for gender wage parity, and foster a robust social safety net comprising unemployment aids, secure pensions, and supportive childcare facilities.
2. **Migration and Integration**
   - **Urgency:** The soaring numbers of individuals forced to migrate due to armed conflicts, environmental shifts, and sociopolitical reasons necessitate urgent attention to migrant rights and their integration into host societies.
   - **Policy Recommendation:** Formulate human rights-centric migration guidelines, facilitate smoother cultural integration through language acquisition and vocational training, and bolster public campaigns countering xenophobia.
3. **Universal Healthcare**
   - **Urgency:** With diseases transcending borders and new health challenges arising, universal access to healthcare is more crucial than ever.
   - **Policy Recommendation:** Pave the way for a unified healthcare approach or a versatile model that underscores preventive measures, integrates psychological health provisions, and guarantees healthcare accessibility and affordability across socioeconomic spectrums.
4. **Education for All**
   - **Urgency:** A well-informed populace is indispensable for navigating and resolving present-day global challenges, driving innovation, and underpinning economic advancement.
   - **Policy Recommendation:** Champion comprehensive education by waiving primary and secondary school

tuition. Infuse curriculums with essential life skills, environmental awareness, and technological competencies. Amplify teacher professional development to enrich instructional quality.

5. **Climate Resilience and Environmental Justice**
   - **Urgency:** Climate change repercussions, such as forced relocations and threats to food supplies, are intensifying. Proactive steps are vital, especially to shield the most vulnerable populations.
   - **Policy Recommendation:** Channel investments into eco-friendly infrastructure and sustainable energy ventures, while sculpting strategies to aid and compensate communities at the frontline of environmental challenges.
6. **Access to Clean Water and Sanitation**
   - **Urgency:** Despite advancements, the global quest for achieving Sustainable Development Goal 6 remains challenging. Water shortages and inadequate sanitation can catalyze health crises, societal disputes, and forced relocations.
   - **Policy Recommendation:** Chart out national water conservation blueprints, optimize water distribution, and buttress infrastructural endeavors. Encourage collaborations between public sectors and industries to pioneer advances in water treatment and sanitation practices.
7. **Affordable Housing and Urban Development**
   - **Urgency:** With cities swelling rapidly, the quest for sustainable urban living and affordable housing is more pronounced.
   - **Policy Recommendation:** Promote green housing ventures through fiscal incentives. Foster urban designs accentuating pedestrian-friendly zones, recreational green belts, and seamless public commuting systems.
8. **Digital Inclusion**
   - **Urgency:** The digitization wave is omnipresent, making digital inclusivity imperative for societal progress and individual empowerment.
   - **Policy Recommendation:** Launch countrywide digital infrastructure enhancement projects. Augment digital literacy drives, particularly targeting regions lagging in

digital access, to ensure holistic societal participation in the digital age.

9. **Labor and Employment**
   - **Urgency:** The job landscape is undergoing a metamorphosis, influenced by technological advancements like AI. Addressing the rights and securities of the workforce is paramount.
   - **Policy Recommendation:** Foresee and navigate automation's impact via rigorous reskilling and upskilling initiatives. Extend protective measures to gig economy participants, assuring them of rights and benefits paralleling conventional job roles.
10. **Human Rights and Governance**
    - **Urgency:** A society's strength lies in its governance structures and commitment to human rights. Fragile institutions could jeopardize broader societal goals.
    - **Policy Recommendation:** Bolster independent judicial frameworks and bodies combatting corruption. Champion governmental transparency, fortify press freedoms, and ensure human rights considerations are paramount in international diplomacy and trade deliberations.

Prioritizing these urgencies can vary depending on regional contexts, but in a globalized world, challenges in one region can quickly have repercussions elsewhere. For the new sustainability agenda beyond 2030 to be effective, it's crucial to consider a participatory approach that includes stakeholders from various sectors: government, civil society, private sector, academia, and most importantly, the general populace. These are just a few of the many urgencies and social policy priorities. Nevertheless, integrating these and other urgent social policies with a clear vision and concrete targets will enable societies to progress towards a more inclusive, equitable, and sustainable future.[12]

7.8 Social Mindset Shift Priorities

In advancing the social sustainability agenda, the call to shift our social mindset is not just urgent—it's an ethical imperative. This shift requires a profound re-envisioning of our values and practices, demanding that we do more than acknowledge systemic challenges; we must actively dismantle them. We are tasked with creating a sustainability ethos that seamlessly integrates social equity and inclusivity at its core.[13] It is not enough to address environmental concerns; we must also champion the causes of those marginalized by socioeconomic disparities and racial injustices, especially Black, Indigenous, and People of Color (BIPOC) communities that endure the heaviest impacts of environmental degradation. The Diversity, Equity, and Inclusion (DEI) movement must mature from passive representation to a dynamic and conscious reformation that critically examines power structures, privileges, and the intersectionality of identities. This is a transformative journey toward equitable employment and an acknowledgment of the diverse cultural, skill-based, and experiential contributions vital to our shared future's rich tapestry.

A company's sustainability is intrinsically linked to its genuine embrace of diversity and inclusion—not as a checklist for public image but as a substantive part of its identity. The pervasive problem of "diversity washing"—where firms publicize a commitment to DEI yet fail to practice it within their workforce composition—erodes the potential for real transformation and misguides stakeholders.[14] A radical shift towards radical inclusion and unyielding transparency is essential to move beyond this. This shift would see companies sharing detailed reports on their DEI impact and progress and setting clear, actionable goals. Furthermore, integrating non-executive directors to provide impartial oversight ensures DEI becomes more than a veneer—it becomes a core principle of the corporate ethos. By embracing these changes, we can safeguard that the integration of diversity, equity, and inclusion in all societal and corporate domains is substantial, driving forward sustainability strategies and ESG ratings with integrity.

The following is an initial list of fundamental elements that should take precedence in transforming our societal mindset towards a more inclusive and authentic paradigm, particularly for companies and communities striving to foster social inclusivity.

1. **Realizing True Diversity:** Diversity must be reimagined beyond quotas; it should reflect a holistic representation of diverse identities, experiences, and perspectives. This means valuing not just demographic diversity but cognitive and

experiential diversity that drives innovation and inclusive decision-making.

2. **Equity—The Bedrock of Inclusion:** Equity involves more than equal treatment—it's about proactively removing barriers and ensuring all individuals have the resources needed to thrive, thus fostering a society where equity is lived and experienced by every member.
3. **Cultivating a Culture of Belonging:** True inclusion demands active engagement with diverse groups, ensuring that all voices are not only heard but are integral to an organization's strategy and culture, promoting a deep sense of belonging and contribution.
4. **Combatting "Diversity-Washing":** Organizations must go beyond lip service, substantiating their DEI claims with transparent reporting and accountability measures, setting benchmarks for progress and openly addressing shortcomings.
5. **Embedding DEI in ESG Ratings:** DEI should be a cornerstone in the assessment of ESG ratings, with a clear focus on how deeply these principles are woven into the fabric of a company's operations and culture.

In summary, promoting diversity, equity, and inclusion represents a holistic effort that extends beyond quantifiable metrics. It entails cultivating a societal awareness that incorporates these principles across all levels of society and within the framework of organizations, thereby fostering the development of societies and businesses that not only embrace diversity but also embody genuine equity and sustainable inclusivity, aligning with the social and well-being priorities of a new sustainability agenda.

7.9 Resources

As we have seen throughout Chapter 7, social well-being sustainability involves ensuring that current and future generations meet their basic needs, live with dignity, have opportunities for personal and collective growth, and are empowered to participate fully in societal activities. Understanding and promoting social well-being requires a multidimensional approach, and several significant studies over the years have shaped our understanding of this facet of sustainability. Fortunately, the last few decades have seen the establishment and development of alternative indexes to measure well-being beyond economic indicators. The following frameworks review the priority indicators for a comprehensive well-being measurement for social sustainability.

1. **SDSD World Happiness Report:** Published annually by the United Nations Sustainable Development Solutions Network, this report ranks countries based on various well-being indicators, including income, social support, healthy life expectancy, freedom, trust, and generosity. It offers a comprehensive snapshot of global well-being and its various determinants. Read more at https://worldhappiness.report/.
2. **UNDP Human Development Report:** An annual publication of the United Nations Development Programme (UNDP) exploring different themes through the human development approach, which places people at the center of the development process. It presents data from the HDI which evaluates countries based on three fundamental dimensions: health (reflected by life expectancy at birth), education (captured by mean and expected years of schooling), and economic prosperity (represented by Gross National Income per capita). While the HDI encompasses more than just social well-being, it offers valuable perspectives on key factors that enhance it. Explore further at https://hdr.undp.org/.
3. **OECD Better Life Index:** For nearly a decade, the OECD has expanded its focus from just the economic system to the diverse living conditions and experiences of individuals and households. One of its significant endeavors in this area is the "OECD Better Life Initiative," introduced in May 2011. This initiative consolidates data from across the OECD into two primary components: "How's Life?" and "Your Better Life Index." The "How's Life?" report offers a detailed view of well-being in OECD nations, examining both material and quality of life aspects. "Your Better Life Index" is an online interactive platform enabling users to evaluate and contrast well-being across nations based on their personalized criteria for well-being dimensions. Read more at www.oecdbetterlifeindex.org.
4. **NEF Happy Planet Index:** The Happy Life Index (HPI), published by The New Economics Foundation (NEF), offers a unique perspective on national progress, focusing on sustainable well-being for all. Instead of conventional

metrics, the HPI evaluates countries based on three central factors: individuals' self-reported well-being, life expectancy as a standard health measure, and the ecological footprint reflecting the environmental impact of consumption patterns within a country. Well-being is assessed by asking people in a country how they feel about their lives. In essence, the HPI aims to determine how efficiently nations produce long, contented lives relative to their environmental consumption. Explore further at https://happyplanetindex.org/.

5. **Human Development and Capacity Approach (HDCA):** The capabilities approach by Amartya Sen and Martha Nussbaum is an influential framework that emphasizes the importance of enhancing people's capabilities, meaning their freedom to lead lives they have reason to value. While this approach is more of a conceptual framework than a specific study, it has informed various empirical research endeavors on well-being and development. See *Creating Capabilities: The Human Development Approach* by Martha Nussbaum (2011). Read more at https://hd-ca.org/.
6. **Social Progress Index (SPI):** As we reviewed earlier, SPI is developed by the non-profit Social Progress Imperative, and measures the social and environmental outcomes directly rather than the economic factors. The index covers many societal needs, including health, safety, access to education, and individual rights, providing a broader view of social well-being. Read more at www.socialprogress.org.
7. **Gross National Happiness (GNH):** Known as a primary challenge to GDP, the GNH originated in Bhutan as a holistic approach to development. It measures prosperity through formal indicators not only of the economy but also of cultural, spiritual, and environmental well-being. It is based on four pillars: sustainable and equitable socioeconomic development, conservation of the environment, preservation and promotion of culture, and good governance. Read more at www.gnhcentrebhutan.org.

Notes

1 United Nations (2020). *World Social Report 2020*. United Nations. https://www.un.org/en/desa/world-social-report-2020#:~:text=UN%20Secretary%2DGeneral%20Ant%C3%B3nio%20Guterres,a%20deeply%20unequal%20global%20landscape.

2 Soubbotina, T.P. (2004). *Beyond Economic Growth: An Introduction to Sustainable Development*. Ukraine: World Bank.
3 Robeyns, I. (2017). *Well-Being, Freedom and Social Justice: The Capability Approach Re-Examined*. United Kingdom: Open Book Publishers. See also: Sen, A. (2011). *Development as Freedom*. United Kingdom: Knopf Doubleday Publishing Group.
4 Grin, J., Veraart, F., Lintsen, H., & Smits, J. (2018). *Well-Being, Sustainability and Social Development: The Netherlands* 1850–2050. Germany: Springer International Publishing. See also: Rauschmayer, F., Omann, I., & Frühmann, J. (2012). *Sustainable Development: Capabilities, Needs, and Well-being*. United Kingdom: Taylor & Francis.
5 Dorji, T. (2018). *Gross National Happiness. Bhutan's Goal of Develpment*. Germany: GRIN Verlag.
6 Stiglitz, J. (2019). *For Good Measure: An Agenda for Moving Beyond GDP*. United Kingdom: New Press.
7 McGillivray, M. (2006). *Human Well-Being: Concept and Measurement*. United Kingdom: Palgrave Macmillan.
8 Stiglitz, J., Fitoussi, J.P, & Durand, M. (2018). *For Good Measure: Advancing Research on Well-being Metrics Beyond GDP*. France: OECD Publishing.
9 OECD (2020). *How's Life? 2020: Measuring Well-being*. France: OECD Publishing.
10 United Nations (n.d.). *Intersectionality And Working Together To Achieve The SDGs*. https://social.desa.un.org/sdn/intersectionality-and-working-together-to-achieve-the-sdgs#:~:text=The%20Sustainable%20Development%20Goals%20(SDGs,aspects%20of%20the%202030%20Agenda.
11 United Nations (n.d.). *Goal 6: Ensure Access to Water and Sanitation For All*. https://www.un.org/sustainabledevelopment/water-and-sanitation/
12 Dodds, F., Laguna-Celis, J., & Thompson, L. (2014). *From Rio+20 to a New Development Agenda: Building a Bridge to a Sustainable Future*. United Kingdom: Taylor & Francis.
13 Gonçalves, S. P., Figueiredo, P. C. N., Tomé, E. L. S., & Baptista, J. (Eds.). (2023). *Developing Diversity, Equity, and Inclusion Policies for Promoting Employee Sustainability and Well-being*. IGI Global.
14 Baker, A., Larcker, D.F., McClure, C., Saraph, D., & Watts, E.M. (2022). Diversity washing. *Chicago Booth Research Paper No. 22–18*.

8 Economic Prosperity Priorities

> Now is the time to correct a glaring blind spot in how we measure economic prosperity and progress. When profits come at the expense of people and our planet, we are left with an incomplete picture of the true cost of economic growth. As currently measured, gross domestic product (GDP) fails to capture the human and environmental destruction of some business activities. I call for new measures to complement GDP, so that people can gain a full understanding of the impacts of business activities and how we can and must do better to support people and our planet. [...] We must urgently find measures of progress that complement GDP, as we were tasked to do by 2030 in target 17.19 of the Sustainable Development Goals. We know that GDP fails to account for human well-being, planetary sustainability and non-market services and care, or to consider the distributional dimensions of economic activity. Absurdly, GDP rises when there is overfishing, cutting of forests or burning of fossil fuels. We are destroying nature, but we count it as an increase in wealth. Such discussions have been ongoing for decades. It is time to collectively commit to complementary measurements. Without that fundamental shift, the targets that we have fixed in relation to biodiversity, pollution and climate change will not be achievable.
>
> (Statement by UN Secretary-General António Guterres in *Our Common Agenda: Report of the Secretary-General*[1])

Overview

This chapter explores the necessity of rethinking economic paradigms to align with sustainable development principles. It expands on the notion of well-being to advance alternative economic models that bring prosperity for all along creating and maintaining regenerative values. Key priorities include sustainable and inclusive growth, reducing income inequality, fostering economic resilience, and integrating economic policies with environmental and social objectives.

DOI: 10.4324/9781003494676-11

8.1 Prosperity Beyond Profit

We begin our exploration of economic priorities related to sustainable development with a discussion that navigates through the avenues of contrasting economic paradigms: the traditional profit-only model and the more inclusive prosperity-focused approach.

The profit-only economic model has traditionally reigned supreme, focusing on financial gain. This model has been the driving force behind much of the economic growth seen in the past century. Under this paradigm, success is primarily measured by economic indicators (such as GDP as stated earlier), with societal or environmental factors often diminished. This quest for profitability is viewed narrowly, disregarding the broader impacts on society and the environment. Consequently, this has led to economic growth but with costs, such as increased inequality, environmental degradation, and social dislocation.

Conversely, the prosperity-inclusive economic approach considers economic growth as a means to an end rather than just an end to itself. This model broadens the definition of success beyond monetary measures to include overall well-being, equality, and environmental sustainability. It emphasizes the need for economic activities to provide shared benefits, enhance social cohesion, reduce disparities, and preserve natural resources for future generations. It is a model where the economy serves society and the environment rather than vice versa.

In the context of sustainable development, the profit-only model often falls short. While it can generate wealth, it often fails to distribute it equitably or to ensure long-term sustainability. It tends to view natural resources as unlimited, and it often externalizes environmental and social costs, which can lead to overconsumption, pollution, and other forms of environmental degradation.

The prosperity-inclusive model aligns more closely with sustainable development principles, embracing the triple bottom line of social, environmental, and economic performance. It recognizes that long-term economic prosperity is intertwined with environmental stewardship and social inclusion. Economic activities are seen as interdependent with ecological systems, and economic policies are designed to promote fair distribution, social justice, and environmental sustainability.

Ultimately, while the profit-only model has driven economic growth in the past, it's increasingly clear that a shift toward a prosperity-inclusive approach is crucial to meet the present and future needs of society and the planet. Shaping an economy that is sustainable, inclusive, and equitable requires transformative change in the way we understand and pursue economic prosperity.

8.2 Stakeholders Beyond Shareholders

In the context of sustainable development, companies are increasingly required to move beyond a narrow shareholder-only focus to encompass a broader stakeholder-orientated approach. Traditional CSR initiatives prioritizing shareholders often fail to address the complexities of sustainable development, as they tend to focus mainly on maximizing profits and improving shareholder value.

Shareholder-centric models of corporate governance often limit the scope of responsibility to the economic returns for shareholders, largely excluding the interests of other stakeholders such as employees, customers, local communities, and the environment. This narrow focus can lead to practices that undermine social equity and environmental sustainability, thereby contradicting the principles of sustainable development.[2]

Conversely, a stakeholder-inclusive approach in corporate governance promotes transparency, accountability, and broad-based participation. It considers the interests and well-being of all parties impacted by a company's activities, acknowledging that businesses are a part of a larger societal and environmental system. This broader view reflects a more accurate understanding of the role businesses play in society, and their potential for contributing to, or detracting from, sustainable development.

In a stakeholder-transparency model, companies actively engage with a wide range of stakeholders, seek their inputs, and make decisions that balance different interests. They are transparent about their operations, impacts, and strategies, and are accountable for their social, environmental, and economic performance. This not only enhances their credibility and public trust, but it also can lead to better decision-making, innovation, and long-term viability.

Stakeholder participation further broadens this approach by actively involving different stakeholder groups in decision-making processes. This may include employee participation in management decisions, customer input on product development, community involvement in project planning, and public input on corporate policies. By giving voice to those affected by corporate activities, stakeholder participation can lead to more equitable, sustainable, and resilient business models.

In conclusion, shifting from a shareholder-only CSR model to a stakeholder-transparency and participation model can be a powerful strategy for aligning corporate behavior with SDGs. It is not just about mitigating harm or managing risk but about creating shared value and contributing positively to the social, environmental, and economic systems within which businesses operate.

Several initiatives have emerged prioritizing stakeholders in economic models for a more equitable and sustainable economy. These include B Corporations, which are companies certified to meet high social and environmental standards; the Equator Principles, a risk management framework for assessing environmental and social risk in projects; and the Global Reporting Initiative (GRI), which assists organizations in communicating their impacts on sustainability issues. In addition, the UNGC is a CEO-led initiative for implementing universal sustainability principles, and the SDGs guide companies towards enhancing their social, economic, and environmental impacts. Furthermore, shareholder activism is rising, with shareholders demanding increased transparency and accountability on environmental, social, and governance issues. Finally, employee ownership and cooperative models offer direct business stakes to employees or customers. Collectively, these initiatives signify a shift towards stakeholder capitalism that balances the needs of shareholders with other stakeholders to foster sustainable development and a more inclusive economy.

8.3 CSV Beyond CSR

In the economic priorities post-2030, it's vital to facilitate the legal formation of new business structures that inherently intertwine profit-making with social and environmental considerations, such as Benefit Corporations and social enterprises. These models represent a marked shift from the traditional business approach that often puts profits first and treats social and environmental concerns as secondary or even optional considerations.

Benefit Corporations and social enterprises are designed to create social or environmental benefits alongside profit. This stands in contrast to conventional corporations, which primarily aim to maximize shareholder returns. A Benefit Corporation, for example, has an expanded purpose beyond profit maximization and must consider the impact of decisions on all stakeholders, including workers, the community, and the environment.[3]

This concept dovetails with the Creating Shared Value (CSV) philosophy, first proposed by Michael Porter and Mark Kramer. CSV suggests that companies can generate economic value in a way that also produces value for society by addressing its needs and challenges. Instead of treating social and environmental efforts as separate from their business or as a cost, companies incorporate them into their competitive strategy and core operations. This shift toward shared value creation goes beyond the traditional CSR framework, which often involves businesses making separate contributions to society, such as philanthropy or volunteering, rather than integrating social and environmental concerns into their core business strategies.[4]

In the long run, businesses built on CSV principles are likely to be more impactful and sustainable. Rather than seeing societal issues as peripheral to their operations or as problems to be mitigated, they view them as opportunities for innovation, competitiveness, and long-term value creation. This approach has the potential to foster economic prosperity, environmental sustainability, and social well-being simultaneously, which is central to the goals of sustainable development.

Beyond the importance of establishing legal identities for CSV enterprises, certifications play a critical role in advancing impactful practices. One essential certification is the B Corporation (B Corp) certification, conferred by the non-profit B Lab. B Corps are businesses that meet the highest standards of verified social and environmental performance, public transparency, and legal accountability to balance profit and purpose. The rigorous certification process requires businesses to score a minimum on an assessment that examines their impact on workers, customers, the community, and the environment. B Corp certification signals to all stakeholders that a business is committed to CSV and holds itself to a higher standard of performance and accountability.

In addition to certifications, standardized reporting frameworks provide a structure for businesses to measure and communicate their social and environmental performance transparently and comparably. The GRI is one such framework. It promotes sustainability reporting as a way for organizations to become more sustainable and contribute to sustainable development. GRI standards create a common language for organizations and stakeholders to discuss sustainability impacts. Similarly, UNGC reporting, as a voluntary initiative, encourages businesses worldwide to adopt sustainable and socially responsible policies and to report on their implementation. UNGC reporting covers human rights, labor, environment, and anti-corruption.

These certifications and reporting frameworks provide essential tools for promoting and validating CSV practices. They provide benchmarks and guidelines for businesses, ensuring transparency and accountability. They also assure stakeholders, including consumers and investors, that businesses are genuinely committed to social and environmental responsibilities. As a part of post-2030 economic priorities, the continued growth and influence of these certifications and standardized reporting frameworks will be crucial to mainstreaming CSV and sustainable business practices.

Thus, the move towards these new business models and the CSV approach represents an important component of post-2030 economic priorities. It signals a shift from voluntary, often superficial, CSR practices towards systemic integration of social and environmental concerns in businesses' core operations and strategies, resulting in a more sustainable and equitable economy.

8.4 ESG Integration Beyond ROI Maximization

Environmental, Social, and Governance (ESG) integration is crucial to shift economic priorities post-2030 from a singular focus on Return on Investment (ROI) maximization to a more sustainable and inclusive economic model. Models like ESG that integrate multiple dimensions of value creation—not solely financial—offer a richer perspective for assessment and planning, leading towards frameworks like the Social Return on Investment (SROI) that prioritize prosperity-driven, rather than profit-driven, outcomes. ESG integration implies including environmental, social, and governance factors into investment decisions, a change from traditional investing models that only consider financial metrics.[5]

1. **Environmental Responsibility:** Environmental factors consider how businesses interact with the natural world. They may include a company's carbon footprint, waste management, resource conservation, and contributions to climate change. Green investing promotes businesses prioritizing environmentally sustainable practices, driving the transition towards green economies.
2. **Social Responsibility:** Social factors look at a company's relationships with its employees, suppliers, customers, and the communities where it operates. They may include labor standards, data protection, health and safety, and human rights. Impact investing, which seeks to generate specific beneficial social or environmental effects alongside a financial return, supports businesses with strong social performance.
3. **Governance:** Governance factors are concerned with a company's leadership, executive pay, audits and internal controls, and shareholder rights. Ethical investing ensures funds go towards businesses adhering to ethical governance practices.

The integration of ESG factors into investment decisions is a way to promote sustainable and ethical business practices, benefiting not just individual companies and investors but society. Considering these broader impacts, ESG integration encourages businesses to think long term and contribute positively to society and the environment, leading to more sustainable, resilient, and inclusive economies post-2030.

Moreover, research increasingly demonstrates that ESG integration can lead to better financial performance in the long run, making it a win-win for investors, companies, and society. By mainstreaming ESG and impact investing, we can direct significant financial resources toward tackling the most pressing social and environmental challenges of our time, aligning our economic system with the broader goals of sustainable development. These integrations and mainstreaming of ESG approaches are visible across industries and market sectors often making the consideration of economic factors more integral to other levels of environmental, social, and governance factors.[6]

8.5 Sustainability Reporting Integrations

The convergence of sustainability and ESG values within modern economic structures has ushered in the development of tailored accounting mechanisms that aptly echo these sentiments. Traditional accounting methods, although foundational, can often overlook the intricate web of environmental, social, and governance intricacies inherent in businesses today. Recognizing this gap, alternative reporting systems have emerged, paving the way for greater transparency, accountability, and a focus on long-term resilience.[7]

1. **Global Reporting Initiative (GRI):** GRI is a pioneering framework that champions transparency and has become a global standard for sustainability reporting. It provides organizations with a comprehensive set of indicators covering environmental, social, and governance factors to report their impact and performance.
2. **World Business Council for Sustainable Development (WBCSD):** WBCSD is an influential CEO-led organization that works to accelerate the transition to a sustainable world. While not a reporting standard per se, WBCSD collaborates with companies to develop sustainable business strategies and practices, some of which influence or align with other sustainability reporting frameworks.
3. **International Integrated Reporting Council (IIRC):** IIRC has introduced the concept of integrated reporting, which combines financial and sustainability information in a single, unified document. This holistic view enables organizations to present a clear picture of their overall impact and performance.
4. **Sustainability Accounting Standards Board (SASB):** SASB presents businesses with a clear framework to convey financial material sustainability information to stakeholders. SASB's approach is industry-tailored, highlighting the financial ramifications across various sustainability topics and ensuring stakeholders derive actionable insights.
5. **European Sustainability Reporting Standards (ESRS):** Launched by the European Commission, the ESRS aim to redefine how EU-based companies report on climate and ESG actions. Rooted in the European Green Deal and formulated by the European Financial Reporting Advisory

Group, ESRS are designed to evaluate the sustainability endeavors of businesses, positioning the EU at the forefront of sustainability dialogue.

The mosaic of global sustainability demands robust, integrated reporting systems encompassing financial and non-financial facets of ESG and materiality. While SASB provides niche frameworks targeting the financial implications of sustainability, the ESRS offers a more panoramic view, addressing broader sustainability concerns with nuance. Such evolving standards exemplify the integration of sustainability accounting into corporate operations, harmonizing them with global agreements and national economic blueprints.

As we live through an age of rapid economic metamorphosis, propelled by technological advancements and evolving societal norms, our accounting frameworks must be adaptive, comprehensive, and anticipatory. If the global vision leans towards a future marked by sustainability, inclusivity, and resilience, our accounting structures should ideally be the compass guiding this transformation. Perfecting these frameworks can thus offer robust methodologies for understanding the profound repercussions of emerging economic paradigms, underscoring transparency, accountability, and universal comparability.

8.6 Alternative Economic Models Beyond Carbon

As the challenges of the 21st century evolve, traditional economic models are being re-evaluated in favor of more holistic and sustainable approaches. The priorities for the post-2030 economic agenda need to be centered on the principles of sustainability and inclusivity to create resilient, equitable, and future-ready economies. Two emerging economic models that align with these principles are the social economy and the circular economy. Carbon-heavy economies, on the other hand, have proven to be unsustainable and detrimental to our planet and its inhabitants.

1. **Social Economy:** The social economy (SE) encompasses organizations and enterprises prioritizing social, environmental, and community objectives over profit. This economic model, sometimes called the social and solidarity economy (SSE), signifies its principles prioritizing

collaboration over competition and social purpose over profit-making. Examples include cooperatives, mutual societies, non-profit associations, and social enterprises. They often operate in health, education, social services, work integration, and environmental protection sectors. Social economy enterprises contribute to sustainable development by promoting social inclusion, creating jobs, and providing innovative goods and services that meet social needs. They can play a key role in the post-2030 economy by promoting economic democracy, reducing inequalities, and fostering local development.[8]

2. **Circular Economy:** The circular economy (often termed "circularity" or "CE") aims to redesign our linear "take-make-waste" economic model into one that is restorative and regenerative by design. CE represents a revolutionary approach to production and consumption, emphasizing the prolonged lifecycle of materials and products through methods like sharing, leasing, repairing, refurbishing, and recycling. By focusing on these sustainable strategies, the CE model responds to pressing economic challenges such as the judicious use of resources, emission controls, and waste minimization. Above all, CE stands out as a beacon for economic prosperity by fortifying sustainable consumption and enhancing resource efficiency. CE promotes the reduction, reuse, and recycling of resources to minimize waste and make the most of our natural resources. A circular economy not only helps preserve the environment but can also generate new jobs and economic growth. In the post-2030 era, embracing the circular economy can help address critical environmental challenges like resource depletion and climate change, while also driving innovation and economic prosperity [9]

In recent decades, additional new economic models have emerged, underscoring the imperative of crafting alternative, human-centric solutions for economic inclusivity. This is evident in the advent of the caring and sharing economies. When shaped by democratic and inclusive policies, these models can also pave the way for solutions that transcend a carbon-reliant economy.

3. **Caring Economy:** The caring economy emphasizes sectors that revolve around care work, including childcare, elder

care, healthcare, and education. This economic model strives to highlight the importance of such roles, often undervalued, and envisions an economic structure that rewards care as pivotal to societal health and sustainability. By focusing on human well-being, the caring economy inherently supports sustainable development, diverting attention from mere profit-driven motives to long-term societal benefits. Such an approach not only strengthens community bonds but also moves beyond the carbon-intensive industrial models, reducing ecological footprints and promoting harmony with the environment. To truly promote this model, it is crucial for policymakers to implement strategies such as offering adequate compensation, job security, and benefits to care workers. Establishing publicly funded care services can alleviate the burden on families, ensuring all citizens have access to vital care. Furthermore, supporting education and training tailored for roles in the caring economy can further bolster its growth and recognition.[10]

4. **Sharing Economy:** The sharing economy represents an economic system where assets or services are exchanged between individuals, either freely or for a fee, typically facilitated by the Internet. Prioritizing access over ownership, this model fosters efficient resource use and strengthens community ties. By maximizing the utility of already existing resources and minimizing waste, the sharing economy inherently supports sustainable practices and moves away from the carbon-intensive consumption patterns characteristic of traditional economies. Such a shift not only reduces carbon footprints but also promotes a more resilient, localized economy that is less reliant on global supply chains and overproduction. Policymakers aiming to cultivate the sharing economy should consider updating city regulations to support shared spaces and resources, while also offering tax incentives to businesses operating under sharing models. Ensuring user safety and trustworthiness, regulatory measures must be established, holding sharing platforms to stringent standards. Moreover, nurturing partnerships between local governments, businesses, and non-profits can spearhead community-driven sharing initiatives, making the sharing economy more integrated into daily life.[11]

In addition to the "social," "circular," "caring," and "sharing" economic models, several innovative models have emerged, seeking not only to redefine value and growth but also to address the complex interplay between economic systems and environmental and social well-being. Among these are ecological economics, feminist economics, doughnut economics, and regenerative economics each offering a unique perspective on creating a sustainable future beyond carbon reliance.

5. **Ecological Economics:** Ecological economics fuses the principles of ecology and economics, stressing the interconnectedness of nature's systems and human economies. This model recognizes that our economic activities occur within, and are constrained by, the biosphere's limits. It challenges the traditional economic focus on endless growth, emphasizing instead the need for a steady-state economy where material and energy throughout are stabilized at sustainable levels. By placing ecological limits at the center of policy and decision-making, ecological economics offers a roadmap to operate within Earth's boundaries, minimizing carbon footprints and promoting environmental balance.[12]
6. **Feminist Economics:** Feminist economics challenges the patriarchal biases present in traditional economic models, advocating for gender-aware and inclusive approaches to economic analysis. It questions the undervaluing of "women's work," especially in care and domestic spheres, and promotes economic policies that ensure gender equity. This model emphasizes the role of cooperative, rather than competitive, economic behaviors, advocating for systems that consider long-term societal well-being. By prioritizing social equity and de-emphasizing aggressive growth, feminist economics supports sustainable development and offers an alternative to carbon-intensive, exploitative economies.[13]
7. **Doughnut Economics:** Proposed by Kate Raworth, doughnut economics presents a visual framework—a doughnut—to represent the balance between essential human needs and the planet's ecological limits. The inner ring of the doughnut stands for a social foundation, ensuring that no one is left lacking in life's essentials, while the outer ring represents the ecological ceiling that we should not exceed to maintain a stable planet. This model calls for operating within the "safe and just space" between the rings. Doughnut economics,

by design, pushes for policies and practices that address social inequalities while ensuring environmental stewardship, making it a holistic approach to moving beyond carbon-dependent economies.[14]

8. **Regenerative Economics:** Building upon the principles of sustainable and holistic economic systems, the regenerative economy centers on the idea of renewal, restoration, and growth that simultaneously adds value to society and the environment. Unlike models that only seek to maintain or reduce harm, a regenerative approach actively works to repair historical damages to ecosystems, communities, and resources. This model believes in the potential of economies to be forces of healing and restoration. It prioritizes business practices and policy decisions that create conditions conducive for a flourishing life, aiming to replace extractive practices with regenerative ones. By aligning economic activity with natural cycles and systems, the regenerative economy reduces carbon dependence, revitalizes ecosystems, strengthens community bonds, and creates a resilient, adaptive, and thriving socioeconomic landscape [15]

The "regenerative" and "restoring" economic paradigms are associated with the "blue" economy paradigm, which contrasts with the "red" economy and expands on the "green" economy paradigms.

Red Economy Paradigm: The red economy represents a period where the primary concern was progress and innovation without significant regard for the environment or societal inequalities. It adheres to a linear "take-make-waste" model where raw materials are extracted, turned into products, and discarded without much thought for sustainability. This model embodies individualistic values, emphasizing personal achievements and the accumulation of wealth, which often comes at the community's expense. Consequently, wealth becomes concentrated in the hands of a few, leading to pronounced economic disparities. Such an approach also fosters a deep societal reliance on non-renewable resources, underlining the strong dependence on continual consumption to fuel economic growth.

Green Economy Paradigm: Transitioning from this, the green economy arises as a more environmentally conscious model.

Instead of the sheer exploitation characteristic of the red economy, the green economy adopts a protective stance, striving to reduce environmental harm. This model champions a circular approach where waste is minimized, and products are consciously designed for recycling or reuse. Central to the green economy is a collective spirit, emphasizing community solutions, cooperation, and community-driven initiatives. However, it's worth noting that while the green economy is a step forward, it may still resort to practices that, although greener, might not be entirely sustainable. By diversifying energy sources, like harnessing wind and solar power, and leaning into local solutions, the green economy becomes more resilient to external disruptions.

Blue Economy Paradigm: Lastly, the blue economy emerges as an evolution beyond the green model, aiming to reduce harm and actively regenerate and restore ecosystems. Instead of viewing the economy as a mere machine, the blue economy sees it as a living, breathing ecosystem, ready to be nurtured. Drawing deep inspiration from nature, it underscores symbiotic relationships where entities coexist, supporting and benefiting each other without exploitation. Moving away from the scarcity-driven mindset of previous models, the blue economy thrives on a logic of abundance. It continually seeks innovative ways to regenerate resources and value. A distinct characteristic of the blue economy is its emphasis on autonomy, promoting self-sufficiency and decentralization, thus reducing external dependencies and power imbalances.

While the green economy marked a vital departure from the unsustainable tendencies of the red economy, the blue economy pushed the boundaries even further. It envisions a world where economic practices not only cause no harm but actively rejuvenate the environment, tackle social disparities, and generate value for all.

The regenerative economics and blue economy paradigm, similar to ecological, feminist, and doughnut economics, signify a transition from traditional, "red," linear, and often exploitative systems. They illustrate a collective effort to envision an economic future that is equitable, inclusive, and in harmony with the planet. As more industries, policymakers, and societies begin to internalize and implement these models, there is the potential for a profound shift towards a global economy that values all forms of life and their intricate interdependencies.

8.7 Toward a Well-Being Economic Paradigm

In the evolving discourse on alternative economic models prioritizing sustainability and holistic development, another transformative framework merits attention: the well-being economy. Building on the foundational principles of previously mentioned models, the Club of Rome's *Earth for All* publication describes an economy that synergizes various sustainable tenets, culminating in what's known as the well-being economy.[16]

Well-Being Economy: The well-being economy stands as a testament to an economic paradigm that fundamentally centers on the holistic well-being of current and subsequent generations. Within its structure, societal norms and incentives are meticulously crafted to guarantee that every individual enjoys a life of contentment, safety, and joy. It emphasizes environmental prudence, cherishing elements intrinsic to human happiness, such as health, nature, education, and cohesive communities. Moreover, the well-being economy diligently addresses climate change impacts, ensuring a more secure future for nature and humanity.

Rather than perpetuating a ceaseless quest for exponential growth, this economic model advocates for sustainable development, underlining the importance of shared well-being over mere numeric ascendancy like GDP growth. Central to its doctrine is a profound systemic metamorphosis; the paradigm shifts from overemphasizing economic growth to prioritizing holistic well-being. As articulated by the Well-Being Economic Alliance (WeAll), the economy is seen not as the ultimate destination but as a vehicle to uplift societal well-being. The core tenets of this vision are:

- **Dignity:** Affirming that everyone can access ample resources for a fulfilling life encompassing comfort, health, and safety.
- **Nature:** Committing to protecting and revitalizing the environment for the collective benefit of all living beings.
- **Connection:** Nurturing an intrinsic sense of community, anchored in institutions that propel the common welfare.

- **Fairness:** Upholding justice at the heart of economic activities, while diligently working to bridge the chasm between the affluent and the underprivileged.
- **Participation:** Championing a deeply engaged citizenry, where individuals are interwoven into their local communities and economies.

The well-being economy, alongside other alternative economic paradigms, sharply departs from traditional carbon-intensive economies. The latter are often mired in a myopic, linear perspective underpinned by neoliberal values, frequently propelling a relentless pursuit of growth without considering the broader implications for long-term sustainability and the overall well-being of systems and societies. Such economies significantly amplify global greenhouse gas emissions, triggering exacerbated climate change and its associated severe repercussions, from extreme weather events to biodiversity loss. Beyond the environmental ramifications, the economic implications of these myopic strategies are profound and concerning. Moreover, these growth-centric paradigms exacerbate social disparities, with marginalized groups disproportionately shouldering the environmental and societal burdens of unchecked economic expansion. Therefore, a pivot from such linear, short-term-focused economies is not merely an environmental mandate, but also a socioeconomic one.

As we set our sights post-2030, and as suggested by the Club of Rome even post-2050, it's imperative that policy initiatives realign economic objectives. This involves transitioning towards renewable energy, championing energy conservation, and nurturing sustainable industries. Beyond mere economic recalibration, this transformation can spur job creation, fuel innovation, bolster communal health, and underpin resilient economies, while effectively countering climate change. It is crucial, however, that this transition remain grounded in equity, ensuring no community is sidelined or overlooked.

8.8 Other Post-2030 Economic Priorities

In addition to shifting toward stakeholder-oriented economic models, CSV enterprise entities, certification, and reporting, mainstreaming ESG investments, expanding social, circular and other alternative economies while discouraging carbon-heavy industries, there are several other priorities that should be considered for a post-2030 sustainable, resilient, and inclusive economic agenda:

1. **Inclusive Growth and Reducing Inequalities:** Addressing economic inequalities is fundamental for sustainable development. Policies should aim to promote inclusive growth that benefits all sections of society, including the most marginalized and disadvantaged. This includes ensuring equal access to opportunities and resources, fair wage policies, progressive taxation, and robust social protection systems.
2. **Investment in Green Infrastructure:** Investment in green infrastructure such as renewable energy, sustainable transport, and climate-resilient buildings can drive sustainable economic growth, create jobs, and help mitigate and adapt to climate change.
3. **Promotion of Sustainable Consumption and Production:** Economies should aim to transition toward sustainable consumption and production patterns. This includes promoting sustainable agricultural practices, reducing food waste, supporting sustainable supply chains, and fostering sustainable consumer behavior.
4. **Fostering Innovation and Sustainable Industrialization:** Technological innovation and sustainable industrialization can play a key role in addressing many of the challenges of sustainable development. This includes promoting R&D in green technologies, supporting sustainable SMEs, and encouraging digital inclusivity.
5. **Financial System Reform:** The global financial system needs to better align with SDGs. This could involve measures like incorporating climate risk into financial stability monitoring, encouraging green bonds and other sustainable financial products, and ensuring that central bank practices support sustainability objectives.
6. **International Trade and Investment Rules:** International trade and investment rules should be fair, transparent, and supportive of sustainable development. This includes removing trade barriers for low-income countries, enforcing fair labor and environmental standards in trade agreements, and ensuring that investment treaties do not restrict countries' abilities to regulate in the public interest.

7. **Decent Work and Economic Growth:** Ensuring decent work opportunities is a crucial aspect of sustainable development. Policies should aim to promote full and productive employment, decent work for all, and eradicate forced labor, human trafficking, and child labor.
8. **The Idea of Work as a Human Right in the Age of Robotization and Automation:** As we navigate the rapid advancements of AI, robotization, and automation, the vision of prosperity needs to be recalibrated. Economic policies should intertwine with social objectives, placing humans at the center. To foster prosperity that extends beyond mere profit, it is essential to view work not just as a means to an economic end, but as a fundamental human right. By considering work as a human right and recognizing its deeper sociocultural significance, we can create a balanced and prosperous future that harmoniously blends technology with the innate human need for purpose, connection, and well-being.
9. **Lifelong Learning and Reskilling:** As the nature of jobs change, there's a pressing need to invest in continuous learning. Governments and corporations should facilitate programs that allow workers to upskill and reskill, adapting to the changing job market. Governments should plan for incentives and opportunities to access affordable, quality, and relevant educational upgrades.

These priorities represent an integrated and transformative approach that recognizes the interdependence of economic, social, and environmental factors in achieving sustainable development. They underscore the need for systemic change and the importance of cross-sectoral and international cooperation in shaping an inclusive, resilient, and sustainable economic future.

The discourse surrounding economic prosperity is undergoing a significant paradigm shift. As underscored by the reflections from the 2023 World Economic Forum (WEF) and its luminaries, we are at a turning point where the narrative is no longer solely about growth. Rather, it is about redefining the very essence of what growth means in a global context. The wisdom imparted by WEF founder Klaus Schwab resonates this view. He stated, "Growth, while indispensable, must be viewed not just as an increase in numbers or material wealth, but as an embodiment of resilience, equity, and sustainability."[17]

Localization and diversification of supply chains, while offering a fresh geography of growth, bring the benefits of inclusivity to the forefront. They pave the way for small and medium-sized enterprises to thrive, offering diverse job opportunities and empowering new participants in the market. Yet, it is equally crucial to remember that our world thrives on connections. The seamless exchange of goods, services, ideas, and technologies is a cornerstone for ensuring prosperity in developing nations, enhancing living standards universally, and crafting solutions to the pressing climate crisis.

ILO Director-General Gilbert Houngbo's poignant statement at the 2023 WEF illustrates this sobering reminder. He stated, "Poverty anywhere is a threat to prosperity everywhere." Prosperity is not just about individual or national success. It's a collective endeavor. If we leave sections of our global society behind, we're compromising the integrity of our shared future. The priorities of economic prosperity must encompass a holistic view that melds growth with inclusion, resilience, and sustainability, ensuring a brighter, more equitable future for all.[18]

8.9 Economic Mindset Shift Priorities

Advancing economic sustainability and prosperity demands adopting a broader mindset that transcends the traditional emphasis on mere profit maximization. This approach involves integrating values of environmental stewardship, social equity, and long-term viability into the core of economic strategies, thereby ensuring a balanced and sustainable growth that benefits all stakeholders. It requires a shift in understanding our economic value creations through a holistic view of the true value of things. It advocates for a model of economic sustainability that unfolds across four interconnected levels. This expansive framework not only redefines "materiality" by transcending mere financial considerations (economic capital) but also integrates critical elements such as environmental stewardship (environmental capital), human well-being in times of crises and emergencies (human capital), and the appreciation of diverse cultural values and perspectives (cultural capital). Such an approach champions a comprehensive and resilient economic development strategy that acknowledges and values the multifaceted nature of sustainability.

1. **Economic Sustainability Level 1—Rethinking Profit Maximization:** Milton Friedman's perspective positioned profit maximization as the primary goal of businesses.[19] While this approach serves essential financial priorities, it needs to balance its short-term perspectives, which are solely concentrated on monetary gains, with global responsibility and the broader impact of business activities on society and the environment. To achieve genuine economic sustainability, we must adopt a more comprehensive perspective on costs—encompassing direct financial outlays and indirect societal expenses, such as environmental harm and social disparities. By doing so, the true economic impact of products and services can be accurately reflected and addressed.
2. **Economic Sustainability Level 2—Embracing a Multi-Capital Approach:** Building upon Rachel Carson's seminal work *Silent Spring*,[20] which raised alarms about lasting environmental damage, this level advocates for measuring multiple forms of capital—financial, social, and environmental. Such a holistic approach recognizes that economic activities extend their influence beyond immediate financial outcomes, impacting broader ecological and societal domains. A comprehensive valuation of products and services must include the costs associated with environmental externalities and social implications, as neglecting these aspects leads to unsustainable practices with potentially devastating long-term consequences.
3. **Economic Sustainability Level 3—Valuing Time and Crisis Responsiveness:** Inspired by John Elkington's insights in *Green Swans*,[21] this level encourages businesses to look beyond mere profit and risk management, urging them to focus on responsibilities that range from resilience to regeneration. It highlights the importance of valuing goods and services in light of their potential fluctuations during emergencies or global challenges like climate change and pandemics. This perspective underlines the need for adaptability and forward-thinking in business practices, evaluating companies' and economies' capability to respond to and mitigate crises, and prioritizing resilience and long-term sustainability over short-term gains.
4. **Economic Sustainability Level 4—Incorporating Cultural and Non-Material Values:** Drawing from Mariana

> Mazzucato's *The Value of Everything*,[22] this level prompts a re-evaluation of how value is defined and measured, advocating for integrating diverse, cultural, and non-material considerations into our understanding of economic value. It calls for acknowledging and respecting various cultural value systems, including those of Indigenous peoples who often prioritize harmony with nature. This broader, more inclusive perspective on value extends beyond traditional economic metrics, emphasizing the significance of nature's intrinsic value and cultural heritage, which, though challenging to quantify economically, are essential for a comprehensive and genuine approach to economic sustainability.

In essence, embracing the multidimensional model of capital and values described in the four levels of economic sustainability calls for a paradigm shift in our sustainability agenda. This shift focuses on prioritizing collective well-being and identifying shared values that shape a sustainable future for all. Moving beyond the limited perspective of personal gains or profit maximization, a viewpoint historically championed by Milton Friedman, this approach urges a deeper consideration of our economic activities' extensive impacts on society and the environment, echoing the insights of Rachel Carson and other thought leaders. Such a holistic perspective is crucial in forging a balanced and sustainable path forward, where economic decisions are made with an acute awareness of their long-term implications on our world.

By incorporating a diverse spectrum of capital forms—financial, environmental, social, and cultural—we start to address the critical issues highlighted in Garrett Hardin's *Tragedy of the Commons*,[23] where individual actions can lead to the depletion of shared resources. This holistic economic sustainability model not only aims to prevent the overuse of shared resources but also promotes a collective sense of responsibility and public stewardship, resonating with the principles outlined by Elinor Ostrom in her work on "governing the commons."[24]

The multifaceted approach to economic sustainability, emphasizing various forms of capital and shared duties, paves the way for establishing future standards in "dual-materiality" sustainability reporting, as per the most recent European Commission guidelines.[25] This ensures a thorough assessment and reporting of both financial and non-financial impacts.

Moreover, this strategy acknowledges that enduring economic sustainability and resilience, especially when facing global challenges like climate change and pandemics, requires a unified effort and careful management of communal resources. It highlights the necessity for cooperative governance structures that are inclusive and participatory, allowing a range of voices and viewpoints to contribute to the decision-making process.

By redefining the concepts of value and success in this manner, we can foster economic systems that are not only sustainable and equitable but also beneficial for all stakeholders, including future generations and the environment.

8.10 Resources

As we have seen throughout Chapter 8, economic prosperity sustainability is concerned with creating and maintaining economic systems that provide equitable opportunities for all individuals and future generations while ensuring environmental and social well-being. Significant studies have illuminated the paths and challenges in achieving sustainable economic prosperity. Here are some of them:

1. **World Bank's *World Development Reports* (WDR):** These annual reports provide a deep dive into various facets of sustainable development. Over the years, the topics have ranged from agriculture, environment, health, to equity, offering comprehensive insights into the challenges and pathways to sustainable economic prosperity. Read more at www.worldbank.org/en/publication/wdr/wdr-archive.
2. ***Doughnut Economics: Seven Ways to Think Like a 21st-Century Economist* by Kate Raworth (2017):** Raworth introduces the concept of the doughnut as a visual representation of a sustainable economy. The inner ring of the doughnut represents a social foundation—the basic needs that every person should meet—while the outer ring represents an ecological ceiling. The space in-between is the safe and just space for humanity. Raworth argues that current economic models are outdated, and we need to rethink how we conceptualize growth, value, and economic health. Read more at https://doughnuteconomics.org/.
3. ***The Blue Economy 3.0: The Marriage of Science, Innovation and Entrepreneurship Creates a New Business Model That***

Transforms Society **by Gunter Pauli (2017):** Pauli's work on the blue economy is a shift from the business-as-usual economic model to a regenerative model that takes inspiration from natural systems. The book details innovations that are sustainable and regenerative, emphasizing local resources, waste reduction, and increased value creation. It underscores the point that sustainability and economic prosperity are not mutually exclusive but can be symbiotic. Read more at www.theblueeconomy.org/.

4. ***Green Swans: The Coming Boom in Regenerative Capitalism*** **by John Elkington (2020):** In this book, Elkington, a world-renowned thought leader in corporate responsibility and sustainable capitalism, introduces the concept of "Green Swans." Drawing from Nassim Nicholas Taleb's idea of "Black Swans" (rare, unpredictable events with enormous impact), Elkington's Green Swans are similarly rare but represent positive transformative events. He discusses how businesses can evolve to produce solutions that deliver sustainable and equitable growth. Read more at www.oecd-forum.org/posts/out-of-the-blue-green-swans-take-off-in-the-exponential-decade.
5. ***Strategy for Sustainability: A Business Manifesto*** **by Adam Werbach (2009):** Werbach, once the youngest president of the Sierra Club, a leading American environmental organization, presents a strategic approach for businesses to achieve sustainability. He outlines how companies can benefit economically while being environmentally and socially responsible. Werbach introduces a method of categorizing sustainability strategies based on their scale, discussing tactics that range from quick and small scale to large, transformative endeavors. Read more at https://ssir.org/books/reviews/entry/strategy_for_sustainability_adam_werbach.

Notes

1 United Nations (2015). *Our Common Agenda: Report of the Secretary-General*. United Nations. https://www.un.org/en/common-agenda#:~:text=The%20Our%20Common%20Agenda%20report&text=We%20must%20recognize%20that%20humanity's,can%20solve%20its%20challenges%20alone

2 Shams, S.R., Vrontis, D., Weber, Y., Tsoukatos, E., & Galati, A. (Eds.). (2019). *Stakeholder Engagement and Sustainability*. Routledge.

3 Honeyman, R. (2014). *The B Corp Handbook: How to Use Business as a Force for Good*. Berrett-Koehler Publishers.
4 Risso, M., & Testarmata, S. (Eds.). (2017). *Value Sharing for Sustainable and Inclusive Development*. IGI.
5 OECD (2019). *Social Impact Investment 2019: The Impact Imperative for Sustainable Development*. OECD Publishing.
6 Tavanti, M. (2023). *Developing Sustainability in Organizations: A Values-Based Approach*. Palgrave Macmillan.
7 To explore factors contributing to the standardization of sustainability accounting systems, see: Stolowy, H., & Paugam, L. (2023). Sustainability reporting: Is convergence possible?. *Accounting in Europe*, 20(2), 139–165. For an overview of ESF Financial Investing, see: OECD (2020). *Business and Finance Outlook 2020: Sustainable and Resilient Finance*. United OECD Publishing.
8 On the social and participatory economy, see: Connelly, S., Gismondi, M.A., Roseland, M., & Markey, S.P. (2016). *Scaling Up: The Convergence of Social Economy and Sustainability.* AU Press.
9 On the circle economy, see: Wiesmeth, H. (2020). *Implementi ng the Circular Economy for Sustainable Development*. Elsevier Science.
10 On the caring economy, see: Eisler, R. (2008). *The Real Wealth of Nations: Creating A Caring Economics*. Berrett-Koehler Publishers.
11 On the sharing economy, see: Sundararajan, A. (2017). *The Sharing Economy: The End of Employment and the Rise of Crowd-Based Capitalism*. MIT Press.
12 On the ecological economy, see: Daly, H.E., & Farley, J. (2010). *Ecological Economics, Second Edition: Principles and Applications*. Island Press.
13 On the feminist economy, see: Berik, G., & Kongar, E. (2021). *The Routledge Handbook of Feminist Economics*. Taylor & Francis.
14 On the doughnut economy, see: Raworth, K. (2017). *Doughnut Economics: Seven Ways to Think Like a 21st-Century Economist.* Chelsea Green Publishing.
15 On the regenerative economics model, see: Antonino Marvuglia, A., Andreucci, M.B., Baltov, M., & Hansen, P. (2021). *Rethinking Sustainability Towards a Regenerative Economy*. Springer International Publishing.
16 On the well-being economy, see: Club of Rome (2022). *Earth for All: A Survival Guide for Humanity*. New Society Publishers.
17 World Economic Forum (2023). *Growth Summit 2023: Job Creation and Reskilling Must Be Central to Growth in the Age of Uncertainty, Advancing AI and the Green Transition*. https://www.weforum.org/press/2023/05/growth-summit-2023-job-creation-and-reskilling-must-be-central-to-growth-in-the-age-of-uncertainty-advancing-ai-and-the-green-transition/
18 ILO (2023, January 16). *ILO Director-General highlights world of work issues and social justice at the World Economic Forum*. https://www.ilo.org/global/about-the-ilo/how-the-ilo-works/ilo-director-general/news-and-press-releases/WCMS_865512/lang—en/index.htm

19 Friedman, M. (1970). The social responsibility of business is to increase its profits. *The New York Times Magazine.*
20 Carson, R. (1962). *Silent Spring*. Houghton Mifflin.
21 Elkington, J. (2020). *Green Swans: The Coming Boom in Regenerative Capitalism.* Fast Company Press.
22 Mazzucato, M. (2018). *The Value of Everything: Making and Taking in the Global Economy.* PublicAffairs.
23 Hardin, G. (1968). The Tragedy of the Commons. *Science*, 162(3859), 1243–1248.
24 Ostrom, E. (1990). *Governing the Commons: The Evolution of Institutions for Collective Action.* Cambridge University Press.
25 European Commission. (2023). *Corporate Sustainability Reporting.* https://finance.ec.europa.eu/corporate-sustainability-reporting_en

9 Environmental and Climate Priorities

> Human activities, principally through emissions of greenhouse gases, have unequivocally caused global warming, with global surface temperature reaching 1.1°C above 1850–1900 in 2011–2020. Global greenhouse gas emissions have continued to increase over 2010–2019, with unequal historical and ongoing contributions arising from unsustainable energy use, land use and land-use change, lifestyles and patterns of consumption and production across regions, between and within countries, and between individuals (high confidence). Human-caused climate change is already affecting many weather and climate extremes in every region across the globe. This has led to widespread adverse impacts on food and water security, human health and on economies and society and related losses and damages63 to nature and people (high confidence). Vulnerable communities who have historically contributed the least to current climate change are disproportionately affected (high confidence).
>
> (*IPCC Climate Change 2023: Synthesis Report*[1])

Overview

In this chapter, we examine the critical environmental challenges that threaten global sustainability. Priorities range from climate change mitigation, adaptation, and biodiversity conservation to sustainable resource management and pollution reduction. The complex interconnections between environmental health and human well-being are also unpacked.

9.1 Calling for Effective Climate Agenda

As the pages of our calendar move beyond 2030, we stand at a critical moment in our planet's history. The alarming pace of climate emergencies and the unprecedented loss of biodiversity have resonated with a clear and disconcerting message: the Earth itself is under threat. From the melting glaciers of the

DOI: 10.4324/9781003494676-12

polar regions to the receding forests of the Amazon, from the displaced communities due to rising sea levels to the vanishing species that once enriched our ecosystems—the impacts are widespread, profound, and indiscriminate.

Yet, despite this looming shadow, much of our world's decision-making machinery remains myopic. National interests often overshadow the broader, collective needs of our planet. The parochial vision, focused solely on immediate territorial benefits or driven by short-term economic gains, exacerbates the chasm between awareness and action. Such a compartmentalized approach, marked by indifference or denial, contradicts the universality of our environmental crises.

The IPCC has consistently underscored the urgency of these challenges. Their findings, dovetailed with the objectives of SDG 13 (Climate Action), reflect a clarion call for decisive and unified action. However, as we venture into the post-2030 landscape, it's evident that more than merely alignment is needed. Our global agenda requires a more robust integration, a framework that not only merges the priorities of the IPCC and SDG 13 but also institutes mechanisms for collective decision-making.

This chapter delves deeper into these imperatives. As we navigate through it, remember that the Post-2030 Agenda demands more than just commitments. It calls for enforceable actions, globally coordinated efforts, and a renewed pledge to place our planet's health above all else. The future of everything and everyone on Earth hinges on our choices. It's high time we think and act as one.

9.2 Climate Change Priorities

The effects of climate change are projected to intensify in the future. According to the IPCC, here are some key trends and projections:

1. **Increasing Temperatures:** The global temperature is projected to rise by about 1.5 degrees Celsius to 4.5 degrees Celsius by 2100, relative to 1850–1900, depending on future greenhouse gas emissions. This temperature rise is expected to cause more frequent and intense heatwaves. The last decade (2011–2020) has already been the hottest on record.
2. **Changing Rainfall Patterns:** Changes in precipitation patterns are expected, with some areas seeing more rainfall,

leading to increased flood risks, and others experiencing less, leading to droughts.

3. **Rising Sea Levels:** Global sea levels are projected to continue to rise due to the melting of polar ice caps and the thermal expansion of seawater. This poses a serious threat to coastal cities and low-lying island nations. Sea level is projected to rise between 0.26 to 0.77 meters by 2100 under different emissions scenarios.
4. **More Extreme Weather Events:** There is expected to be an increase in the frequency and intensity of extreme weather events such as storms, hurricanes, and heavy rainfall events.
5. **Biodiversity Loss:** Changing climates could result in the loss of many species unable to adapt quickly enough, and affect the function of ecosystems, threatening biodiversity.
6. **Ocean Acidification:** As more CO_2 is absorbed by the world's oceans, their pH is expected to continue to decrease, leading to ocean acidification that threatens marine life, especially coral reefs.
7. **Ice Retreat:** Arctic sea ice, glaciers, and the Greenland and Antarctic ice sheets are projected to continue to shrink.

These projections represent a serious challenge for humanity in the coming decades. They underscore the importance of mitigating climate change by reducing greenhouse gas emissions and adapting to changes that are already inevitable. The need for comprehensive, effective, and rapid action cannot be overstated[2]

Addressing climate change is crucial for the sustainable development and well-being of all life on Earth. The Post-2030 Agenda must reflect our commitment to this task and go beyond the targets set by the Paris Agreement and the SDGs. Here are key climate change priorities to consider for the Post-2030 Agenda:

1. **Mitigation and Adaptation:** The Post-2030 Agenda should build upon existing mitigation strategies to reduce greenhouse gas emissions, aiming for more ambitious targets. It should also emphasize adaptation efforts, helping communities prepare for and respond to the impacts of climate change, particularly in vulnerable regions.
2. **Transition to Renewable Energy:** A swift transition from fossil fuels to renewable energy sources, such as solar, wind,

and hydroelectric power, should be prioritized. This transition should be done to support workers and communities currently reliant on fossil fuel industries.

3. **Nature-Based Solutions:** Investing in and promoting nature-based solutions, such as reforestation, restoration of peatlands, protection of wildlife habitats, and promoting sustainable agriculture and ocean practices. This helps absorb CO_2 from the atmosphere, enhance biodiversity, and improve livelihoods.
4. **Green Finance:** Prioritizing green finance mechanisms to fund both mitigation and adaptation efforts. This includes carbon pricing, green bonds, and incentivizing financial investments in sustainable projects and businesses.
5. **Sustainable Infrastructure and Transport:** The development of low-carbon and resilient infrastructure, including energy-efficient buildings and sustainable transport systems.
6. **Carbon Sequestration Technologies:** Investment in carbon capture, use, and storage (CCUS) technologies and other innovative solutions that can remove CO_2 from the atmosphere.
7. **Global Cooperation and Just Transition:** Emphasizing the need for global cooperation to tackle climate change. This should also ensure a just transition where no communities are left behind, especially those most vulnerable to climate impacts.
8. **Climate Education and Awareness:** Enhancing education and raising awareness about the causes and impacts of climate change and what individuals and communities can do to help.

Addressing climate change in the Post-2030 Agenda requires an integrated approach considering environmental, social, and economic dimensions. It's about reducing emissions and building a fair and resilient society that can withstand and thrive in a changing climate.

9.3 Biodiversity Conservation Priorities

Biodiversity losses are an exponentially challenging issue at their current rate that could become even more dramatic in the future. Biodiversity is the variety of life on Earth and encompasses the entire range of species, their genetic variation, and the ecosystems they inhabit. This natural resource is fundamental not only for the stability of the planet, but also for the goods and services it provides, including those vital for human health such as medicine.

Many of our pharmaceuticals have been derived from nature. For example, around 50% of all drugs used in clinical medicine in the last century were either natural products or derived from natural products, including plants, animals, and microorganisms. This includes life-saving medications such as antibiotics, antivirals, anticancer drugs, painkillers, and various medicines used for heart diseases, mental health, and more.

However, the ongoing loss of biodiversity potentially means the loss of opportunities for the discovery of new drugs. The unknown extent of this damage becomes even more significant when we realize that a large portion of the world's biodiversity remains unexplored. Estimates suggest that less than 10% of species on Earth have been identified, meaning a vast majority of potential medicinal resources are yet to be discovered and understood.[3]

Furthermore, healthy ecosystems and rich biodiversity are also critical in disease prevention. They regulate disease vectors, dilute disease transmission, and regulate climate change, which is increasingly impacting disease spread and human health.

Overall, the loss of biodiversity could mean missing out on yet undiscovered remedies, losing potential models for studying diseases, and disrupting ecosystems that regulate disease spread. Addressing biodiversity loss should therefore be an essential part of our strategies for health security and medical advancements.

In addition, the loss of soil biodiversity could also threaten food production possibly generating unimaginable levels of world hunger. Soil is home to a quarter of our planet's biodiversity. A myriad of organisms including bacteria, archaea, viruses, fungi, prions, protozoa, algae, and nematodes, along with micro-arthropods, mites, springtails, insects (ants, beetles, termites), and larger organisms such as earthworms and rodents, contribute to a complex and dynamic ecosystem below ground.

These organisms play a vital role in soil health and fertility by contributing to key soil functions such as nutrient cycling, organic matter decomposition, soil structure formation and maintenance, disease suppression and water regulation.

In the context of food production, soil organisms enhance nutrient availability for crops, control pests and diseases, and improve soil structure and water-holding capacity, all of which contribute to increased crop productivity. The loss of soil biodiversity can, therefore, have direct impacts on food security.

Furthermore, a rich soil biodiversity also aids in the resilience of soil functions under changing environmental conditions. It provides a buffer against stresses, such as those caused by climate change, making agroecosystems more resilient and sustainable.

Unfortunately, human activities, such as intensive farming practices, deforestation, pollution, and climate change, are threatening soil biodiversity. Maintaining and enhancing soil biodiversity through sustainable soil management practices is essential for long-term agricultural productivity, food security and ecosystem sustainability.

Biodiversity loss is also an alarming phenomenon for species extension, insect decline, coral reefs, deforestation, and wetlands. According to the Intergovernmental Science-Policy Platform on Biodiversity and Ecosystem Services (IPBES) Global Assessment Report in 2019, around one million animal and plant species (more than one in four) are threatened with extinction, many within decades, more than ever before in human history. The worldwide decline in bee populations is a pressing issue, impacting biodiversity and our food systems. Around 75% of global food crops rely on pollinators like bees. Threats like habitat loss, climate change, pesticides, diseases, and invasive species are causing significant bee population declines. This situation underscores the need for sustainable agricultural practices, reducing pesticide use, and protecting natural habitats. Addressing bee decline is vital to preserve biodiversity and ensure sustainable food systems.[4]

According to the IPCC, 70–90% of coral reefs are expected to disappear even with global warming of 1.5 degrees Celsius, and virtually all would be lost at 2 degrees Celsius. The World Bank reported that the Earth lost 502,000 square miles (1.3 million square kilometers) of forest between 1990 and 2016, an area larger than South Africa. The Ramsar Convention has reported that as much as 87% of the global wetland resource has been lost since the start of the modern era in 1700, with 35% of this loss occurring between 1970–2015. This data paints a bleak picture but underscores the urgent need for concerted global action to halt and reverse these trends.[5]

The future challenges related to the loss of biodiversity are immense and complex. As noted, these are interlinked to climate change which alters habitats and can lead to species extinction. Therefore, reducing greenhouse gas emissions is critical, as is research into how climate change will affect specific species and ecosystems so we can try to mitigate its impact. Here are some other key areas that should be prioritized to preserve biodiversity and decelerate biodiversity losses:

1. **Habitat Loss and Degradation:** This is the primary cause of species extinction. Priorities should include preventing deforestation, protecting natural habitats, and implementing restoration efforts in degraded areas. Land-use policies should prioritize the preservation of biodiversity.
2. **Overexploitation:** Overfishing, hunting, logging, and trade of wildlife and plant species should be controlled, and sustainable practices promoted.
3. **Invasive Species:** Efforts to prevent the introduction of and to control and eradicate invasive species that outcompete native species should be intensified.
4. **Pollution:** Reducing all forms of pollution, including plastic waste, toxic chemicals, and excess nutrients, is important to protect species and ecosystems.
5. **Promoting Sustainable Agriculture:** With the growing global population, agriculture is increasingly encroaching on natural ecosystems. Promoting sustainable agricultural practices that conserve biodiversity is essential.
6. **Public Awareness and Education:** It's important to raise public awareness about biodiversity's importance and educate people about what they can do to help conserve it.
7. **Funding and Policy Commitment:** Resources must be allocated for conservation work, and strong, enforceable policies must be implemented.
8. **Conservation Science and Research:** Scientific research into biodiversity and the effectiveness of different conservation strategies should be promoted.
9. **Protected Areas:** Increasing the size and connectivity of protected areas, both on land and in the oceans, is a crucial part of biodiversity conservation.

It is important to note that tackling the loss of biodiversity requires a holistic approach that acknowledges the interconnectedness of the planet's ecosystems. It's not just about preserving individual species, but also about maintaining the ecological processes and the diversity of life that keep our planet habitable.

9.4 Pollution Reduction Priorities

The environmental challenges posed by various forms of pollution are severe and increasingly urgent. **Microplastic** pollution in the oceans is of particular concern. Microplastics, tiny plastic particles less than 5mm in size, accumulate in the marine ecosystem, posing threats to marine life and humans as they enter the food chain. It's estimated that around 8 million tons of plastic end up in our oceans every year, with far-reaching effects on marine biodiversity, economies, and potentially human health.

Atmospheric pollution, particularly the presence of particulate matter, is another critical issue. These particles, often composed of harmful compounds like heavy metals, can lead to various health issues, from respiratory problems to cardiovascular diseases, while also contributing to climate change.[6]

Water pollution, often due to agricultural runoff containing pesticides and fertilizers, can cause severe damage to freshwater ecosystems, affecting both biodiversity and the availability of clean, safe water for human consumption. Nutrient pollution can lead to eutrophication, creating "dead zones" devoid of oxygen where most marine life can't survive.

Another pollution threat comes from "**forever chemicals**"—a term that describes per-and poly-fluoroalkyl substances (PFAS), a group of man-made chemicals used in industry and consumer products worldwide since the 1950s. They earned their nickname due to their powerful molecular bonds, which do not break down naturally in the environment or the human body, hence "forever."[7]

PFAS have been used in many products due to their water-, grease-, and stain-resistant properties. They can be found in everything from non-stick cookware to water-repellent clothing, stain-resistant carpets and fabrics, firefighting foams, and cosmetics.

Their widespread use and persistence mean they have become a global environmental contaminant. PFAS can be found in soil, water, and air, and have even been detected in the bodies of humans and wildlife worldwide.

PFAS exposure has been linked to a variety of health effects. According to the EPA, certain PFAS can accumulate and stay in the human body for long periods. Long-term exposure to these chemicals can potentially result in increased cholesterol levels, effects on the immune system, increased risk of certain types of cancer (like kidney and testicular cancer), and disruptions in hormones and growth, development, learning, and behavior in infants and children.

Addressing forever chemicals will be a significant environmental priority in the Post-2030 Agenda. This includes reducing their use, managing their disposal and cleanup, and conducting further research into their environmental and health impacts. Strong policy and regulation will be needed at national and international levels alongside innovation in developing safer alternatives.

All these pollution issues require a robust, multipronged approach. This might include policies to reduce plastic production and promote recycling, emissions, and agricultural runoff regulations and investment in clean energy and sustainable agriculture. The urgency of these environmental challenges underscores the need for innovative solutions and global cooperation.[8]

9.5 Environmental-Human Health Priorities

Environmental health and human health are deeply interconnected. One particularly salient example of this link is in the case of zoonotic diseases, which are diseases transmitted to humans from animals. The rise of zoonotic diseases often results from environmental changes and human behaviors that disrupt natural ecosystems and bring humans closer to wildlife.

Deforestation, land use changes, intensive farming practices, and climate change all play significant roles in the emergence of zoonotic diseases. These activities not only destroy wildlife habitats but also create conditions where animals, insects, and humans come into closer and more frequent contact, increasing the chances of diseases spilling over from animals to people. The COVID-19 pandemic, thought to have originated in bats, is a prime example, along with other significant disease outbreaks like Ebola, Zika, and H1N1 swine flu.

As we move into the post-2030 era, understanding and addressing this interdependence will be crucial for preventing future pandemics and protecting both environmental and human health. Priorities will include promoting sustainable land use and farming practices, protecting wildlife habitats, and improving surveillance of zoonotic diseases at the human-animal-environment interface. Raising public awareness of the link between environmental and human health can also encourage behavior changes that reduce the risk of zoonotic diseases.

The One Health approach, which recognizes the interconnectedness of human health, animal health, and the environment, is increasingly being advocated as a strategy for preventing and managing zoonotic diseases. It calls for integrating human, animal, and environmental health sectors and promotes a comprehensive, collaborative, and multisectoral approach to achieve optimal health outcomes. As we move forward, such a holistic and integrative approach will be vital for addressing the complex health challenges our changing environment poses.[9]

Several current and future environmental challenges exemplify the profound interdependence of human health with environmental health. Below are a few examples:

1. **Air Pollution:** Air pollution, resulting from industrial emissions, vehicle exhaust, and other anthropogenic sources, contributes to a multitude of health problems such as respiratory illnesses, heart disease, stroke, and lung cancer. The World Health Organization (WHO) estimates that about 7 million people die each year due to exposure to fine particles in polluted air.
2. **Climate Change:** The impacts of climate change, such as extreme weather events, heatwaves, and changing patterns of disease vectors, have significant effects on human health. For example, heatwaves can lead to heat exhaustion and heatstroke, while increased flooding and higher temperatures can enhance the spread of vector-borne diseases like malaria and dengue fever.
3. **Water Pollution:** Contaminated water sources due to industrial waste, agricultural runoff, and inadequate sanitation can lead to the spread of waterborne diseases, such as cholera, dysentery, and typhoid fever. In addition, chemical contaminants like lead and mercury can have long-term

health impacts, including developmental issues in children and various forms of cancer.

4. **Food Security:** Environmental degradation and climate change threaten food security, which can lead to malnutrition and starvation. Changes in temperature and precipitation patterns can affect crop yields, while ocean acidification and overfishing threaten marine food sources.
5. **Mental Health:** Emerging research suggests that environmental degradation and climate change can have significant impacts on mental health. Natural disasters and extreme weather events can cause acute traumatic stress, while longer-term changes, such as rising temperatures and increasing droughts, have been linked to depression, anxiety, and other mental health disorders.

Looking towards the future, addressing these challenges will require comprehensive strategies that recognize and account for the interconnectedness of environmental health and human health. This will involve not only mitigating environmental degradation and climate change but also adapting our health systems to cope with these changing realities.

9.6 Environmental Priorities for Post-2030 Agenda

As we navigate the critical crossroads of our ecological future, the Post-2030 Agenda necessitates a broader vision beyond mere compliance with the existing SDGs. We must foster a forward-thinking approach that comprehends the urgency and magnitude of evolving environmental crises and presents multifaceted priorities to help design a resilient and sustainable future. In addition to the above-mentioned core priorities, other urgent challenges would need to be considered and emphasized in the analysis and identification of environmental priorities for the new Post-2030 Agenda.

1. **Transition to a Circular Economy:** Our current "take-make-waste" linear economy is unsustainable. A transition to a circular economy, where waste is minimized and resources are reused and recycled, can significantly reduce environmental degradation and resource depletion.
2. **Sustainable Agriculture and Food Systems:** Current agricultural practices are responsible for significant biodiversity

loss, deforestation, and water pollution. Adopting sustainable agricultural practices and developing food systems prioritizing local, seasonal, and organic foods can help address these issues.

3. **Net-Zero Emissions:** To limit global warming to 1.5 degrees Celsius above pre-industrial levels, as recommended by the IPCC, we need to reach net-zero carbon emissions by 2050. This will require rapid decarbonization across all sectors, including energy, transport, buildings, and industry.
4. **Nature-Based Solutions:** Protecting and restoring natural ecosystems can provide numerous benefits, including carbon sequestration, biodiversity conservation, and improved human well-being. Investing in nature-based solutions such as reforestation, wetland restoration, and regenerative agriculture should be a priority.
5. **Sustainable Urban Development:** With the global population increasingly living in cities, sustainable urban development is essential. This includes building energy-efficient infrastructure, promoting public transport, and ensuring access to green spaces and cooling features for residents.
6. **Water Security:** With climate change altering precipitation patterns, ensuring water security will become increasingly important. This will involve sustainable water management practices, improved water infrastructure, and equitable water policies.
7. **Ocean Conservation:** Oceans absorb about a third of CO_2 emissions and are a major source of biodiversity. Ensuring sustainable fisheries, reducing ocean pollution, and protecting marine ecosystems are essential for maintaining the health of our oceans.
8. **Environmental Education and Awareness:** Fostering a greater understanding of environmental issues and promoting sustainable lifestyles is crucial for driving societal change towards sustainability.
9. **Sustainable Consumption and Production:** Our current consumption patterns exceed Earth's biocapacity. Promoting sustainable consumption and production patterns is essential to minimize our environmental footprint and ensure long-term planetary health.
10. **Resilience and Adaptation to Climate Change:** With the effects of climate change already being felt, building

resilience and adaptive capacity in all sectors and communities is paramount.

11. **Just Transition:** Transitioning to a green economy should include everyone. A just transition ensures that the shift towards environmental sustainability results in decent work and quality jobs.
12. **Indigenous Rights and Knowledge:** Indigenous communities often serve as the guardians of biodiversity. Recognizing and protecting their rights and integrating their traditional knowledge into environmental management can greatly contribute to conservation efforts.
13. **Regenerative Design:** Beyond sustainability, we need to adopt regenerative approaches that repair and restore ecosystems and create systems that are beneficial for both humans and nature.
14. **Integration of One Health Approach:** One Health is a collaborative, multisectoral, and transdisciplinary approach—working at the local, regional, national, and global levels—with the goal of achieving optimal health outcomes recognizing the interconnection between people, animals, plants, and their shared environment.

In summary, the post-2030 environmental agenda must prioritize systemic and transformative changes that recognize the interconnectedness of environmental, social, and economic systems to ensure the well-being of all life on Earth. A paradigm shift is required in our environmental priorities. The international community must align its strategies, policies, and actions to address climate emergencies and biodiversity loss. Voluntary commitments, while valuable, may not suffice; we need enforceable action.

Recognizing the rights of nature, youth, and future generations in legislation is a positive step, but structural change is essential. The United Nations, with its global influence, should lead this transformation, establishing institutions with greater authority to enforce environmental commitments. Achieving a healthier planet demands collective action, legal imperatives, and unwavering commitment. Let us not merely hope for a brighter future; let us legally, institutionally, and ethically compel ourselves to create it.

9.7 Environmental Mindset Shift Priorities

In reshaping the sustainability agenda to address the urgent environmental and climate challenges of the 21st century, it is crucial to critically reassess the common but limited perceptions and misperceptions of sustainability. Despite advancements in sustainability research and practice,[10] a persistent oversimplification confines sustainability to environmental protection, nature conservation, or individual initiatives like recycling. While these efforts are commendable, they only scratch the surface of environmental sustainability and can inadvertently limit the development and implementation of a more transformative and comprehensive sustainability strategy.

How do we address this limitation? Efforts must be made to include the concept of sustainability at all levels of education and outreach to all sectors to address sustainability. For example, educational institutions and programs are ideally positioned to offer a more rounded and in-depth understanding of sustainability issues. Moving beyond specialized or technical curriculums that lack a comprehensive perspective, these educational entities have the opportunity to cultivate an in-depth understanding of how environmental, social, and economic elements intertwine within the realm of sustainability. This approach broadens the scope of sustainability education and equips individuals and professionals with the knowledge and tools to contribute more effectively to a holistic and sustainable future.

The urgency of adopting a comprehensive sustainability mindset extends beyond individual and educational realms to the critical areas of corporate marketing and media reporting. Such an all-encompassing perspective is vital to preventing the pitfalls of greenwashing. In this deceptive practice, organizations overstate their environmental efforts or sustainability credentials, often due to a limited understanding of sustainability's multifaceted nature. Greenwashing not only misleads consumers and investors but also undermines genuine sustainability efforts. It frequently arises from a narrow awareness of sustainability that needs to consider its intersections with socioeconomic and political aspects. This superficial approach in corporate communication and media coverage can skew public perception and decision-making, emphasizing the need for transparency and depth in addressing sustainability. By advocating for and embracing a broader understanding of sustainability, organizations and media entities can more accurately represent their sustainable practices and impacts, fostering a more informed and conscientious public dialogue. This shift is vital for ensuring that sustainability efforts are genuine, effective, and aligned with the broader goal of creating a balanced and equitable future for all.

1. **Consequences of Limited "Green-Only" Sustainability Approaches:** The limitations of a "green-only" approach to sustainability can have far-reaching consequences across various sectors. Economically, this narrow focus may lead to policies that neglect broader economic implications, potentially resulting in job losses in specific industries without offering sustainable alternatives, thereby deepening economic inequalities. From a social standpoint, such an approach often overlooks critical social issues, potentially exacerbating challenges like poverty, educational disparities, and health inequities. In terms of governance and the rule of law, a lack of attention to these aspects in sustainability strategies can lead to the creation of policies that are either difficult to enforce or are implemented unfairly, ultimately undermining public trust and adherence. Additionally, a purely environmentally focused strategy risks overlooking the pivotal role of technological innovation in sustainability, particularly in areas such as the development and equitable distribution of clean energy technologies. This comprehensive view underscores the necessity of integrating multiple perspectives and efforts to avoid adverse outcomes while promoting sustainability mindsets for the common good and our common future.[11]
2. **Advocating for a Holistic and Comprehensive Approach:** Embracing a holistic mindset and integrated approaches in sustainability efforts is vital for addressing our world's complex and interconnected challenges. This approach expands on the principles of the SDGs and their encompassing 5Ps framework—People, Planet, Prosperity, Peace, and Partnership. Such a mindset acknowledges the necessity of not only prioritizing environmental sustainability but also ensuring economic viability, social equity, and technological advancement. For companies and organizations, this means moving away from selective "cherry-picking" of convenient

sustainability goals, which often leads to greenwashing, and instead adopting comprehensive and transparent practices. This could involve integrated reporting that reflects performance across all sustainability dimensions, engaging a broad range of stakeholders for diverse perspectives, conducting thorough impact assessments, establishing collaborative partnerships, and continually adapting to evolving sustainability standards. By adopting such an integrated approach, businesses and organizations can make significant contributions to the global sustainability agenda, creating economic systems that are sustainable, equitable, and beneficial for all, including future generations and the planet. This holistic view is crucial for fully realizing the interconnected nature of our world's challenges and effectively navigating them.

In essence, cultivating and promoting a sustainability mindset are imperative for the success of the new sustainability agenda. This mindset begins with recognizing that the concept of sustainability extends beyond just environmental concerns. It encompasses a profound understanding of the interplay between ecological balance, social equity, and economic prosperity. Such a comprehensive perspective is essential not only for mitigating the risks of greenwashing in corporate and media spheres but also for fostering informed decision-making and responsible actions across all sectors of society.[12] By integrating this holistic view of sustainability into education, policymaking, business strategies, and personal behaviors, we can ensure that our actions today do not compromise the ability of future generations to meet their own needs. In doing so, we lay the foundation for a more sustainable, just, and prosperous world where our planet's health and its inhabitants' well-being are in harmonious balance. This is not just an aspiration but a necessary evolution of our collective approach to living and working on this planet, a change that is urgent and vital for the long-term survival and thriving of humanity and the natural world.

9.8 Resources

As we have seen throughout Chapter 9, environmental climate sustainability emphasizes maintaining and protecting our planet's ecosystems, biodiversity, and climate systems. Given climate change's increasing challenges, many resources have been dedicated to addressing these issues. Here are a few valuable reports and seminal resources:

1. **IPCC (Intergovernmental Panel on Climate Change) Reports:** The IPCC produces periodic assessment reports, considered the gold standard in climate science. They offer comprehensive insights into the state of the climate, future projections, and adaptation and mitigation strategies. Read more at www.ipcc.ch/reports/.
2. ***Climate Justice: Hope, Resilience, and the Fight for a Sustainable Future* by Mary Robinson (2018):** Robinson, former Irish president and UN Special Envoy on Climate Change, shares stories of frontline activists battling climate impacts and championing sustainability in their communities, particularly women.
3. ***Regeneration: Ending the Climate Crisis in One Generation* by Paul Hawken (2022):** Hawken offers a hopeful perspective on the climate crisis. He provides an action-oriented guide that explores practical solutions individuals, businesses, and governments can implement to regenerate ecosystems and reverse climate change.
4. ***The Climate Book: The Facts and the Solutions* by Greta Thunberg (2023):** From a pivotal figure in the youth-led climate movement, this book comprehensively explores the climate crisis. It includes the insights of over a hundred professionals—from geophysicists and meteorologists to philosophers and Indigenous leaders—to present a well-rounded understanding of imminent climatic threats. The book emphasizes the extent of the global community's lack of understanding of the crisis. Yet, she also clarifies that awareness is a beacon of hope. The message of the book is clear: we stand at a critical juncture in human history, and we must pivot towards a sustainable future.
5. ***The Sixth Extinction: An Unnatural History* by Elizabeth Kolbert (2014):** Journalist Elizabeth Kolbert examines the ongoing mass extinction event driven by human actions, intertwining research with on-the-ground investigations. She delves into how our activities, particularly those

contributing to climate change, are leading to a dramatic loss in biodiversity.

Notes

1 Lee, H., & Romero, J. (Eds.) (2023). IPCC, 2023: Sections. In: *Climate Change 2023: Synthesis Report. Contribution of Working Groups I, II and III to the Sixth Assessment Report of the Intergovernmental Panel on Climate Change*, pp. 35–115. Geneva, Switzerland: IPCC. https://www.ipcc.ch/report/ar6/syr/downloads/report/IPCC_AR6_SYR_SPM.pdf
2 Ohara, K.D. (2022). *Climate Change in the Anthropocene.* Netherlands: Elsevier Science.
3 Ozturk, M., Egamberdieva, D., & Pešić, M. (Eds.). (2020). *Biodiversity and Biomedicine: Our Future.* Academic Press.
4 Brondizio, E.S., Settele, J., Díaz, S., & Ngo, H.T. (Eds.) (2019) *Global Assessment Report on Biodiversity and Ecosystem Services of the Intergovernmental Science-Policy Platform on Biodiversity and Ecosystem Services.* Bonn, Germany: IPBES secretariat. https://doi.org/10.5281/zenodo.3831673
5 Masson-Delmotte, V., Zhai, P., Pirani, A., Connors, S.L., Péan, C., Berger, S., Caud, N. et al. (Eds.) (2021) *Climate Change 2021: The Physical Science Basis. Contribution of Working Group I to the Sixth Assessment Report of the Intergovernmental Panel on Climate Change.* Cambridge University Press, Cambridge and New York, NY: IPPC. https://doi.org/10.1017/9781009157896. For the WB deforestation data, see: *Five Forest figures for the International Day of Forests* (2016, March 21). World Bank Blogs. https://blogs.worldbank.org/opendata/five-forest-figures-international-day-forests. For the Ramsar studies, see: *Wetlands—World's Most Valuable Ecosystem—Disappearing Three Times Faster Than Forests, Warns New Report* (2018). https://www.ramsar.org/news/wetlands-worlds-most-valuable-ecosystem-disappearing-three-times-faster-forests-warns-new
6 Gardiner, B. (2019). *Choked: Life and Breath in the Age of Air Pollution. United States: University of Chicago Press.*
7 Kempisty, D. M., & Racz, L. (Eds.) (2021). *Forever Chemicals: Environmental, Economic, and Social Equity Concerns with PFAs in the Environment.* CRC Press.
8 McGee, T.K., & Penning-Rowsell, E.C. (Eds.) (2022). *Routledge Handbook of Environmental Hazards and Society.* Routledge.
9 Prata, J.C., Ribeiro, A.I., & Rocha-Santos, T. (Eds.) (2022). *One Health: Integrated Approach to 21st Century Challenges to Health.* Academic Press.
10 Rimanoczy, I. (2020). *The Sustainability Mindset Principles: A Guide to Developing a Mindset for a Better World.* Routledge. See also: Kassel, K., & Rimanoczy, I. (Eds.) (2018).

Developing a Sustainability Mindset in Management education. Routledge.

11 Ritz, A.A., & Rimanoczy, I. (Eds.). (2021). *Sustainability Mindset and Transformative Leadership: a Multidisciplinary Perspective.* Springer Nature.

12 Ven, H.v.d. (2019). *Beyond Greenwash: Explaining Credibility in Transnational Eco-Labeling.* United States: Oxford University Press.

10 Governance and Legal Priorities

> We want to change our world. And we can. We want to give the world a more humane face. And we can. That is what the 2030 Agenda is for. To this end, we are adopting new goals which cover the entire spectrum of global development and which apply to all, industrial and developing countries alike. If we are to achieve these goals, we need a new global partnership. In order to establish such a global partnership, we need, firstly, efficient structures at all levels—national, regional and global. [...] Seventy years after its foundation, the United Nations as a whole, with its unique legitimacy, is still indispensable when it comes to resolving the issues facing humanity. But it, too, needs to adapt to new challenges. [...] The 2030 Agenda provides the right framework for this. It balances economic, ecological and social aspects of development. Each and every one of us should, indeed must, work to implement this Agenda—so that people the world over can live a life in dignity. This must be our shared aspiration. By agreeing on the Agenda we are setting the course for efforts to tackle the causes. The priority now is to work towards this end at all levels—national, regional and global.
>
> (Speech by Dr. Angela Merkel, Chancellor of the Federal Republic of Germany, at the United Nations Sustainable Development Summit in New York, September 25, 2015[1])

Overview

This chapter examines how governance and legal systems can support or hinder sustainable development. The focus is on transparency, accountability, rule of law, and inclusive participation. Also explored are global governance challenges and the role of international law in shaping sustainability trajectories.

10.1 Governing the Commons for Polycentric Systems

Central to the ethos of sustainable development lies the intricate concept of the "commons"—these are natural resources, such

DOI: 10.4324/9781003494676-13

as forests, fisheries, and the air we breathe, which are not only shared among communities but are often under joint management. The significance of effective governance in safeguarding these environmental assets and championing sustainable development is undeniable. It is a bulwark against what ecologist Garrett Hardin famously described as "the tragedy of the commons." In this scenario, individuals, driven by self-interest and working independently, undermine the collective good, leading to the overexploitation and eventual depletion of the shared resource.[2]

However, Nobel Laureate and Distinguished Professor Elinor Ostrom constructively challenged this bleak view of the commons. In her pioneering work, *Governing the Commons*, Ostrom refuted this theory and described the potential of communities to oversee shared resources without succumbing to the anticipated tragedy. Her belief was anchored in the power of collective institutions crafted with thought and care.[3] Her model for governance of Common-Pool Resources (CPRs) radically transformed how we understand and address the management of shared resources. Her groundbreaking insights indicated that local communities could effectively manage shared resources under certain conditions without external intervention or privatization. Ostrom proposed eight "design principles" for fostering successful collective management of CPRs, especially within polycentric systems (systems where governance is undertaken by multiple overlapping authorities rather than a single centralized entity). These principles are:

1. **Clearly Defined Boundaries:** The resource and its user group should have clearly defined boundaries. This helps avoid confusion and conflicts over rights and responsibilities. For example, a specific fishing area might be designated for a certain community.
2. **Proportional Equivalence:** The benefits derived from the resource should be proportional to the effort invested by the users. This principle promotes fairness and can motivate members to use and protect the resource sustainably. It means that if a person contributes more to maintaining a shared resource, they should benefit more.
3. **Collective Decision-Making:** All individuals affected by the resource rules should have a voice in modifying those rules. Giving users a voice fosters a sense of ownership and

responsibility. This principle is seen in Indigenous communities where collective decisions regarding forest use or water sources are made.

4. **Monitoring:** Monitors, who are part of or accountable to the users, should regularly check the resource's condition and the behavior of its users. Monitoring ensures that rules are followed and that the resource is not overexploited. For instance, community-appointed guards might monitor a shared pasture to ensure no one overgrazes.
5. **Graduated Sanctions:** Implement a system of sanctions for rule violators, where the severity of the punishment corresponds to the severity of the violation. This discourages overexploitation and fosters community norms around sustainable usage. This could be seen in a community garden where those who fail to maintain their plots might initially receive a warning, followed by fines or expulsion for repeated offenses.
6. **Conflict Resolution Mechanisms:** Accessible and low-cost mechanisms should be available for resolving disputes among users or between users and officials. Prompt resolution of conflicts helps maintain trust and cooperation among community members. For instance, village elders might mediate disputes over water usage in a shared well.
7. **Local Autonomy:** The rights of users to design their own institutions should be recognized by higher-level authorities. This means that state or national governments should not interfere with local resource management practices without a very good reason. External intervention or overriding rules by higher authorities can disrupt locally tailored solutions.
8. **Nested Enterprises:** For larger resources that span multiple communities or even countries, governance should be organized in multiple layers, with small, local institutions nested inside larger ones. This recognizes the complexity of larger systems and supports governance at scales appropriate to the specific resource in question. An example is river basin management, where local user groups manage tributary sections, but a larger overseeing body manages the whole basin.

These design principles are timelier than ever for today's challenges, including climate change, biodiversity loss, and increasing demands on natural resources. Many contemporary environmental problems are, at their core, collective action problems. Ostrom's principles provide a roadmap for fostering cooperation, building trust, and ensuring sustainable management in a complex, interconnected world. They serve as a foundation for understanding that local, adaptive solutions, driven by the very users of the resources, can offer viable alternatives to top-down regulatory or market-driven approaches.

Yet, the journey of environmental protection and steering towards sustainable development is laden with multifaceted challenges. These span from the often-encountered lack of political resolve and inadequate enforcement of environmental laws to broader challenges like insufficient public awareness about environmental issues and the unequal allocation of resources. Complicating matters further is the inherent global dimension of many environmental dilemmas. These vast challenges, such as climate change or biodiversity loss, require a harmonized, collective response. However, this is frequently hampered by conflicting national interests, which can impede the global efforts needed.

10.2 Governing Sustainable Choices through Carrots and Sticks

Addressing intricate environmental and sustainability challenges necessitates a clear governance framework that emphasizes both incentives ("carrots") and deterrents ("sticks"). This dual approach provides a strategic pathway, safeguarding the sanctity of our shared resources—the commons—and promoting sustainable development for the broader community.

The Carrots of Sustainable Governance: These represent positive reinforcements to motivate sustainable choices and actions:

1. **Financial Incentives:** Governments may provide tax breaks, subsidies for renewable energy projects, or reduced fees for eco-friendly products and services.
2. **Grants and Research Funding:** Investment in research for sustainable technologies can be furthered through government or international grants.
3. **Recognition and Certification:** Certifying businesses for their eco-friendly operations or products can enhance their market reputation and encourage sustainable practices.

Individuals can also benefit, for instance, through rebates for energy-efficient appliances or credits for rainwater harvesting.

The Sticks of Sustainable Governance: These embody the punitive measures and regulations aimed at curbing environmentally harmful behaviors:

1. **Fines and Penalties:** Activities like overfishing, illegal logging, or exceeding carbon emission limits can result in significant fines.
2. **Sanctions:** Companies found polluting natural resources may face operational restrictions or other punitive measures.
3. **Regulations and Standards:** Governments can enforce stringent environmental standards and might penalize entities failing to meet them.
4. **Environmental Taxes:** Imposing taxes, like carbon taxes, based on environmental impact encourages companies to adopt greener alternatives.

By combining incentives and deterrents, governance structures can strike a delicate yet imperative balance between inspiration and regulation. In such an environment, choosing sustainability is transformed from a mere optional endeavor to a profoundly ingrained ethical obligation and a calculated, beneficial strategy. This combined approach amplifies the allure of responsible choices and amplifies their tangible benefits, be they financial, social, or reputational. Concurrently, it sets up a clear differentiation, signaling that actions detrimental to our shared ecosystem will not only be discouraged but will also incur consequences. Thus, by meticulously weaving rewards and penalties into the fabric of governance, we can shape a future where the ethos of sustainability is celebrated and becomes the norm, ensuring the well-being of our planet and its inhabitants for generations to come.

10.3 Environmental Global Governance Priorities

In the complex and evolving dynamics of environmental global governance, the significance of environmental justice, multilateral collaboration, and solid governance frameworks has become more pronounced, setting the path for the post-2030 environmental and global agenda. The intertwined fates of nations, magnified by shared environmental challenges, underscore the indispensable nature of multilateralism. This becomes especially evident when considering complex, borderless issues like climate change, biodiversity loss, and widespread pollution. Such challenges defy the constraints of geography, rendering unilateral solutions insufficient. Instead, they compel nations to work together, uniting their efforts to devise holistic strategies and solutions. Historically, the success and impact of multilateral agreements, such as the landmark Paris Agreement and the CBD, stand as a testament to the potential of cooperative international action. These successes signify the effectiveness of joint initiatives and emphasize the mounting need to amplify such collaborative endeavors in the future. As we delve deeper into the myriad challenges and emerging processes, it becomes clear that a strategic rethinking and reinforcement of multilateralism in environmental governance is imperative. To guide our journey forward, we present a curated list of pivotal governance priorities specifically tailored for sustainable development, which should take center stage in multilateral deliberations and agreements:

1. **Strengthening Institutions, Regulations, and Multilateral Institutions:** Efficient governance across local, national, and global levels is essential. Pakistan's Ministry of Climate Change is a notable example. Moreover, robust institutions are vital for effective multilateralism, with the Environmental Goods Agreement (EGA) under WTO acting as an exemplar.
2. **Transparency, Accountability, and Enhanced Cooperation:** An example of this is the Extractive Industries Transparency Initiative (EITI), which fosters openness in managing oil, gas, and mineral resources. Accountability mechanisms, such as the Voluntary National Reviews (VNRs) for the SDGs, highlight transparent reporting. Agreements like the Montreal Protocol and the Paris Agreement underscore global cooperative achievements.
3. **Participation, Inclusivity, and Global Representation:** Instruments like the UN Declaration on the Rights of Indigenous Peoples (UNDRIP) and the Paris Agreement prioritize inclusivity. Ensuring diverse representation, as seen with the IPCC, brings varied perspectives to decision-making.

4. **Integration of Environmental Concerns into Other Policies:** The European Union's Green Deal showcases the holistic integration of environmental considerations across policy sectors.
5. **Promoting Sustainable Practices and Capacity-Building:** Laws like the German Renewable Energy Act (EEG) pave the way for sustainable practices. Capacity-building initiatives, such as the Capacity-Building Initiative for Transparency (CBIT) and the Green Climate Fund (GCF), enhance the capabilities of nations, especially those in the Global South.
6. **Participation of Non-State Actors:** Groups like civil society organizations, Indigenous communities, and the private sector bring depth to environmental governance, as showcased by the UNGC.

Furthermore, legal actions, such as California's September 18, 2023 lawsuit against major oil corporations, including BP, ExxonMobil, Chevron, Shell, ConocoPhillips, and the influential American Petroleum Institute, "for decades long deception" stands as a strong reminder of the increasing urgency for environmental justice and the pressing need for corporate accountability. Such lawsuits highlight the tenuous balance between industrial advancement and environmental preservation, showcasing the changing dynamics where states and jurisdictions are taking formidable stances against entities perceived as environmental transgressors. Moving forward into the post-2030 landscape, it becomes imperative for the global community to embed deeply the principles of justice, sound governance, and collaborative multilateralism when framing environmental strategies and policies. Only by combining these core tenets can we hope to construct a comprehensive and cohesive blueprint that effectively navigates the intricacies of global environmental challenges, propelling humanity toward a more sustainable and harmonious future.

10.4 Accounting Global Governance Shifts

Significant global, political, and economic shifts have occurred since the 1972 Stockholm Conference. The balance of power and influence has transformed with the rise of India's and China's economies. They have emerged from being developing nations to global powerhouses. These changes have ramifications for the framing and realization of the Post-2030 Agenda.

At the 1972 conference, More Developed Countries (MDCs), led by Sweden, attempted to set the environmental agenda. However, they were met with resistance from the Less Developed Countries (LDCs) who formed a block to counter this dominance. Notably, India and China were part of this resistance.

Fast-forward to the present day, the dynamics of global cooperation have shifted dramatically. South-South cooperation, which was once a counterweight to the dominance of the North, has lost ground to the new reality of South-North cooperation. This change is partly attributable to the economic rise of nations in the Global South, who are now increasingly involved in North-South partnerships.

This new political economy implies a reshaping of global cooperation and a redefinition of traditional roles. It challenges us to reconsider conventional wisdom about "developed" and "developing" countries in the context of sustainable development.

Therefore, a Post-2030 Agenda needs to acknowledge these changes. It must account for the shifts in economic and political power and the resulting implications for global cooperation. Understanding this new context is critical to ensuring that the next set of SDGs is both relevant and practical.

10.5 Citizens' Participation in the Post-2030 Agenda

The Post-2030 Agenda must prioritize citizens' engagement and empowerment in sustainability's governance and decision-making processes. This approach recognizes citizens as agents of change who hold the potential to drive sustainable development from the grassroots level. The rise of technology has facilitated the growth of this "Citizen's Agenda," with social media and digital platforms allowing for increased communication, awareness, and participation.

Democratic and participatory methods of agenda-setting can lead to more effective and equitable outcomes, as they involve input from diverse groups of people with different perspectives and experiences. This could include participatory budgeting initiatives, community-led environmental projects, and public consultations on policy decisions.

In addition, prioritizing the "Citizen's Agenda" implies the need for substantial education and capacity-building initiatives. Citizens must be well-informed and equipped with the necessary skills and knowledge to engage in decision-making processes effectively.

Finally, this approach also calls for strengthening and enforcing laws and policies that protect the rights of citizens to participate in environmental decision-making. This could include measures to protect environmental activists, policies to ensure access to environmental information and laws to ensure that corporations are transparent and accountable to the communities in which they operate.

Therefore, the future of environmental governance and sustainable development hinges on a shift towards a Citizen's Agenda that emphasizes participation, inclusivity, and empowerment. This should be a crucial priority for the Post-2030 Agenda.

10.6 Global Governance Institutional Realignment

The necessity for a global governance institutional realignment is born out of the recognition that the existing institutions were formed in a context that is no longer relevant. The first Bretton Woods Agreement was established in the aftermath of World War II and at the height of the Cold War. It set the stage for the contemporary global economic system. But the economic, political, and environmental landscape has changed significantly since that time.

In the post-2030 era, the new economic system will necessitate a more balanced, inclusive, and sustainable economic system that can better address the challenges of the 21st century. This could include rethinking the roles of the International Monetary Fund and the World Bank, strengthening regional development banks, and creating new financial mechanisms to support sustainable development.

New and future environmental planetary challenges will require strengthening international environmental governance. Transforming UNEP into a World Environmental Organization could be one way to achieve this. This new organization could have a stronger mandate and more resources to coordinate global environmental policies, ensure compliance with international environmental agreements, and promote sustainable practices.

The idea of converting the UN Trusteeship Council into a Citizens Council reflects the growing recognition of the need to involve civil society in decision-making processes at the UN. This could ensure that the voices of diverse groups, including Indigenous peoples, women, youth, and other marginalized communities, are heard in global governance.

Implementing these changes would be challenging and require substantial political will and cooperation among nations. However, such a global governance institutional realignment could provide a stronger and more effective framework for implementing the Post-2030 Agenda, addressing emerging challenges, and promoting sustainable development.

10.7 Rule of Law and Sustainability

The profound relationship between the rule of law and sustainability is rooted in the belief that sustainable development can only be achieved within an environment where laws are clear, equitable, and consistently enforced. The principles of the rule of law—such as equality, predictability, and transparency—are foundational for building a thriving and sustainable future. Here are four priorities where the rule of law exemplifies its capacity to promote sustainable development outcomes.

1. **Legal and Institutional Reforms:** The essence of sustainable development lies in the continual adaptation and reform of legal and institutional systems. Such reforms ensure that our legal frameworks are current, relevant, and capable of addressing the evolving challenges of our times. For instance, Brazil's Forest Code, which underwent a significant transformation in 2012, showcases this point. The primary objective of this reform was to protect the Amazon rainforest, a pivotal carbon sink for our planet. This code's consistent and proper enforcement is vital for environmental sustainability in the region.
2. **Protection of Rights:** The rule of law shines a spotlight on protecting individual rights, especially those of vulnerable populations. By doing so, it facilitates social sustainability by fostering an environment of social inclusion, equity, and justice. The Forest Rights Act of 2006 in India serves as a prime example. This act acknowledges and respects the rights of Indigenous communities over forest lands and

resources. Effective implementation of such laws ensures a balance between environmental conservation and Indigenous peoples' rights, leading to social and environmental sustainability.

3. **Access to Justice:** Access to justice is essential for the rule of law and sustainability. If individuals are denied this access, they cannot effectively seek redress or assert their rights, undermining the efficacy of sustainable policies at the grassroots level. Some countries, recognizing the importance of this, have taken proactive measures. For example, Kenya established the Environment and Land Court specifically to address disputes related to environmental laws, ensuring quick and equitable resolution of such issues.
4. **Legal Empowerment Strategies:** Legal empowerment is not just about laws and regulations; it's about equipping communities and individuals with the knowledge and tools to benefit from and uphold the rule of law. In the Philippines, this principle has been brought to life through community-based paralegal programs. By providing communities with legal knowledge, these programs empower them to challenge wrongful land acquisitions or advocate for their environmental rights, thus fostering social and environmental sustainability.

Overall, when rightly championed and enforced, the rule of law can be a beacon for sustainable development. However, it demands ongoing evaluation and reform to ensure its effectiveness. This iterative process requires vigilance, a willingness to learn from past experiences, and an unwavering dedication to intertwining the rule of law with all facets of sustainable development.

10.8 Environmental Justice for the Post-2030 Governance Agenda

Justice remains paramount in the post-2030 governance agenda, specifically concerning environmental justice, the rights of nature, and animal rights. These concerns echo the increasing acknowledgment of the intrinsic worth of the natural world and the imperative to address historical and ongoing environmental injustices.[4]

Environmental justice intends to provide equitable access to environmental benefits and protection, irrespective of race, ethnicity, or socioeconomic status. It recognizes the need to address the environmental degradation often disproportionately experienced by marginalized communities. In light of the post-2030 era, the drive for environmental justice must tackle systemic disparities, encourage inclusive decision-making processes, and roll out policies that center the welfare of all communities.[5]

The notion of the rights of nature posits that nature has inherent rights, comparable to human rights, necessitating protection and reverence. This perspective challenges the traditional view that perceives nature merely as a resource. Incorporating these rights into governance can lead to groundbreaking shifts, like granting legal personhood to ecosystems, and promote our duty to safeguard the natural world.

Furthermore, the rights of animals play a significant role in crafting a just and sustainable society. Advocates argue for humanely treating animals, highlighting their ability to experience pain and asserting their entitlement to a life free from unwarranted suffering. Upcoming progress may see heightened legal protections for animals, the endorsement of cruelty-free methodologies, and innovative techniques in animal agriculture and testing.

Countries are progressively integrating the rights of nature into their legal frameworks. For example:

Ecuador: In 2008, Ecuador became the inaugural country to endorse the rights of nature in its constitution, recognizing the irrefutable rights of the ecosystem.

Bolivia: In 2010, Bolivia adopted the Law of the Rights of Mother Earth, presenting the rights of Mother Earth with an ombudsman dedicated to these rights.

New Zealand: The Whanganui River was accorded legal personhood in 2017.

Colombia: Colombia's Constitutional Court recognized the rights of the Atrato River and the Amazon Rainforest.

India: In 2017, the Ganges and Yamuna rivers in India were decreed as legal entities.

Adopting the rights of nature in legal doctrines is a budding and dynamic area of law. Future developments might include establishing dedicated courts for environmental offenses, integrating Indigenous wisdom into decision-making, and espousing sustainable, ethical industrial practices. Grassroots initiatives and civil society's push for environmental justice, rights of nature, and animal rights will continue influencing and reforming governance methodologies.

In sum, integrating justice into the post-2030 governance blueprint underscores the interrelatedness of social, environmental, and economic sustainability aspects. By positioning justice at the heart of our governance approach, we strive for a world where the rights of humans, nature, and animals are intertwined and revered.

10.9 Other Governance Priorities for the Post-2030 Agenda

Special considerations should guide the assessment and formulation of future global governance structures and solutions, especially in the context of post-2030 challenges. Peace and security, along with technological integrations, are important subjects and priorities that we will consider more specifically in the following chapters. Specifically for governance:

1. **Technological Integration:** The increasing pervasiveness of technology in every aspect of our lives should be considered. Global governance mechanisms must evolve to address the digital divide, data privacy, cybersecurity, artificial intelligence, and other technology-related issues.
2. **Peace and Security:** Ongoing conflicts and security issues pose significant challenges to sustainable development. Global governance structures should aim to prevent conflicts, support peacebuilding, and address the root causes of violence, including poverty, inequality, and social exclusion.

Other interconnected global governance priorities that should be part of the Post-2030 Agenda are:

3. **Global Health Governance:** Given the experience of the COVID-19 pandemic, there is a need to prioritize the strengthening of global health governance. This might involve empowering the WHO, enhancing international cooperation on health issues, and improving the capacity to prevent, detect, and respond to future pandemics and other health emergencies.

4. **Climate Justice and Equity:** Global governance mechanisms should emphasize fairness, given that the impacts of climate change are disproportionately borne by those who contribute least to the problem. This would involve addressing issues related to climate finance, technology transfer, capacity-building, and loss and damage.
5. **Interconnectedness of Issues:** Recognize the interconnectedness of various global issues like climate change, biodiversity loss, health, poverty, inequality, and peace. A siloed approach is unlikely to be effective. Hence the necessity to create interagency collaborations and new entities that truly represent the complexity of these intersectional issues.
6. **Empowerment of Marginalized Groups:** Greater efforts must be made to ensure that women, Indigenous communities, and other marginalized groups can meaningfully participate in global governance processes. Technology and frugal innovation solutions could be instrumental in creating mechanisms of representation, decision-making, and consultation.
7. **Robust Monitoring and Accountability Mechanisms:** Global governance structures need robust monitoring and accountability mechanisms to ensure that countries and other actors deliver on their commitments. Standardized and publicly available mechanisms for reporting and disclosure could be instrumental in increasing accountability and transparency.
8. **Resilience and Adaptation:** With ongoing and future challenges such as climate change, future governance structures must be designed with resilience and adaptability in mind to respond effectively to changing circumstances and crises. This includes the capacity to respond to crises, including resilient recoveries.

The post-2030 era will confront enduring challenges, such as climate change, biodiversity loss, social inequities, and the impacts of technological advancement, necessitating a reimagining of our global governance systems.

Our discussions have underscored the imperative for more democratic, inclusive, and accountable governance structures, ones that guarantee representation and participation from all nations and stakeholders. Key priorities include fortifying institutions and regulations, championing transparency and accountability, and fostering participation and inclusivity.

Moreover, there is a clear need to enhance cooperation and integrate environmental concerns into policymaking.

Multilateralism remains the most promising avenue, with the potential to mobilize collective action and promote shared responsibility. Success stories we've examined exemplify the potential of this approach when combined with capacity-building, global representation, transparency, and inclusion of non-state actors.

However, as we enter the post-2030 era, it's evident that more than incremental changes are required. Profound transformations, including establishing a new Bretton Woods Agreement to reshape the global economic order, are necessary for institutional realignment that formalizes civil society's participatory roles.

The future governance landscape must acknowledge and address the intricate links among global issues, prioritize justice and equity, and actively involve marginalized communities. It should incorporate robust monitoring and accountability mechanisms to steer us towards our common objectives. However, these endeavors and priorities would prove fruitless without a coordinated, multilateral focus on cultivating and safeguarding the right mindsets and mechanisms essential for accountability, democracy, participation, and good governance.

10.10 Governance Mindset Shift Priorities

To effectively shape governance priorities for the Post-2030 Sustainability Agenda, it is essential to recognize the critical role of the global community's collective mindset. Fundamental mindset shifts must address several pressing issues: eroding trust in institutions, waning support for democratic principles, insufficient focus on civic education, widespread skepticism towards governance and public regulations, and the rise of conspiracy theories and misinformation.

1. **Rebuilding Trust in Institutions:** Restoring faith in governmental and international bodies is central to these shifts. Achieving this requires these entities to demonstrate transparency, accountability, and responsiveness. Highlighting their positive societal impacts can also be crucial in rebuilding trust.
2. **Rekindling Faith in Democracy:** To combat the diminishing support for democratic values, a concerted effort is needed to educate citizens about the benefits and principles of democracy. Integrating civic education in schools and

community programs can empower individuals to engage actively in their governance systems.

3. **Strengthening Civic Education:** Enhanced civic education is vital in equipping citizens with the necessary skills and knowledge for meaningful civic and political discourse engagement. This approach is a potent tool against misinformation and ensures a well-informed electorate.
4. **Promoting Inclusive Governance:** Governance must prioritize inclusivity, ensuring that all voices, primarily those that are marginalized, are heard and considered. This approach is key to achieving social equity and sustainable development.
5. **Enhancing Regulatory Trust:** Building trust in public regulations is crucial. Governments and regulatory bodies should focus on transparent decision-making, clear communication about regulatory objectives, and public participation mechanisms.
6. **Building Community Relations:** Strengthening community bonds is essential to combat the isolation that breeds susceptibility to conspiracy theories and manipulation. Initiatives that promote community engagement can foster a sense of belonging and counteract misinformation.
7. **Encouraging Critical Thinking and Media Literacy:** Educating individuals in critical thinking and media literacy is vital to discern credible information from falsehoods, thus diminishing the influence of conspiracy theories.
8. **Fostering Open Dialogue:** Encouraging respectful dialogue among diverse groups can bridge societal divides, foster understanding and empathy, and reduce polarization.
9. **Promoting Ethical Leadership:** Leaders in all sectors should exemplify ethical conduct, prioritizing the common good over self-interest. Such leadership can inspire collective action and rebuild trust.
10. **Advocating Global Cooperation and Solidarity:** Recognizing our interconnectedness and fostering global cooperation, especially in addressing challenges like climate change and resource management, is crucial for effective commons governance.

The proposed mindset shifts are more than mere suggestions; they are essential catalysts for a sustainable future. By directly addressing the foundational issues that undermine effective governance, we lay the groundwork for a framework rooted in equity, sustainability, and collective welfare. In the emerging post-2030 landscape, these governance priorities must become the cornerstones upon which we build our strategies, informing and guiding our concerted efforts to navigate toward a future that is not only sustainable but also resilient and inclusive.

In the epoch of the Anthropocene, where humanity's footprint is indelibly shaping the planet, the imperatives of global governance and robust multilateral mechanisms become ever more critical.[6] The escalating emergencies borne of climate change and other planetary challenges compel us to transcend parochial national interests and reconsider libertarian approaches that often eschew the collective responsibility vital for governance. Only through a unified, collaborative global framework can we muster the concerted action and shared accountability necessary to safeguard our planet for current and future generations. These commitments require a mindset shift centered around public service and global responsibility for our common good.[7]

As we venture into the uncertain terrains of the future, it is imperative that these priorities and principles light our path, enabling us to maneuver through the complexities of global challenges with agility and foresight. Our collective destiny hinges on our willingness to evolve governance into a dynamic force that can withstand the trials of global adversities and harness them into opportunities for sustainable growth and shared prosperity. In this spirit, we must commit to a transformation journey that will redefine our interactions, our systems, and ultimately, our world.

Resources

As we have seen throughout Chapter 10, governance and legal sustainability focus on ensuring that societal systems, laws, and institutions are designed and operated in ways that support long-term environmental, social, and economic well-being. The recognition and incorporation of Indigenous rights, rights of nature, and other equity-focused principles are central to this concept. Here is a review of some essential resources in this area:

1. **Reports by the World Commission on Environmental Law (WCEL):** The WCEL, an arm of the International Union for Conservation of Nature (IUCN), frequently publishes reports on various aspects of environmental law, considering both ecological protection and human rights. Their publications

cover topics from biodiversity conservation to climate change and provide insights into evolving legal perspectives on sustainability. Read more at www.iucn.org/our-union/commissions/world-commission-environmental-law.

2. ***Governing the Commons: The Evolution of Institutions for Collective Action* by Elinor Ostrom (1990):** Ostrom's seminal work explores how communities around the world have successfully managed shared resources without resorting to either privatization or government regulation. She introduces the concept of "polycentric governance," emphasizing that local solutions and institutions can effectively manage and sustain common resources.
3. ***Framework for Assessing and Improving Law for Sustainability* by Ben Boer, Paul Martin, and Lydia Slobodian (2016):** This work underscores the importance of effective legal systems in achieving sustainability goals. The authors present a systematic approach to analyze the effectiveness of legal systems and instruments in different contexts, guiding researchers and policymakers in the development and evaluation of sustainability-oriented laws.
4. ***The Rights of Nature: A Legal Revolution That Could Save the World* by David R. Boyd (2017):** The author delves into the transformative legal movement that recognizes the rights of ecosystems and non-human entities. Several countries and communities aim to ensure environmental protection and balance human-centric legal systems by granting legal rights to nature.
5. ***Indigenous Peoples, Customary Law and Human Rights – Why Living Law Matters* by Brendan Tobin (2014):** Tobin addresses the intersections of Indigenous customary law, or "living law," with international human rights norms. The book considers how recognizing Indigenous legal systems can contribute to global sustainability and justice efforts. It addresses important principles such as "Free, Prior, and Informed Consent" (FPIC) asserting Indigenous rights in large-scale development projects.

Notes

1 The Federal Chancellor of the Federal Republic of Germany (2024). *Speech by Chancellor Angela Merkel to the United Nations General Assembly*. https://www.bundeskanzler.de/bk-en/news/speech-by-chancellor-angela-merkel-to-the-united-nations-general-assembly-476140

2 Hudson, B., Cole, D., & Rosenbloom, J. (2019). *Routledge Handbook of the Study of the Commons*. United Kingdom: Taylor & Francis.
3 Ostrom, E. (2015). *Governing the Commons: The Evolution of Institutions for Collective Action*. United Kingdom: Cambridge University Press.
4 Boyd, D.R. (2017). *The Rights of Nature: A Legal Revolution that Could Save the World*. Canada: ECW Press.
5 Sze, J. (2020). *Environmental Justice in a Moment of Danger.* United States: University of California Press.
6 Seyedsayamdost, E. (2019). Global Governance in the Age of the Anthropocene: Are Sustainable Development Goals the Answer? *Global Environmental Politics*, 19(2), 169–174.
7 Westra, L. (Ed.). (2016). *The Common Good and Environmental Governance for the Support of Life*. Cambridge Scholars Publishing.

11 Peace and Security Priorities

> The collective security system that the United Nations embodies has recorded remarkable accomplishments. It has succeeded in preventing a new global conflagration. International cooperation—spanning from sustainable development, disarmament, human rights and women's empowerment to counter-terrorism and the protection of the environment—has made humanity safer and more prosperous. Peacemaking and peacekeeping have helped to end wars and prevent numerous crises from escalating into full-blown violence. Where wars broke out, collective action by the United Nations often helped shorten their duration and alleviate their worst effects. Nonetheless, peace remains an elusive promise for many around the world. Conflicts continue to wreak destruction, while their causes have become more complex and difficult to resolve. This may make the pursuit of peace appear a hopeless undertaking. However, in reality, it is the political decisions and actions of human beings that can either sustain or crush hopes for peace. War is always a choice: to resort to arms instead of dialogue, coercion instead of negotiation, imposition instead of persuasion. Therein lies our greatest prospect, for if war is a choice, peace can be too. It is time for a recommitment to peace.
>
> (United Nations—*A New Agenda for Peace*[1])

Overview

This chapter evaluates the linkages between peace, security, and sustainable development. Priorities include conflict prevention and resolution, humanitarian response, disarmament, and post-conflict reconstruction. The chapter investigates how sustainable development can contribute to peacebuilding and conflict resilience.

11.1 Environmental Factors in Conflicts

Environmental factors can play a significant role in conflicts, both as contributing factors and as potential triggers. Some examples of environmental factors in conflicts include:

DOI: 10.4324/9781003494676-14

1. **Resource Scarcity:** Competition over limited natural resources, such as water, land, minerals, or energy, can lead to conflicts between different groups or communities. Disputes over access to resources can exacerbate tensions and contribute to violent conflict.
2. **Land Degradation and Displacement:** Environmental degradation, such as deforestation, desertification, and soil erosion, can result in the displacement of communities and the loss of livelihoods. Displaced populations may be forced to migrate to other areas, leading to competition and potential conflicts over resources in the receiving areas.
3. **Water Scarcity and Access:** Water scarcity is a pressing global issue, and conflicts can arise when there is a lack of access to clean water for drinking, agriculture, or industrial use. Competing demands for water resources can result in tensions and disputes between different user groups or even between nations sharing transboundary water sources.
4. **Climate Change Impacts:** Climate change is increasingly recognized as a potential driver of conflicts. Rising temperatures, changing precipitation patterns, sea-level rise, and extreme weather events can lead to increased vulnerability, displacement, and social unrest. Climate-induced migration and competition over scarce resources can further exacerbate existing tensions and trigger conflicts.

Environmental factors have played a role in various recent conflicts throughout history. Here are some notable examples:

1. **Darfur Conflict (2003–2010):** The conflict in Darfur, Sudan was partly driven by competition over scarce natural resources, particularly water and grazing land. Droughts and desertification in the region led to increased tensions between nomadic herders and settled farmers, resulting in violent clashes and mass displacement.
2. **Syrian Civil War (2011–Present):** While the Syrian civil war has complex causes, environmental factors such as prolonged drought and water scarcity have been identified as contributing factors. A severe drought that lasted from 2006 to 2011 led to crop failures, loss of livelihoods, and mass migration from rural areas to urban centers, exacerbating social and economic pressures and contributing to the conflict.

3. **Niger Delta Conflict (2003–Present):** The Niger Delta region in Nigeria has been marred by oil extraction and environmental degradation conflicts. Oil spills, pollution, and land degradation have caused significant harm to local communities and their livelihoods, leading to protests, sabotage of oil infrastructure, and violent clashes between communities, militant groups, and security forces.
4. **Ukraine-Russia War (2022–Present):** The "special military operation" as Russia called it has military and expansionistic origin but the interest in resource grabbing is also clearly present. Ukraine is a large producer of wheat and corn largely exported to Africa and West Asia. In addition, Ukraine has the second-biggest known gas reserves in Europe, apart from Russia's gas reserves in Asia, and it has numerous mineral resources, including lithium, titanium, and precious metals.
5. **Conflict over the South China Sea (1947–Present):** The South China Sea, a region fraught with territorial disputes, has seen multiple countries vying for control, primarily motivated by its rich maritime resources, including fish stocks and potential offshore oil and gas reserves. Beyond its environmental and resource value, the sea holds significant geopolitical importance. Notably, China has been assertive in its desire to dominate this region, leading to increased tensions and geopolitical standoffs with neighboring countries.

Future conflicts over water scarcity are a growing concern as population growth, climate change, and unsustainable water management practices put increased pressure on freshwater resources. Here are some regions where water scarcity could potentially lead to conflicts:

1. **Middle East:** The Middle East is already a water-stressed region, and tensions over shared water resources, particularly the Jordan, Euphrates, and Tigris rivers, have been a source of conflict. As water availability decreases due to climate change and population growth, the competition for limited water resources may intensify existing political and social conflicts in the region.
2. **Sub-Saharan Africa:** Many countries in sub-Saharan Africa face water scarcity challenges, with increased demand for water due to population growth and agricultural

development. The potential for conflicts over shared river basins, such as the Nile River, which traverses multiple countries, remains a concern.

3. **South Asia:** In South Asia, the Indus River basin, shared by India and Pakistan, faces water stress due to population growth, climate change impacts, and upstream water diversion projects. Disputes over water sharing have the potential to escalate into conflicts between these nuclear-armed nations.
4. **Central Asia:** The Aral Sea basin, shared by Kazakhstan, Uzbekistan, Turkmenistan, Tajikistan, and Kyrgyzstan, has experienced significant water scarcity and environmental degradation. Competition over water resources, particularly for irrigation and hydropower projects, could lead to tensions among the countries in the region.

To mitigate potential conflicts over water scarcity, effective water management strategies, cooperation among riparian countries, and international water agreements are crucial. Investing in sustainable water infrastructure, promoting water conservation and efficiency, and addressing the underlying social and political factors that contribute to conflicts are essential for ensuring water security and preventing future conflicts.[2]

These examples highlight how environmental factors can intersect with political, social, and economic factors to exacerbate conflicts. Addressing environmental issues, promoting sustainable resource management, and finding equitable solutions are essential for mitigating conflicts and fostering peace and stability.

Looking at the uncertainties and probable crises of the near future, it is expected that environmental factors will continue to play a significant role in conflicts. The impacts of climate change, coupled with population growth and resource scarcity, are likely to increase the pressure on ecosystems and communities, potentially leading to heightened conflicts. However, it is important to note that environmental factors alone do not directly cause conflicts. Socioeconomic, political, and historical factors also interact with environmental issues, shaping the dynamics of conflicts.

Addressing environmental factors in conflicts requires integrated approaches that combine environmental management, sustainable resource use, conflict prevention, and peacebuilding efforts. It is crucial to promote sustainable development, enhance resource management, foster cooperation, and invest in climate adaptation and resilience to mitigate the potential risks of environmental conflicts in the future.

11.2 Sustainable Development for Peacebuilding

The connection between sustainable development and peacebuilding is closely intertwined, as they both contribute to creating a more peaceful and stable society. Sustainable development focuses on meeting the needs of the present without compromising the ability of future generations to meet their own needs, while peacebuilding aims to prevent and resolve conflicts to establish lasting peace.

Sustainable development is essential for peacebuilding because it addresses the root causes of conflicts, such as poverty, inequality, social exclusion, and environmental degradation. By promoting inclusive economic growth, social development, and environmental protection, sustainable development can help reduce grievances and inequalities that often fuel conflicts. It also fosters the conditions for social cohesion, trust, and resilience, which are vital for building peaceful and resilient societies.

In addition, peacebuilding efforts create a conducive environment for sustainable development by establishing political stability, promoting social cohesion, and resolving conflicts peacefully. Peacebuilding processes often involve political negotiations, transitional justice, disarmament, demobilization, and reintegration of ex-combatants, and fostering reconciliation among communities. These measures contribute to creating an enabling environment for sustainable development to thrive.

In terms of peace and security priorities, the relation between sustainable development and peacebuilding calls for:

1. **Conflict Prevention:** Addressing the root causes of conflicts, such as poverty, inequality, and environmental degradation, through sustainable development strategies can help prevent the outbreak or recurrence of conflicts.
2. **Inclusive Governance:** Promoting inclusive and participatory governance systems that respect human rights, ensure rule of law, and provide equal access to justice and services is crucial for building peaceful societies and achieving sustainable development.

3. **Social Cohesion and Reconciliation:** Promoting social cohesion, trust-building, and reconciliation among communities affected by conflicts is essential for sustainable peace and development.
4. **Economic Recovery and Livelihoods:** Supporting economic recovery, job creation, and livelihood opportunities for conflict-affected populations is critical for fostering stability, reducing grievances, and preventing the resurgence of conflicts.
5. **Environmental Sustainability:** Protecting and restoring ecosystems, managing natural resources sustainably, and addressing environmental challenges are vital for both sustainable development and peacebuilding. Environmental degradation can exacerbate conflicts, while environmental conservation and sustainable resource management can contribute to peace and stability.

In particular, the relationship between sustainable development and peacebuilding highlights the importance of integrated and holistic approaches that address social, economic, environmental, and governance dimensions to facilitate long-term peace, security, and sustainable development.

The Post-2030 Agenda should prioritize several key implications and priorities to promote sustainable development and peacebuilding:

1. **Integrated Approach:** The Post-2030 Agenda should emphasize the need for an integrated approach that addresses the interconnected challenges of sustainable development and peacebuilding. It should recognize the interdependencies between social, economic, environmental, and governance dimensions and promote coordinated actions across sectors.
2. **Conflict prevention and Resolution:** Efforts to prevent conflicts and resolve existing conflicts should be prioritized. This includes addressing the root causes of conflicts, promoting dialogue, fostering social cohesion, and strengthening institutions for conflict prevention and resolution.
3. **Inclusive and Participatory Governance:** Ensuring inclusive and participatory governance systems that respect human rights, promote transparency, accountability, and the rule of law is crucial for sustainable development and peacebuilding. This includes empowering marginalized

groups, promoting gender equality, and enhancing citizen engagement in decision-making processes.

4. **Social Equity and Justice:** Prioritizing social equity and justice is essential for building peaceful and inclusive societies. This includes addressing inequalities, promoting social cohesion, and ensuring access to basic services, education, healthcare, and employment opportunities for all.
5. **Environmental Sustainability:** Environmental sustainability should be a core priority, recognizing the close linkages between environmental degradation, resource scarcity, and conflicts. The Post-2030 Agenda should emphasize sustainable resource management, climate action, biodiversity conservation, and the protection of ecosystems as key components of peacebuilding and sustainable development.
6. **Resilience and Risk Reduction:** Building resilience to shocks, disasters, and climate change is critical for sustainable development and peacebuilding. This involves investing in disaster risk reduction, climate adaptation, and promoting the resilience of communities and institutions.
7. **Partnerships and Cooperation:** The Post-2030 Agenda should prioritize partnerships and cooperation among governments, civil society, the private sector, and international organizations. Collaborative efforts are needed to mobilize resources, share knowledge, and coordinate actions to achieve sustainable development and peacebuilding goals.
8. **Data and Monitoring:** Strengthening data collection, monitoring, and evaluation systems is essential for tracking progress, identifying gaps, and making evidence-based decisions. The Post-2030 Agenda should prioritize the availability of reliable and disaggregated data to support evidence-based policies and interventions.

Overall, the Post-2030 Agenda should emphasize the transformative nature of sustainable development and peacebuilding, recognizing their interlinkages and the need for integrated approaches. It should strive for a more inclusive, equitable, and sustainable world, promoting peace, security, and prosperity for all.

11.3 Sustainable Development and Human Rights

Sustainable development and human rights are intrinsically linked concepts. The United Nations' 2030 Agenda for

Sustainable Development explicitly recognizes the strong interconnection between these two areas and seeks to promote both.[3]

1. **Interdependence:** Sustainable development cannot be achieved without the realization of human rights, and vice versa. Human rights offer a legal and ethical framework that ensures that development is not just about economic growth, but about enabling all people to live with dignity. Development processes that fail to address human rights can exacerbate inequalities, discrimination, and exclusion.
2. **People-Centered Approach:** Both concepts place the human being at the center. Sustainable development aims at "meeting the needs of the present without compromising the ability of future generations to meet their own needs." Additionally, human rights law seeks to protect individuals' fundamental needs and freedoms.
3. **Inclusive Development:** Sustainable development requires the inclusion of all people, including the most vulnerable and marginalized, which is a key principle of human rights law. Human rights law also requires non-discrimination and equality, which are crucial for sustainable development.
4. **Participation and Accountability:** Both frameworks emphasize the importance of participation and access to information. In human rights terms, individuals and communities have the right to participate in decision-making processes that affect their lives. In sustainable development, stakeholders' involvement, transparency, and accountability are essential for the legitimacy and effectiveness of development initiatives.

As we approach the Post-2030 Agenda, the following may be critical implications to consider:

1. **Human Rights-Based Approaches to Development:** More emphasis should be placed on human rights-based approaches to development. This includes developing policies and programs that are explicitly designed to realize human rights and promote equality.
2. **Climate Justice:** With the increasing threat of climate change, a focus on climate justice will be needed. This includes recognizing and addressing the disproportionate impact of climate change on the rights of vulnerable and marginalized communities.

3. **Economic Inequality and Social Rights:** Addressing economic inequality will be a priority, with implications for the realization of social, economic, and cultural rights. This might involve a greater focus on progressive taxation, social protection, and living wages.
4. **Digital Rights:** As digital technology becomes increasingly integral to our lives and economies, protecting digital rights will become more important. This could involve, for example, ensuring access to the internet as a fundamental right and protecting privacy in the digital age.
5. **Gender Equality:** Despite progress, gender equality remains an unfulfilled promise. Post-2030, there will need to be a continued focus on women's rights and gender equality, including through initiatives designed to promote women's economic empowerment and combat gender-based violence.
6. **Protecting Civic Spaces:** With rising authoritarianism worldwide, protecting civic space and the right to dissent will be critical. This includes protecting the rights of activists and civil society organizations, which play a key role in both promoting human rights and sustainable development.
7. **Global Governance and Cooperation:** Achieving both sustainable development and human rights will require global cooperation. This includes reforming international institutions to make them more representative and effective, and strengthening international law to better address global challenges.

Ultimately, the Post-2030 Agenda should recognize the interdependence between sustainable development and human rights and take a holistic, integrated approach to these issues.

11.4 Climate Refugees and Environmental Migrants

Climate change contributes to forced migration and the creation of climate refugees in several significant ways:

1. **Environmental Disasters:** Increased frequency and intensity of environmental disasters such as hurricanes, floods, and wildfires can directly displace people from their homes. For example, the Internal Displacement Monitoring Centre estimated that between 2008 and 2014, an average of

26.4 million people per year were displaced by disasters brought on by natural hazards.

2. **Sea-Level Rise:** Rising sea levels due to melting ice caps can inundate low-lying islands and coastal areas, forcing inhabitants to relocate. Countries like the Maldives and Kiribati are already grappling with this threat.
3. **Droughts and Desertification:** Changes in weather patterns can lead to prolonged droughts and desertification, making some areas uninhabitable and affecting agricultural practices. This can force farmers and rural populations to migrate to urban areas or other countries in search of livelihoods.
4. **Resource Scarcity:** Climate change can exacerbate resource scarcity, particularly water and fertile land. This can lead to conflicts over these resources, forcing people to move to safer locations.

The concept of "climate refugees" or "environmental migrants" is not currently recognized under international refugee law, specifically the 1951 Refugee Convention, which defines a refugee as a person fleeing persecution due to race, religion, nationality, membership of a particular social group, or political opinion. However, the growing impacts of climate change have sparked debates on the necessity of expanding this definition or creating new legal instruments to protect the rights of people displaced by environmental factors.[4]

The recognition of these rights is critical for several reasons:

1. **Legal Protection:** Recognizing climate refugees would provide them with legal protections under international law, such as the right not to be returned to a place where their life or freedom would be threatened.
2. **Support Mechanisms:** Recognition would enable more systematic support for climate refugees, including humanitarian aid, resettlement options, and assistance in achieving sustainable livelihoods.
3. **Responsibility Sharing:** It could lead to more equitable sharing of responsibilities among nations, rather than leaving the burden to the countries most affected by climate change or those geographically closer to the crises.
4. **Planned Relocation:** Recognition could enable better planning for relocation and reduce the risk of human rights

abuses during forced displacement. This includes ensuring that relocation processes respect the rights of the displaced, including rights to housing, education, healthcare, and livelihood.

5. **Preventive Measures:** It can also help drive global action to mitigate climate change. Acknowledging that climate change displaces people underscores the human costs of inaction and could spur greater efforts to reduce greenhouse gas emissions.

As we move forward, it's clear that the international community will need to develop new legal, policy, and practical solutions to protect people displaced by climate change, recognizing their rights, and addressing the root causes of their displacement.

11.5 Expanding SDG 16 for the Post-2030 Agenda

United Nations' Sustainable Development Goal 16 (SDG 16) is about promoting peace, justice, and strong institutions. It underlines the importance of peace, justice, and effective institutions to sustainable development. As we approach the Post-2030 Agenda, there are several ways SDG 16 could be expanded and prioritized:

1. **Interconnectedness of SDGs:** More focus could be put on emphasizing the interconnectedness of SDG 16 with all other SDGs. Peace, justice, and strong institutions are not only goals but also crucial enablers for achieving other SDGs. Their importance to areas such as health, education, climate action, and economic growth should be highlighted.
2. **Climate Justice:** Given the increasing recognition of the link between climate change and conflict, climate justice could be incorporated more explicitly into SDG 16. This could involve promoting peacebuilding strategies that also address climate change and protect the rights of people affected by climate-related displacement.
3. **Digital Governance and Cyber Peace:** The digital space is becoming an important area for peace, justice, and effective institutions. SDG 16 could be expanded to address challenges like cybercrime, misinformation, digital inequality, and threats to privacy and freedom of speech online.

4. **Inclusion and Equity:** While SDG 16 already seeks to promote inclusive societies, more emphasis could be placed on the intersectional nature of exclusion and discrimination. This might involve a greater focus on the rights and inclusion of groups who face multiple forms of discrimination, such as women from ethnic or religious minorities.
5. **Preventive Diplomacy and Peace Education:** Efforts can be intensified to emphasize preventive diplomacy, conflict prevention, and resolution strategies. The promotion of peace education to foster a culture of peace from a young age can also be a priority.
6. **Resilience-Building:** The concept of resilience can be integrated more into SDG 16, focusing on the ability of communities, institutions, and states to withstand and recover from shocks and crises without lapsing into conflict.
7. **Reforming International Institutions:** A focus could be added on reforming international institutions to make them more representative, effective, and able to address global challenges, including peace and justice.
8. **Recognition and Support for Local Peace Efforts:** There could be a stronger emphasis on recognizing and supporting local and community-led peace and justice initiatives. Often, local actors are best placed to understand and address the specific dynamics of their contexts.
9. **Monitoring and Accountability:** More robust and comprehensive indicators for monitoring progress towards SDG 16 could be developed. Greater accountability mechanisms can also be put in place to hold governments and international institutions accountable for their commitments under this goal.
10. **Global Cooperation and Partnership:** Lastly, more emphasis on the importance of global cooperation and partnership in achieving peace, justice, and strong institutions should be included.

These are just potential directions, as the specific priorities for the Post-2030 Agenda will be determined through international negotiations involving UN member states and other stakeholders. However, all these areas could potentially contribute to an expanded and prioritized focus on SDG 16 in the Post-2030 Agenda.

11.6 Sustainable Human Security

Sustainable human security (SHS) presents an evolved perspective on traditional security paradigms by focusing on the fundamental rights and freedoms of individuals and communities, acknowledging the complex interplay of various dimensions of human life, and understanding the deep interconnectedness of human security with social, economic, political, and environmental systems. Here's an explanation of the four dimensions of sustainable human security:

1. **Freedom from Fear:** This dimension of SHS is about ensuring physical safety and security for all people. It includes protection against violence, conflict, and man-made or natural disasters. In practical terms, it could involve measures like conflict prevention and resolution, disaster risk reduction, law enforcement reform, and violence prevention programs. It implies the creation of conditions where individuals and communities can live without the constant threat of violence, conflict, or disaster.
2. **Freedom from Want:** This dimension focuses on ensuring that all people can meet their basic needs and fully participate in society. It includes combating extreme poverty, systemic poverty, and recurring poverty. This could involve measures such as social protection programs, inclusive economic policies, and efforts to ensure access to essential services like healthcare and education. It acknowledges that poverty is not just a lack of income, but also a form of deprivation and exclusion that can undermine human security.
3. **Freedom from Shame:** This dimension is about promoting human dignity and respect for all aspects of diversity. It involves the recognition and protection of the fundamental human rights of every individual. This could include measures to combat discrimination, promote social inclusion, protect the rights of marginalized and vulnerable groups, and ensure that all people can participate in social, economic, and political life without discrimination or stigma.
4. **Freedom from Vulnerability:** This dimension is about promoting resilience and sustainability. It involves protecting people from both immediate and long-term threats, particularly those related to environmental degradation and climate change. This could involve measures like climate

adaptation and mitigation, environmental conservation, and sustainable development policies. It acknowledges that our long-term security is deeply interconnected with the health of our planet.

These four pillars are embedded into political, economic, social, and environmental responsibility. They are addressed through a rights-based approach, recognizing that human rights are a crucial foundation for human security, and a sustainable capacity approach, acknowledging that our ability to achieve human security depends on our capacity to manage social, economic, political, and environmental systems in a sustainable way.[5]

The SHS paradigm provides a roadmap for creating a world where all people can live with dignity, safety, and freedom, protected from fear, want, shame, and vulnerability. It's an integrated approach that recognizes the interconnected nature of the challenges we face and the importance of addressing them holistically and comprehensively.

The SHS paradigm reflects the need of integrating sustainability with a comprehensive human rights value. It also integrates traditional conceptions of security to emphasize the importance of human rights for sustainable development practices at individual and community levels. It focuses on the interconnectedness of various threats to human security and argues for a more holistic, integrated approach. Integrating this paradigm into the Post-2030 Agenda could involve the following elements:

1. **Holistic Approach:** Recognize that threats to human security are interconnected and need to be addressed in a holistic manner. This means not only addressing immediate threats but also underlying vulnerabilities and systemic issues that can undermine human security. For example, poverty is not just an economic issue, but can also affect personal security, health, education, and other areas.
2. **Prevention and Resilience:** Focus on prevention and resilience-building rather than just crisis response. This could involve, for example, addressing the root causes of conflict, promoting social cohesion, strengthening community resilience, and implementing climate adaptation measures. A preventive approach can save lives, resources, and preserve human dignity.

3. **Sustainable Development and Human Rights:** Acknowledge that sustainable development and human rights are essential for human security. This means integrating sustainable human security considerations into all aspects of the Post-2030 Sustainable Development Agenda. Prioritizing the rights of the most vulnerable and marginalized is a crucial aspect of this approach.
4. **Climate Change and Environmental Security:** Recognize that climate change and environmental degradation are major threats to human security. This can involve integrating climate action into all aspects of the Post-2030 Agenda and recognizing the rights of climate refugees.
5. **Inclusive Governance and Participation:** Promote inclusive, accountable, and participatory governance. This includes ensuring that all individuals and communities, particularly the most vulnerable and marginalized, can participate in decision-making processes affecting their security.
6. **Gender Sensitivity:** Incorporate a gender perspective, acknowledging that men, women, and gender-diverse individuals may face different security threats and have different security needs. Empowerment of women and gender equality should be integrated as key aspects of sustainable human security.
7. **Global Cooperation and Solidarity:** Emphasize the importance of global cooperation and solidarity in addressing threats to human security. Many of these threats, such as climate change and pandemics, are transnational and can only be effectively addressed through international cooperation.
8. **Innovative Solutions and Technology:** Encourage the use of innovative solutions and technology to enhance human security. Digital technology, for instance, can provide new ways to enhance access to services, improve accountability, and facilitate participation.
9. **Measurement and Accountability:** Develop robust mechanisms for measuring progress towards sustainable human security and holding governments and other actors accountable for their commitments.

Incorporating a sustainable human security paradigm into the Post-2030 Agenda could ensure that this agenda is not only about promoting economic growth or protecting the environment but also about enhancing the security, rights, and well-being of all people, particularly the most vulnerable and marginalized. It also emphasizes that these goals are interconnected and mutually reinforcing.

In advocating for a paradigm shift towards peace as the bedrock of sustainable human security, we recognize the resonant demand for a world liberated from the shackles of poverty, hunger, disease, fear, and violence. This vision of human security, inextricably linked with the principles of sustainability, dignity, development, and safety, transcends the realm of policy; it is a moral imperative. We are called upon to uphold a covenant—a profound commitment to ensuring that every person is endowed with the fundamental rights and the inherent dignity that define our shared humanity. This is not merely an ideal to aspire to; it is the very essence of a just and thriving global community, and it demands a collective shift in our perceptions, our values, and our actions to cultivate a peaceful and secure future for all.

11.7 The Peace Mindset Shift Priorities

As we contemplate the imperatives of the new sustainability agenda, it becomes increasingly evident that achieving lasting peace is not merely the absence of conflict; it is also about addressing the root causes of discord. Central to these causes are issues of sustainability, including resource scarcity, unequal access to opportunities, and the pursuit of a better quality of life. To foster a world where peace and sustainability go hand in hand, we must prioritize a series of mindset shifts that tackle these fundamental challenges head-on.

1. **Resource Equity:** A cornerstone of the peace mindset shift is recognizing that equitable access to resources is essential for peace and sustainability. By addressing resource scarcity through fair distribution and sustainable management, we can mitigate one of the primary drivers of conflicts.
2. **Global Interconnectedness:** Embracing a mindset that acknowledges our global interconnectedness is paramount. Actions in one region can have far-reaching consequences elsewhere. Understanding this interdependence is crucial in promoting cooperative solutions to global challenges.

3. **Conflict Prevention through Development:** Shifting the focus from reactive conflict resolution to proactive conflict prevention is essential. This involves investing in sustainable development, poverty alleviation, and access to education and healthcare, which can reduce the conditions that breed conflict.
4. **Inclusivity and Equality:** Peace can only be sustained when societies are inclusive and equitable. Prioritizing social justice, gender equality, and minority rights ensures that no group is marginalized or left behind, reducing the potential for grievances that lead to violence.
5. **Environmental Stewardship:** Recognizing the intrinsic link between environmental sustainability and peace is crucial. A mindset shift that values the protection of ecosystems and biodiversity as essential for global stability can help prevent conflicts arising from resource competition.
6. **Diplomacy and Conflict Resolution:** Elevating diplomacy and peaceful conflict resolution as the primary means of addressing disputes reinforces the importance of dialogue over violence. Prioritizing diplomatic efforts fosters a culture of negotiation and cooperation.
7. **Youth and Education:** Empowering youth through education and meaningful participation in decision-making processes can break the cycle of violence and provide opportunities for positive contributions to society.
8. **Cultural Understanding:** Fostering a mindset of cultural understanding and respect promotes tolerance and reduces the potential for conflicts rooted in cultural or religious differences.
9. **Humanitarianism:** Prioritizing humanitarian principles in all aspects of governance and international relations emphasizes the value of human life and the duty to protect vulnerable populations in times of crisis.
10. **Global Solidarity:** Embracing the principle of global solidarity underscores the shared responsibility of nations and individuals in addressing the challenges of our time, promoting cooperation as the path to peace and sustainability.

These peace mindset shift priorities underscore the need to view peace and sustainability as interconnected objectives. By addressing the root causes of conflicts in the context of resource scarcity and unequal access to opportunities, we can build a more harmonious world where both peace and sustainability thrive.

11.8 The New Agenda for Sustainable Peace

The path to sustainable peace mandates a proactive and preventive approach, one that transcends immediate conflict resolution and delves into the strategic mitigation of risks and geopolitical fissures. This entails a steadfast dedication to combating the roots of human insecurity, which include climate change and social inequality. Peace, therefore, must be reimagined as a foundational stance, a deliberate and ongoing effort to maintain harmony and preempt discord.

Within the domain of Peace Operations, the fortification of missions and peace enforcement strategies is imperative. Such operations must encompass a spectrum of initiatives, including conflict prevention, peacekeeping, peace enforcement, peacemaking, peacebuilding, the protection of civilians, and the provision of humanitarian aid. These endeavors, while diverse and complex, are designed to be nimble and adaptive, mirroring the intricate and ever-changing landscape of global relations. Although they may not be a panacea for enduring peace, they are instrumental in cultivating the fertile ground necessary for peace to take root and flourish. Moreover, these operations must account for the environmental underpinnings and repercussions that intertwine with both nascent and prolonged conflicts.

The advancement of the new agenda necessitates a pivotal focus on gender equality and the amplification of women's roles in peace and security processes. The involvement of women and girls is not a supplementary aspect but a cornerstone of sustainable peace and security. Their participation in peacemaking, conflict prevention, and peacebuilding not only deepens the impact of these processes but also ensures they are more equitable, inclusive, and successful.

The conceptualization of the New Agenda for Peace represents a quantum leap in our perception of peace. It intertwines social and economic rights with the right to a clean, healthy, and sustainable environment, asserting that peace is not simply the negation of war but the affirmation of justice, equity, and ecological balance.

The peace and security priorities for the Post-2030 Agenda set before us are both a challenge and an inspiration. They represent not just an aspiration but a tangible blueprint—an action-oriented guide demanding our collective resolve, unwavering dedication, and boldness to act. As our gaze shifts to the horizon beyond 2030, our ambition should not be limited to a world where nations coexist in superficial unity. Instead, we must endeavor to sculpt a reality founded upon a revitalized global peace and security agenda, one where the resonances of social, environmental, economic, governance, and technological considerations are felt in every corner of the globe, from the heart of each individual to the policies of every nation.

11.9 Resources

As we have seen throughout Chapter 11, peace and security are fundamental prerequisites for the achievement of sustainable development. To sustain peace means to proactively foster and support the political, social, and structural environments in which sustainable peace can emerge and thrive. Human security broadens the understanding of security to focus on the protection of individuals rather than just states. It encompasses issues related to economic security, food security, health security, environmental security, personal security, community security, and political security. Here are key resources that focus on the nexus of peace, security, and sustainability:

1. **The Global Partnership for the Prevention of Armed Conflict (GPPAC):** GPPAC is a member-led network of civil society organizations active in conflict prevention and peacebuilding worldwide. Its publications, toolkits, and reports provide guidance on how civil society can play a pivotal role in fostering sustainable peace. It addresses emerging threats like climate security. Read more at www.gppac.net.
2. **Reports by the Institute for Economics & Peace (IEP):** Particularly the Global Peace Index, which assesses the state of peace in countries based on varied indicators. This annual report captures the essence of peace from both a traditional and human-centric security perspective. Read more at www.economicsandpeace.org/reports/.

3. **UNDP's Human Development Report (1994):** A pivotal report entitled *New Dimensions of Human Security* introduced and thoroughly explored the human security concept, emphasizing its significance beyond just protecting states and highlighting its seven primary dimensions. See also the *Human Security Now* published by the Commission on Human Security (CHS) in 2003, it is a deep dive into the concept, implications, and applications of human security in diverse sectors, suggesting strategies to safeguard human rights, protect people in conflict and post-conflict situations, and promote human development. Read more at the UN Trust Fund for Human Security. www.un.org/humansecurity/.
4. **Reports by the UNU Institute for Environment and Human Security (UNU-EHS):** This institute's research delves into the environmental facets of human security. Their work sheds light on how aspects like climate change, environmental degradation, and natural disasters can pose significant threats to human security. Read more at www.unbonn.org/UNU-EHS.
5. **United Nations' *Summit of the Future* (Website):** The United Nations' 2024 documents "Summit of the Future" and the policy brief "Summit of the Future: What Would It Deliver?," available on the website, provide comprehensive insights into the strategies and goals of the United Nations for maintaining and promoting global peace and security in the context of emerging global challenges including cyberspace, outer space, lethal autonomous weapons, AI, and biorisks. The policy brief argues for stronger collective security that would include a reformed Security Council, a revitalized General Assembly, and an enhanced Peacebuilding Commission. www.un.org/en/summit-of-the-future.

Notes

1 United Nations (2023). *Our Common Agenda Policy Brief 9: A New Agenda for Peace*. https://www.un.org/sites/un2.un.org/files/our-common-agenda-policy-brief-new-agenda-for-peace-en.pdf

2 Murphy, C., Nizkorodov, E., & Matthew, R.A. (2021). *Routledge Handbook of Environmental Security.* United Kingdom: Taylor & Francis.

3 Tavanti, M., & Sfeir-Younis, A. (2013). Human Rights Based Sustainable Development: Essential Frameworks for an Integrated Approach. *The International Journal of Sustainability Policy and Practices*, 8(3), 21–35. http://ijspp.cgpublisher.com/product/pub.274/prod.38

4 Behrman, S., & Kent, A. (Eds.). (2018). *Climate Refugees: Beyond the Legal Impasse?* Routledge.

5 Tavanti, M., & Stachowicz-Stanusch, A. (2014). *Sustainable Human Security: Corruption Issues and Anti-Corruption Solutions*. United States: Common Ground Publishing LLC.

12 Technology and Innovation Priorities

> We can do this now. We don't have to wait. At the same time, we recognize that our current technology alone won't get us where we need to be. So, it must also be a decisive decade for innovation: developing, demonstrating, and commercializing new clean energy technologies by 2030 so that we can—they can be widely deployed in time to meet our 2050 net-zero goals.
>
> Clean hydrogen, long-duration energy storage, next-generation renewables and nuclear, carbon capture, sustainable agriculture, and so much more. We need to invest in breakthroughs, and I welcome the UK's leadership on the Glasgow Breakthrough agenda.
>
> Innovation is the key to unlocking our future. That's why the United States is working to quadruple funding for clean energy research and development over the next four years. And we will lead a year of action in 2022 to advance clean technologies globally.
>
> (Remarks by President Biden at COP 26 Climate Summit in Glasgow—"Accelerating Clean Technology Innovation and Deployment" event—November 2, 2021[1])

Overview

The final chapter in this second part explores the role of technology and innovation in sustainable development. Priorities include fostering digital inclusivity, managing technological risks, promoting green and social innovation, and leveraging technology for sustainable solutions.

12.1 From Earth to Space and Back

In the wake of the 2030 Agenda and the challenges we face in the post-2030 world, a salient question is how we can leverage technology and innovation to carve out a sustainable, inclusive, and resilient future for all. Building on the insights from *Post*

DOI: 10.4324/9781003494676-15

2030-Agenda and the Role of Space: The UN 2030 Goals and Their Further Evolution Beyond 2030 for Sustainable Development,[2] this chapter delves into the pertinent technology innovation priorities required for sustainable development.

Harnessing technologies ranging from AI and machine learning to biotechnology to renewable energy and space infrastructure, we can fundamentally change our approach to some of the most pressing global issues. Furthermore, the novel application of technologies, such as the integration of blockchain technology in space activities and the use of satellite data for broad administrative applications, sets a course for a future where accountability and transparency are at the core of global institutions.

In this intricate dance of innovation and sustainability, the digital divide should not be overlooked. Prioritizing digital inclusivity ensures that the fruits of technological advancement are accessible to all, contributing to the equitable advancement of societies. Additionally, navigating the risks associated with these technologies is as important as exploiting their benefits.

This chapter, therefore, sets the stage to explore how technological empowerment can serve communities and how innovation can be directed towards green and socially conscious endeavors. With the right priorities and commitments, we can indeed turn technology and innovation into powerful tools that bring us closer to achieving our sustainability objectives.

12.2 Technology as Community Empowerment

As we embark on this exploration, it is essential to grasp the transformative potential of technological advancements and innovations across a range of fields. From artificial intelligence and machine learning to biotechnology and renewable energy, technology holds the potential to reshape our world. Indeed, these technologies can revolutionize the way we approach systemic problems, providing new tools to understand, adapt to, and mitigate global crises such as climate change, while also paving the way towards a more sustainable, inclusive, and resilient development paradigm.

Yet, the power of technology goes beyond mere problem-solving. It carries the promise of empowerment, of enabling communities to take their futures into their own hands, and of democratizing access to the resources and opportunities necessary for sustainable development. From blockchain providing transparency and reducing corruption to the Internet of Things enabling smart, livable cities, technology can play a pivotal role in enhancing individual and collective agency.

But harnessing this potential is not without its challenges. The march of technology can also exacerbate inequalities, disrupt societies, and create new risks if not managed wisely and equitably. The onus, therefore, is on us to guide the integration of these transformative technologies with foresight and responsibility, ensuring they serve as levers of progress for all of humanity.

In the realm of technology and innovation, there are several groundbreaking developments that show tremendous potential for shaping the future, fostering community empowerment, and driving sustainable development.

1. **Artificial Intelligence (AI) and Machine Learning (ML):** AI and ML technologies offer unprecedented opportunities for analyzing large datasets, predicting outcomes, automating tasks, and enhancing decision-making processes. In the context of community empowerment, they can help democratize access to information, improve public services, facilitate personalized education, and support health diagnostics. For sustainable development, they can help optimize resource use, improve energy efficiency, and provide vital insights into climate change patterns and biodiversity.
2. **Internet of Things (IoT):** IoT can enhance connectivity and data collection, with applications ranging from smart homes to smart cities. In terms of community empowerment, IoT can help create connected, livable, and inclusive urban environments, with real-time data enhancing public services, transportation, and security. In sustainable development, IoT can support efficient energy management, waste reduction, and water conservation.[3]
3. **Blockchain Technology:** Blockchain can provide secure, transparent, and decentralized systems for various transactions. This can empower communities by enhancing trust, reducing corruption, and enabling peer-to-peer interactions. Applications in sustainable development include transparent supply chains, peer-to-peer renewable energy trading, and secure land rights registration.

4. **Renewable Energy Technologies:** Innovations in solar, wind, and other renewable technologies are crucial for a sustainable future. They democratize access to energy, particularly in off-grid rural communities, leading to social and economic empowerment. They also are an entry to a sustainable, low-carbon development pathway.
5. **Biotechnology:** Advances in biotech can transform healthcare and agriculture, empowering communities by enhancing food security and health outcomes. From lab-grown meat to CRISPR gene editing, these technologies can also contribute to sustainable development by reducing environmental degradation and improving resilience to climate change.
6. **5G and Future Connectivity Technologies:** These will facilitate faster and more reliable internet, empowering communities through improved access to information, e-services, and opportunities for remote work and learning. These technologies are also crucial for enabling other innovations (like AI, IoT) and can support sustainability through improved efficiencies.
7. **Green Technologies:** From carbon capture and storage to materials recycling, green technologies are critical for a sustainable future. They can empower communities by creating green jobs and reducing environmental health risks.
8. **Digital Fabrication and 3D Printing:** These technologies can democratize manufacturing, empowering local communities, and promoting a shift towards a circular economy. They can reduce the environmental footprint of manufacturing and make it more sustainable by using recycled materials and reducing transportation needs.

As we integrate these technologies, it's essential to do so responsibly, ensuring that they promote inclusion, equity, and sustainability. This means considering issues like digital literacy, privacy, ethical AI, technology accessibility, and the potential environmental footprint of these technologies. Through a thoughtful, inclusive, and forward-looking approach, technology and innovation can be powerful drivers of community empowerment and sustainable development.

12.2 Technology for Conscious Communication

The exponential rise of digital communication technologies has transformed how societies function, offering unprecedented opportunities for information sharing, collaboration, and social connection. However, alongside these benefits come significant challenges, particularly with the rise of misinformation, disinformation, fake news, and deepfakes—artificially generated images or videos that depict events or actions that never actually occurred.

Given these developments, it's crucial to prioritize the following technological advancements for future communication needs:

1. **Enhanced Fact-Checking and Verification Tools:** With AI-generated fake news and deepfakes becoming increasingly sophisticated, there's a pressing need for more robust and advanced fact-checking and verification tools. These might incorporate machine learning algorithms to detect anomalies and inconsistencies that suggest a piece of content has been artificially generated or manipulated. They could also cross-reference information against trusted databases or use blockchain technology to trace the origin and modification history of digital content.
2. **Media Literacy Education Tools:** Technology can also play a critical role in educating the public about media literacy. Interactive online platforms could be developed to teach users how to critically evaluate the reliability and credibility of different sources of information, recognize signs of misinformation and disinformation, and verify the authenticity of digital content.
3. **Secure and Private Communication Platforms:** With growing concerns about privacy and data security, there is an increasing need for communication technologies that prioritize these aspects. This could involve end-to-end encrypted communication platforms, decentralized networks that reduce reliance on a single authority, and stronger user control over personal data.
4. **Advanced Natural Language Processing (NLP) Systems:** As communication increasingly takes place through digital platforms, the need for advanced NLP systems will grow. These can assist in deciphering and understanding the nuances of human language, including sentiment analysis, text summarization, and language translation, which can be used to improve communication effectiveness and bridge language barriers in a globally connected world.
5. **AI-Assisted Content Moderation:** Given the sheer volume of digital content generated every second, AI can assist in

content moderation. While it's currently used to flag and filter out inappropriate content, future developments could improve the ability to detect and remove harmful content, including hate speech, harassment, or misinformation.

6. **Inclusive and Accessible Technologies:** Future communication technologies should be designed with inclusivity and accessibility in mind. This includes text-to-speech and speech-to-text conversion for people with visual or auditory impairments, easy-to-use interfaces for older adults or individuals with limited digital literacy, and affordability considerations to ensure widespread access.
7. **Decentralized Social Media Platforms:** To combat the concentrated power of current social media platforms, the development of decentralized platforms should be prioritized. These platforms can give users more control over their data and help to prevent the spread of misinformation by creating transparency and trust.

Addressing these technological priorities can go a long way toward ensuring that the digital revolution in communication serves to enhance, rather than undermine, the quality of public discourse and societal cohesion in our increasingly interconnected world.

The Post-2030 Agenda should unequivocally recognize the pivotal role technology can play in nurturing consciousness, fostering critical thinking, and empowering citizens to actively engage in shaping their societies. Technology, when leveraged thoughtfully, has the potential to democratize information access, deepen understanding of complex issues, and spur collective action.

Here are several ways the Post-2030 Agenda could champion these transformative aspects of technology:

1. **Promote Digital Literacy:** The agenda should emphasize the importance of digital literacy as a fundamental skill for the 21st century. Digital literacy extends beyond the ability to use digital devices and involves understanding how to evaluate information, discern reliable sources, and safeguard one's privacy online. Support should be given to initiatives and technologies that aim to enhance digital literacy, such as educational programs, interactive apps, and online platforms.

2. **Encourage Development of EdTech:** Educational technologies (EdTech) have tremendous potential to foster critical thinking and consciousness. AI-driven personalized learning platforms, virtual reality environments, and online collaboration tools can provide immersive, interactive experiences that challenge learners to think deeply and critically about various academic subjects and issues. Funding and policy support for EdTech research, development, and implementation should be a priority.
3. **Advocate for Transparency and Accountability in AI:** AI systems have immense influence over what information we see and how we perceive the world. The agenda should advocate for greater transparency and accountability in AI, ensuring these systems promote a diverse range of perspectives, respect user autonomy, and do not perpetuate bias or misinformation.
4. **Support Civic Tech:** Civic technologies aim to empower citizens and improve government transparency, accountability, and responsiveness. Platforms for digital voting, online public consultations, and crowdsourcing policy ideas can enhance civic engagement and political consciousness. The agenda should support the development and deployment of such technologies.
5. **Facilitate Accessible and Affordable Public Utilities, Including the Internet:** Public utilities such as electricity, water, and the internet are vital infrastructures for accessing information, services, and opportunities. The agenda should champion efforts to make these utilities, including the internet, more affordable and accessible, especially in underserved communities. This will ensure everyone can benefit from modern advancements and essential amenities, recognizing the importance of the internet alongside traditional utilities.
6. **Recognize the Role of Social Media:** Social media has become a significant platform for civic discourse and social mobilization. The agenda should recognize this role and support efforts to make social media platforms safer, more inclusive, and more conducive to constructive dialogue.
7. **Develop Regulations for Digital Rights:** Finally, the Post-2030 Agenda should recognize digital rights as human rights. This includes the right to privacy, freedom of expression,

and access to information online. Policymakers should be encouraged to develop regulations that protect these rights in the digital age.

By emphasizing these priorities, the Post-2030 Agenda can help to harness the transformative potential of technology for consciousness, critical thinking, and citizen empowerment, thus shaping a more democratic, informed, and engaged global society.

12.3 Technology for Economic Leapfrogging

Technology could advance economic leapfrogging for developing countries and for promoting social innovation, sustainability innovation, and frugal innovation.

12.3.1 Economic Leapfrogging

Economic leapfrogging refers to the opportunity for developing countries to skip less efficient, more costly stages of technological development and move directly to more advanced technology solutions. The most well-known example is the widespread adoption of mobile phones in Africa, bypassing the need for extensive landline infrastructure.

Technology can enable economic leapfrogging in several ways:

1. **Digital Economy:** Through digital platforms, e-commerce, mobile money, and other digital financial services, developing countries can foster financial inclusion, create new economic opportunities, and accelerate their transition to digital economies.
2. **Renewable Energy:** Developing countries can bypass traditional, polluting forms of energy and move directly to clean and renewable energy technologies like solar and wind, avoiding the costs and environmental damage associated with fossil fuels.
3. **Smart Agriculture:** Innovative technologies such as precision farming, remote sensing, and AI-powered predictive analytics can help developing countries enhance their agricultural productivity and sustainability, bypassing more resource-intensive and less efficient agricultural practices.

12.3.2 Promoting Social Innovation

Technology can promote social innovation—novel solutions to social problems—in various ways:

1. **Connectivity and Collaboration:** Digital platforms can connect people across geographies, fostering collaboration, knowledge exchange, and collective problem-solving.
2. **Data-Driven Insights:** Technologies such as AI and big data can provide new insights into social problems, helping to design more effective interventions.
3. **Direct Social Impact:** Technologies like telemedicine, online education, and mobile health apps can directly address social challenges such as healthcare access, education, and well-being.

12.3.3 Sustainability Innovation

Sustainability innovation is about using technology to reduce environmental impact and promote sustainable practices:

1. **Resource Efficiency:** Technologies like IoT and AI can improve efficiency in resource use, reducing waste and minimizing environmental impact.
2. **Clean Technology:** Clean technologies such as renewable energy, electric vehicles, and carbon capture and storage can help to decarbonize economies and mitigate climate change.
3. **Circular Economy:** Technologies like blockchain and AI can support circular economy models, facilitating better tracking, recycling, and repurposing of materials.

12.3.4 Frugal Innovation

Frugal innovation involves creating simple, cost-effective solutions to address the needs of resource-constrained environments.

1. **Low-Cost Solutions:** Technology can facilitate the development of low-cost solutions, from affordable medical devices to cheap renewable energy solutions, serving the needs of the economically disadvantaged.
2. **Localized Solutions:** Digital platforms, mobile technologies, and AI can help to develop solutions tailored to local needs and contexts, making them more affordable, relevant, and effective.

In sum, technology holds significant potential to accelerate economic leapfrogging, promote social and sustainability innovation, and foster frugal innovation, contributing to sustainable development in all its dimensions. However, to harness these benefits, it's crucial to address challenges like digital inequality, privacy and security concerns, and the need for relevant regulatory frameworks and digital literacy.

12.4 Technology for Social Inclusion

Technology for social inclusion, also known as inclusive technology, refers to the design, development, and application of technology specifically aimed at improving the lives of marginalized, disadvantaged, or excluded groups. It encompasses efforts to ensure equitable access to technology, as well as the use of technology to promote social, economic, and political inclusion.

Here are a few examples of how technology can promote social inclusion:

1. **Assistive Technologies:** These are designed to help people with disabilities perform tasks that might otherwise be difficult or impossible. Examples include speech recognition software for individuals with mobility impairments, screen readers for visually impaired individuals, and hearing aids compatible with digital devices for the hearing impaired.
2. **Digital Platforms for Financial Inclusion:** Digital financial services like mobile money, online banking, and microloan platforms can provide access to financial services for those who are traditionally excluded from the formal banking system. An example is M-Pesa, a mobile money platform in Kenya that has significantly improved financial inclusion.
3. **Online Education Platforms:** These can provide quality educational resources to underserved areas or disadvantaged groups. Platforms like Coursera, Khan Academy, and edX bring high-quality education content to anyone with an internet connection, promoting educational inclusion.
4. **Health Tech for Underserved Communities:** Telemedicine platforms can bring healthcare services to remote or underserved communities. Apps for tracking health indicators or providing health information can also promote health inclusion.

5. **Social Media for Marginalized Voices:** Social media platforms can give marginalized or underrepresented groups a platform to voice their experiences and perspectives, fostering social and political inclusion.

Making technology for social inclusion a priority in the Post-2030 Agenda is crucial for several reasons:

1. **Reducing Inequalities:** By ensuring that marginalized and disadvantaged groups can access and benefit from technology, we can reduce social, economic, and political inequalities.
2. **Empowering Individuals:** Inclusive technology can empower individuals by giving them the tools and resources they need to improve their lives and participate fully in society.
3. **Fostering Innovation:** Diverse perspectives fuel innovation. We can tap into a wider range of ideas and experiences by including traditionally excluded groups.
4. **Promoting Human Rights:** Access to information and communication technology is increasingly recognized as a basic human right. Promoting technology for social inclusion is, therefore, also about upholding human rights.
5. **Enhancing Social Cohesion:** Technology can help build more cohesive, harmonious societies by fostering inclusion and reducing inequalities.

In conclusion, prioritizing technology for social inclusion in the Post-2030 Agenda can help to realize the Sustainable Development Goal of "leaving no one behind," contributing to a more equitable, inclusive, and sustainable world.

12.5 Technology for Sustainability Innovation

The value of innovation in facilitating sustainability is multifold. As suggested earlier, it can spark a considerable progression in various sectors, cultivating a more stable, flourishing, and fair society.

1. **Resource Management:** Inventive solutions can enable us to fabricate systems and approaches that optimize resource utilization, curtail excess, and advance a regenerative economy.
2. **Sustainable Alternatives:** Progressiveness allows us to devise substitutes for prevailing processes that detrimentally affect

the environment or are unsustainable. For example, renewable energy mechanisms such as wind or solar power lessen our dependency on fossil fuels.

3. **Endurance:** Innovations targeted at sustainability can augment resistance to ecological adversities such as changes in climate, forest reduction, and water scarcity.
4. **Economic Prospects:** Striving for sustainability uncovers fresh markets and encourages employment opportunities, invigorating economic evolution and prosperity.
5. **Social Fairness:** Sustainable resolutions can aid in the equitable allocation of resources, shrinking societal gaps and fostering an enhanced life quality for all.

This perspective provides a unique take on the role of innovation in driving sustainability, distinct from the given narrative that revolves around sustainability innovation, and the emphasis on technologies like IoT, AI, and clean technologies to promote sustainable practices and reduce environmental impact.[4]

The Post-2030 Agenda is to generate priority areas building on the successes of the 2030 target and to identify intersectional and new goals and targets for the next 20 years or so. Post-2030, there will be a continued need to address the persisting challenges and emerging issues in sustainable development. Innovation will remain crucial in accelerating progress, particularly in these areas:

1. **Climate Change Mitigation and Adaptation:** Even as we make progress, the impacts of climate change will continue to evolve and necessitate innovative responses.
2. **Energy Transition:** Despite advancements, there is a need for innovation in energy storage and distribution and clean energy technologies.
3. **Food Systems:** Innovation is needed to ensure food security, enhance agricultural efficiency, reduce food waste, and move towards more plant-based diets.
4. **Water Security:** Water scarcity is a pressing issue in many parts of the world. Innovations in water conservation, purification, and desalination technologies can help ensure water security.
5. **Circular Economy:** This involves the transition from a linear "take-make-dispose" model of consumption to one

that values reuse and recycling. Innovative technologies and business models are needed to make this transition possible.

6. **Sustainable Cities:** As urban populations continue to grow, there is a need for innovation in sustainable urban planning, public transportation, and energy-efficient buildings.
7. **Health and Well-Being:** Innovations in healthcare delivery, pandemic response, and promoting mental health are vital for a sustainable future.

Innovation for sustainability is not just about technology; it is also about innovative policies, financing models, and partnerships. The Post-2030 Agenda calls for a multifaceted, integrated approach that aligns with the principles of sustainable development, and innovation is at the heart of that approach.

12.6 Harnessing Technologies for the Post-2030 Agenda

In conclusion, it is imperative to consider how various forms of technology, including carbon capture and intelligent agriculture, among others, could significantly shape the Post-2030 Agenda and our collective sustainability trajectory.

1. **Carbon Capture and Storage (CCS):** As the impacts of climate change become increasingly dire, the need for effective carbon reduction strategies will be more urgent than ever. Carbon capture and storage technologies, which capture carbon dioxide emissions from sources like power plants and industrial processes and store them underground, are critical. They mitigate the impacts of existing emissions and enable the utilization of captured carbon in various industries. However, for CCS technologies to be viable and sustainable, we need further innovation to lower costs, increase efficiency, and ensure safe and permanent storage. The Post-2030 Agenda must, therefore, emphasize the research, development, and large-scale deployment of effective CCS technologies.
2. **Intelligent Agriculture:** As the global population continues to rise, meeting the increasing demand for food in a sustainable manner presents a significant challenge. Intelligent or smart agriculture, which integrates advanced technologies like AI, IoT, big data, and remote sensing, can revolutionize

how we farm. These technologies can enhance crop yields, optimize resource use, reduce environmental impacts, and enable adaptation to climate change. Examples include precision farming systems that apply the optimal amount of water and fertilizers, AI-based predictive models for pest and disease management, and remote sensing for real-time monitoring of crop health. Recognizing and supporting these advancements should be an integral part of the Post-2030 Agenda.

3. **Energy Technology:** Advancements in energy technology, particularly in areas such as nuclear fusion, could be transformative in our quest for sustainable development. The inclusion of such cutting-edge technologies in the Post-2030 Agenda can certainly be seen as an ambitious, yet necessary, step toward meeting our global energy needs and combating climate change. Unlike nuclear fission, which involves splitting an atom's nucleus and is used in current nuclear power plants, nuclear fusion combines light atomic nuclei to form heavier ones. The process releases significant amounts of energy and is the same reaction that fuels the sun.

The future entails bolstering international collaboration to facilitate access to clean energy research and technology. This encompasses a wide spectrum, ranging from renewable energy and energy efficiency to advanced and cleaner fossil fuel technology. It also calls for substantial investments in energy infrastructure and clean energy technology.[5]

Nuclear fusion, if successfully harnessed, boasts several remarkable advantages, including an abundant fuel supply, absence of greenhouse gases, minimal radioactive waste, and inherent safety without the risks associated with nuclear meltdowns. Incorporating nuclear fusion and other emerging energy technologies into the Post-2030 Agenda would symbolize a bold commitment to innovative solutions for our energy future.

While the agenda primarily focuses on expediting the deployment of well-established renewable energy technologies such as wind and solar power, it should also lend support to research and development in promising fields like fusion. This balanced approach can play a pivotal role in fostering a diverse, resilient, and sustainable energy system for the future, underpinning our efforts to address the world's energy challenges.

Beyond these, we must also consider technologies that support circular economies, renewable energy, water and waste management, biodiversity conservation, and more. The Post-2030 Agenda must prioritize technological advancements and ensure they are accessible and beneficial to all, fostering inclusivity and leaving no one behind.

Additionally, as we harness the power of technology, it is essential to navigate the associated risks and challenges, including digital inequality, privacy and security concerns, and the ethical implications of advanced technologies. Robust governance frameworks, public-private partnerships, multi-stakeholder collaboration, digital literacy, and education, and user-centric design are crucial in this regard.

In essence, the potential of technology to drive sustainable development and peace is immense. But to unlock this potential, we need a shared vision, concerted action, and a commitment to innovation, inclusivity, and sustainability. The Post-2030 Agenda provides a valuable opportunity to shape this trajectory and build a future where technology truly serves humanity and the planet.

12.7 Technology Mindset Shift Priorities

In an era of unprecedented technological advancement, our shared global agenda must evolve, particularly in the realm of artificial intelligence (AI). As we navigate the AI age, we must shift our collective mindset to harness its vast potential while ensuring sustainability, equity, and benefits for all.[6]

1. **Purposeful and Responsible Innovation:** Embracing AI requires a mindset that values purposeful and responsible innovation. AI should not solely drive economic growth but also serve as a catalyst for societal betterment and environmental stewardship.
2. **Ethical Guardrails:** Our pursuit of AI must be guided by ethical frameworks that prioritize human dignity and rights. Global norms and standards should govern AI development, addressing biases, safeguarding privacy, and preventing misuse.
3. **Equitable Access and Inclusion:** Cultivating a mindset advocating for equitable AI access is essential. Bridging the digital divide and providing inclusive opportunities will

prevent technology disparities from exacerbating existing inequalities.

4. **Public Accountability:** Prioritizing international mechanisms for public accountability in AI is essential. This entails transparent reporting, regulatory oversight, and public participation in AI governance, ensuring these technologies serve the common good.
5. **Collaborative Innovation:** A collaborative approach to AI innovation is paramount. Nations, industries, and academia must cooperate, sharing resources and knowledge to drive innovations aligned with global sustainability goals.
6. **AI for Environmental Solutions:** Recognizing AI's potential in addressing environmental challenges is crucial. Investing in AI applications for climate change mitigation, biodiversity conservation, and resource management is a step toward sustainability.
7. **AI Literacy:** Equipping all generations with AI literacy is imperative. Educational systems must adapt to provide the skills and knowledge needed to navigate, innovate, and govern in an AI-driven world.
8. **Human-Centric AI:** AI systems should be designed with a human-centric approach, amplifying human potential and aligning with human values and societal needs.
9. **Shared Economic Benefits:** Strategies must ensure widespread economic benefits from AI, contributing to global economic resilience and prosperity.

As we stand on the brink of a new agenda, incorporating these mindset priorities is pivotal and essential in unlocking the transformative potential of AI and other technologies. The rapid pace of technological innovation demands a global response that is as coordinated as it is visionary. By fostering a global consensus on the ethical, inclusive, and sustainable deployment of AI, we set the stage for a resilient future in the face of change and challenges.

Advocating for globally coordinated solutions ensures that the benefits of AI do not become the exclusive privilege of a few but are instead shared across borders, societies, and economies. This approach helps to mitigate the risk of widening the inequality gap and instead uses AI as a leveler, a tool for empowerment, and a bridge to opportunity for people everywhere.

By embedding the values of sustainability and public good at the core of technological advancement, we ensure that our journey forward with AI is not just about what technology can do but what it should do for the betterment of humanity. It's about steering AI to address the most pressing challenges of our times—from climate change and environmental degradation to healthcare and education.

In this context, the Post-2030 Agenda emerges as a manifesto for change, an actionable blueprint that calls upon nations, industries, and individuals to collaborate in unprecedented ways. It is an invitation to innovate responsibly, to harness the power of technology not as an end but as a means to create a world where sustainability is the default setting, and everyone enjoys the prosperity it generates.

As we move towards this future, it's crucial to remember that technology reflects the values of those who create and manage it. Therefore, our global policies, educational programs, and governance structures must be designed to ensure that the architects of tomorrow's AI are as diverse, inclusive, and ethically grounded as the world we aspire to create.

In conclusion, the Post-2030 Agenda is more than just a framework for the next phase of sustainable development; it is a clarion call for a renaissance in our relationship with technology. By placing AI and other innovations at the service of humanity, we can cultivate a future that respects the planet and enriches the lives of its inhabitants, propelling humanity towards a horizon of more significant equity, justice, and shared prosperity. This is the promise and the challenge of the Post-2030 Sustainability Agenda, which we must embrace with foresight, determination, and an unwavering commitment to the common good.

12.8 Resources

As we have seen throughout Chapter 12, the role of technology and innovation in sustainability is crucial, especially in the face of global challenges like climate change, overpopulation, and resource depletion. Both technological advancements and innovative thought processes are required to create sustainable solutions for our planet's future. Here are some of the primary resources on technology and innovation sustainability:

1. ***Biomimicry: Innovation Inspired by Nature* by Janine M. Benyus (2009):** This groundbreaking work highlights the idea of looking to nature for innovative solutions. Benyus provides examples of how natural processes have inspired

technological advancements, from energy solutions to building designs.

2. ***How to Avoid a Climate Disaster: The Solutions We Have and the Breakthroughs We Need* by Bill Gates (2022):** Gates outlines a comprehensive plan for how the world can get to zero greenhouse gas emissions in time to avoid a climate catastrophe. He addresses the technological advancements needed in various sectors and underscores the importance of innovation in this journey.
3. ***The Third Industrial Revolution: How Lateral Power Is Transforming Energy, the Economy, and the World* by Jeremy Rifkin (2011):** Rifkin explores how internet technology and renewable energy are merging to create a powerful platform for a new era of economic growth, introducing the concept of lateral power which can be harnessed by small groups to produce and share sustainable energy.
4. ***The Upcycle: Beyond Sustainability—Designing for Abundance* by William McDonough and Michael Braungart (2013):** A continuation of their earlier work *Cradle to Cradle*, this book focuses on how products can be designed from the outset to be repurposed, reused, and upcycled, rather than discarded. It's a deep dive into the concept of circular economy and design thinking.
5. ***Sustainable Innovation: Strategy, Process and Impact* by Cosmina L. Voinea and Nadine Roijakkers (2021):** This book delivers a critical overview of sustainable innovations, examining their inception, strategic processes, and impact for businesses and society. With a keen focus on the nuanced relationship between innovation and sustainability, it presents insights into the role of open innovation in both the public sector and SMEs. Notably, it investigates how sustainability is intertwined with strategic business processes and the significance of entrepreneurial ecosystems in driving sustainable innovations.

Notes

1 The White House. (2021, November 2). *Remarks by President Biden in Meeting on the Build Back Better World Initiative*. The White House. https://www.whitehouse.gov/briefing-room/speeches-remarks/2021/11/02/remarks-by-president-biden-in-meeting-on-the-build-back-better-world-initiative/

2 Froehlich, A. (2018). *Post 2030-Agenda and the Role of Space: The UN 2030 Goals and Their Further Evolution Beyond 2030 for Sustainable Development*. Germany: Springer International Publishing.
3 Salam, A. (2019). *Internet of Things for Sustainable Community Development: Wireless Communications, Sensing, and Systems*. Germany: Springer International Publishing.
4 Adenle, A.A., Chertow, M.R., Moors, E.H., & Pannell, D.J. (Eds.). (2020). *Science, Technology, and Innovation for Sustainable Development Goals: Insights from Agriculture, Health, Environment, and Energy*. Oxford University Press.
5 Leal Filho, W., Marisa Azul, A., Brandli, L., Lange Salvia, A., & Wall, T. (Eds.). (2021). *Affordable and Clean Energy*. Springer International Publishing.
6 Hoek, M. (2023). *Tech For Good: Imagine Solving the World's Greatest Challenges*. Taylor & Francis.

Conclusion

Throughout the chapters of this book, we have identified vital trajectories, current challenges, and prospects within each of the priority areas, building a comprehensive understanding of the multidimensional nature of sustainable development. From the analysis of the trajectories that emerged from the 1972 Stockholm Conference to the 2015 SDG Agenda for 2030, core issues intersected with core priorities to be considered in the Post-2030 Agenda.

In summary, we have seen how the 2030 Agenda with the SDGs set by the United Nations in 2015 has made significant strides in uniting nations around common developmental aspirations. We have seen how this time in history has evolved from numerous trajectories from past conversations and commitments. We have seen how the 2030 Agenda includes priorities for people, prosperity, the planet, governance, peace, and technology.

While these priorities are essential, it is also critical to acknowledge and address the underlying social, economic, and political factors that influence environmental sustainability and human well-being, including poverty, inequality, education, and governance. Tackling these challenges will require integrated, holistic approaches and the active engagement and collaboration of governments, businesses, communities, and individuals worldwide. Future leaders must be prepared to navigate a complex and dynamic landscape, making informed and ethical decisions that consider the needs of both current and future generations.

Forefront Priorities for the Post-2030 Agenda

In developing the Post-2030 Agenda, it's imperative to scrutinize our achievements and failures in current goals, addressing persistent challenges while anticipating upcoming global issues crucial to our joint agenda. Essential priorities include **Climate**

DOI: 10.4324/9781003494676-16

Change Mitigation and Adaptation, considering the severe threats it poses to the global environment and societies, necessitating immediate, cooperative action and significant investment. **Sustainable Resource Management** is pivotal due to escalating pressures on natural resources from population growth and consumption, requiring a commitment to conservation, efficient consumption models, and equitable governance. The importance of **Global Health and Pandemic Preparedness** has been accentuated by the COVID-19 pandemic, underscoring the need for robust health infrastructures and a focus on the One Health concept, as new diseases often emerge at the intersection of human, animal, and environmental health.

Furthermore, in our digital age, **Cybersecurity and Data Privacy** are paramount, necessitating protective measures from governments, corporations, and individuals alike, alongside new policies for emerging technologies. The rapid development of technologies like AI also prompts ethical and societal concerns, making it crucial to ensure responsible development and deployment while considering potential risks and benefits to society. **Global Security and Peacekeeping** are increasingly complex and vital, demanding international cooperation to address various severe threats to global stability, including the rise of non-state actors and cyber warfare, while promoting disarmament and conflict prevention.

Additionally, the unprecedented levels of **Forced Displacement** and the need for **Refugee Rights Protection** call for immediate action and long-term solutions, upholding legal frameworks and providing adequate support to host countries. With ongoing globalization and environmental changes, the development and implementation of **Humane Migration Policies** are crucial for individuals' safe and legal movement, addressing the root causes of displacement and supporting integration in destination countries. The fight against **Human Trafficking and Exploitation** is also crucial, requiring international cooperation, legal frameworks enhancement, and victim support while addressing systemic contributing issues.

Tackling migration and refugee rights issues necessitates a holistic approach and global cooperation to protect rights and acknowledge contributions, fostering empathy and integration. Addressing these complex, interconnected challenges requires visionary, collaborative leadership at national, regional, and international levels, with leaders promoting inclusive policies and social cohesion, diligently working towards societies where everyone's rights and dignity are upheld, irrespective of their migration status. Reflecting on past shortcomings is essential as we envision future priorities, emphasizing areas needing more focus as global circumstances evolve.

New Perspectives for the Post-2030 Agenda

As we look beyond 2030, it is evident that the world stands at a crucial turning point. We are armed with lessons from the past and are equipped with aspirations for the future. The path to a sustainable world is not linear but sporadic efforts of interconnected challenges and successes. To navigate this intricate journey, fresh perspectives are needed. These perspectives should reflect the changing dynamics of our global community and resonate with the collective spirit of building a harmonious, equitable world for all.

We suggest three necessary perspectives for a Post-2030 Sustainability Agenda that recognize the importance of local and Indigenous cultures, the democracy challenges and opportunities of technology, and the holistic and integrated dimensions of sustainability.

1. **Local and Indigenous Cultural Context:** While the SDGs aim for universality, there could be a stronger emphasis on recognizing and integrating local and Indigenous knowledge and practices. Tailoring strategies to specific cultural, social, and economic contexts can make them more effective and inclusive. In this regard, it is also important to better integrate the wisdom of Indigenous peoples. Indigenous peoples, having taken care of their lands for millennia, possess a deep reservoir of knowledge integral to sustainable development. Their practices, rooted in harmony with nature, offer insights into sustainable agriculture, water management, and biodiversity preservation. Around 80% of the world's biodiversity exists within Indigenous territories, making their bio-cultural heritage a key to holistic conservation strategies.

   Moreover, their rights to land and resources ensure both their survival and the protection of vital ecosystems. Embracing Indigenous worldviews, emphasizing the interconnectedness of humans, nature, and the spiritual realm, can lead to more cohesive sustainability policies. As communities that have skillfully adapted to environmental changes over generations, their knowledge is pivotal for enhancing global resilience, especially in the face of challenges like climate change. Recognizing and integrating Indigenous wisdom in the Post-2030 Sustainability Agenda can foster a more inclusive and effective path towards global sustainability.

The richness of local and Indigenous knowledge underscores the fact that true sustainability cannot be copied but must be nuanced, tailored, and deeply rooted in cultural contexts. This first necessary perspective is about prioritizing local voices, and integrating time-tested practices can pave the way for solutions that are both ecologically sound and culturally resonant.

2. **Future Technological Impacts and Democratic Integration:** As we advance into an era dominated by technologies such as AI, biotechnology, and nanotechnology, their potential to revolutionize sustainability is undeniable. These technological advancements hold promise not just as tools to solve complex environmental problems but as mechanisms to democratize the process of sustainable development itself. When technology is made accessible and integrated at all levels, it empowers a diverse range of stakeholders—from global organizations to local communities, from pioneering individuals to collaborative networks. By democratizing technology, we enable grassroots innovations and solutions that are sensitive to local needs, thereby ensuring that the progress toward sustainability is both inclusive and diverse.

Furthermore, the measurements of progress toward sustainability goals can be significantly enhanced with technology. Advanced analytics, sensors, and real-time data collection can give a comprehensive picture of where we stand in our sustainability journey. When this technology is democratized, it allows organizations, communities, individuals, and other stakeholders to contribute to, monitor, and validate the collective progress. This not only instills a sense of collective ownership but also ensures transparency and accountability in the pursuit of sustainable objectives.

Moreover, by actively integrating these technologies into our sustainability strategies, we can anticipate and navigate the challenges and opportunities they present, ensuring that our efforts are proactive rather than reactive. For instance, AI can help in the predictive analysis of environmental changes, biotechnology can offer breakthroughs in sustainable agriculture, and nanotechnology can lead to more efficient energy solutions. Thus, a forward-looking perspective on technology not only shapes our understanding of future economies, societies, and environments but also redefines the very way in which we engage with the sustainability agenda.

The second necessary perspective for a Post-2030 Sustainability Agenda must recognize that leaps in technology offer boundless potential, but they also come with the responsibility of equitable access and democratic integration. By ensuring that advancements in AI, biotechnology, and other fields are available and beneficial to all, we can craft a future where technology serves as a great equalizer, driving both innovation and inclusion.

3. **Holistic Integration and the Imperative of Interconnectedness:** Sustainability isn't a compartmentalized concept—it's a deeply interwoven tapestry of challenges and solutions. Each SDG, while representative of specific aspirations, derives its potency from its interconnected nature. Since the seminal 1972 Stockholm Conference, there has been a growing acknowledgment of this holistic approach. Yet, contemporary practices sometimes present a skewed representation of sustainability, with "greenwashing" and "rainbow-washing" masking the absence of genuine commitment.

Challenging the oversimplified perceptions of sustainability as being strictly environmental, financial, or social is pivotal. In truth, these dimensions are mutually inclusive. An environmental setback has repercussions on societal structures and economic vitality, while socioeconomic disparities can reciprocate with adverse environmental impacts.

The SDGs, with their 5Ps—People, Planet, Prosperity, Peace, and Partnership—provide a macro lens to view the entire perspective. The accompanying 17 goals highlight its varied ecosystems, while the 169 targets and 232 indicators take us closer to the individual actions, detailing their uniqueness. But the future of sustainability demands more than recognizing these elements in isolation; it calls for understanding their interwoven relationship.

As we transition towards a post-2030 world, a "bird's-eye" perspective becomes indispensable. This viewpoint equips us to seamlessly integrate the broader macro challenges with the specific micro-level intricacies, anchoring global strategies in localized realities.

In sum, the post-2030 sustainability vision mandates a departure from siloed approaches. It implores us to align the overarching principles of the 5Ps with the granular details of the goals, targets, and indicators. By fostering such an expansive and yet nuanced perspective, we position ourselves better to tackle the multifarious challenges of our era, steering our planet towards an authentically sustainable trajectory.

Ethical Leadership for the Post-2030 Agenda

As we step into the post-2030 era, ethical leadership is at the forefront, emphasizing our collective responsibility to create a sustainable and inclusive future. This isn't just about executing strategies; it's a firm commitment to taking responsible actions that not only address current needs but also pave the way for future generations. Our leadership approach should be guided by principles of unity, innovation, and turning sustainability goals into realities for all.[1]

Principle-based leadership is essential, especially in engaging with a diverse range of stakeholders. The challenges we face are global, and solving them requires collaborative efforts that transcend borders and sectors. Leaders need to be open to partnerships with various stakeholders, including governments, the private sector, non-profits, and civil society. This approach facilitates a broader understanding of the issues, pooling of resources, and formulation of comprehensive and effective strategies in addressing the multifaceted challenges at hand.

Furthermore, engaging with diverse stakeholders brings multiple perspectives, fostering innovation and creative problem-solving. Principle-based leadership ensures collaborations are grounded in shared values and goals, promoting trust and mutual respect among partners. This trust is crucial for building strong alliances and commitments that are both multilateral and sustainable over the long term. When leaders and stakeholders work together under a framework of shared principles, it enhances the legitimacy and acceptance of their initiatives, leading to more substantial support and more successful implementation of global solutions.

The journey ahead is more than deploying advanced solutions or setting strategic goals. It's about acting with a deep sense of duty and responsibility that considers the long-term impacts of today's decisions. Our actions should leave a positive legacy, providing a foundation for those who follow.

The vision for post-2030 is more than just a symbol of progress. It represents our shared ethical values and commitment to leadership that is resilient and regenerative. This vision is more than an action plan—it's a declaration of our commitment to ethical practices and values guiding us toward the future.

As we move forward, our guiding principles should focus on sustainability and peace and actively promote equity, justice, and dignity. We find the strength to lead within our shared commitment to humanity. Our ethical commitments light our path, and our collective efforts bring the possibility of change into sharper focus, providing hope for the future. This journey should embody ethically grounded leadership, responsibly carried out, resilient in the face of challenges, and visionary in its approach to regeneration, as this is the type of leadership required for the future we hope to build.

Note

1 Sfeir-Younis, A. & Tavanti, M. (2020). *Conscious Sustainability Leadership: A New Paradigm for Next Generation Leaders*. Planet Healing Press.

Epilogue

Our Moral Imperative Beyond 2030

Alfredo Sfeir-Younis

Understanding Our Moral Imperative

The history of international relations and deliberations on sustainable development of the past half a century—as presented in this book—have been rich in content and transformational in human empowerment. The review and analysis carried out point out the key landmarks we face today, the true frontier of the debate on sustainability we are to push forward, and the type of interventions the present situation demands. These are often related to how our vision embraces issues of human development and collective awareness—*the Human Factor*, and what type of institutional governance we need to address the management of our global public goods at the planetary level—*the Institutional Factor*. Both are intertwined with economic, political, social, and other considerations. It is not just a matter of defining new goals or proposing more physical interventions. There is an urgent necessity to arrive at a "consensual planetary vision" of humanity's collective future. To agree on such a vision is our true moral imperative.

The change we are to promote is far more complex than most people believe. There are some variables influencing our ability to reach a consensus: (1) A "Planetary Society" where, for the first time in human history, we live in a society within which all manifestations of life are totally interdependent (humans' and nature's), with no boundaries any longer. (2) A different "World Geopolitics," where the geopolitics around the issues of sustainable development and environment has changed dramatically by comparison to the power distribution during the Stockholm Conference (1972) as expressed within international organizations today. (3) An "Empowerment of Citizens," when we have moved from the era of governments to the era of citizens, and where no vision or solutions will bypass the strategic consent of citizens' organizations before

DOI: 10.4324/9781003494676-17

being agreed upon. (4) A transitioning "From Markets to Rights," where we are moving to a right-based development, including Civil and Political Rights, Economic, Social, and Cultural Rights and the Right to Development—also including the Right of Nature and all sentient beings.[1] (5) A "Governance of Global Public Goods," where the management and governance structures of our common heritage are extremely deficient, leading to the demise, for example, of biodiversity and native forests and the depletion of fragile ecosystems. (6) An inescapable "Planetary Constraint," which is now essentially biological in nature, with its corresponding human and social impacts.[2] And (7) an undisputable role for our "Human Collective Consciousness," where our awareness about sustainability has increased with a marked public recognition that the outer ecology is collapsing.

Thus, it is prudent to address some fundamental questions: What is the gross and subtle contents of the moral imperative in this 21st century? What are we willing to accept (to abstain from) in order to change the present course of humanity? What are we willing to let collapse, deplete, or disappear from this multifaceted system of life? What are we willing to leave untouched for future generations to enjoy? What are we willing to do now, in order to avoid a major structural planetary collapse?

Today, our moral imperative goes deep into defining and choosing humanity's new form of planetary collective livelihood, with the aim to re-establish the balance between development and the environment that we have already lost. Consequently, we must push the existing political limits to bring about a form of planetary governance that ensures a high-quality development and transformation for all forms of life. This is why this planetary governance must go beyond the self-interest of individual countries, demanding an eco-planetary-democracy and ensuring the unfolding of ideas such as eco-efficiency, eco-competitiveness, and eco-accounting. The proposed eco-democracy must empower citizens, everywhere, leading to a number of ecological responsibilities. One, avoiding unacceptable forms of theft, like the unnecessary overexploitation of nature and, another, embracing a shift from a market-designed and governed-led economic system, to a nature-designed and citizens-led economic system and principles.

A Rudder Stroke

The term "development progress" must go beyond "material individualism," so that the economy and the practice of economics possess attributes that ensure the highest forms of human self-realization. We already know how our "collective planetary welfare" is affected by health pandemics, human insecurity (war, conflict), climate change, water shortages, migration, poverty... To evaluate whether we are better off or worse off, interventions must be appraised in relation to the economy, state of nature (sustainability), society (empowerment), and well-being (happiness). This is vital for market-oriented economies, which do not have an automatic trigger mechanism to address the joint social and environmental effects of transactions.[3] These demand important changes in mindset. For example, fiscal policy and taxation, where we should tax the "bads" (pollution) and not the "goods" (textbooks). Thus, our imperative is to find a proper planetary livelihood to improve collective planetary welfare and not just individual countries' welfare. Today, many countries consume more than one planet Earth to maintain their level of material welfare![4]

Nothing anew should be implemented without a revolution in collective values: interdependence, cooperation, solidarity, justice, equity, love, compassion...[5]

We must construct and support the foundations of a New Eco-Morality everywhere, to become the code of conduct in bilateral and multilateral institutions on how to treat nature.

We have neither planetary institutions nor organizational spaces that are essential to construct a truly planetary vision. Thus, a new institutional system has to emerge out of a "bottom-up structure," with the full engagement of world citizens. It must be an empowering framework in order to harmonize our inner ecology and outer ecology.[6]

Macroeconomic and social interventions via traditional macro policies, investments, regulations, incentives are not neutral as regards our collective ability to reach the aims of sustainable development. Macro policies affect the nature and accumulation of all forms of capital (both material and non-material capitals). We cannot continue assuming that the impacts of development interventions are only on some forms of capital (like man-made capital) but not on all other capitals (like natural, cultural, and spiritual).[7] Growth targets, prices, taxes, subsidies, income, interest rates, public expenditures, monetary interventions, competitiveness must all be evaluated against their effects on nature.

Sustainable development must be distinct from its social setting. The environmental crises and social crises we witness today are two sides of the same reality.[8] We cannot decouple them. Today, we witness ecological poverty and ecological migration. The constant change in the quantity and quality of our natural endowments has significant human and social consequences. Measuring the social returns of environmental interventions is vital to gaining support for a sustainable planetary vision.

Canvas for Our Human Future

Quantity and Quality of Life

Suppose one compares the statistics of the last 50 years. In that case, there is no doubt that there is more "quantity" in the world (measured by Gross National Product) than "quality" of life (measured by environmental quality factors). Thus, we have sacrificed our health, happiness, and inner welfare to attain higher and higher levels of material welfare. This must be reversed soon.

Path to Interdependent Togetherness

Constructing a path in which our interdependence strengthens, nurtures, and transforms us is imperative. Practicing and self-realizing togetherness will enable all forms and manifestations of life to attain their maximum expression of consciousness. This is the spirituality of the other: all human beings, sentient beings, and nature. It is a state of consciousness within which a relationship of mutuality and all possible interactions make each and every one involved better off, and no one worse off.

New Bretton Woods Agreement

The original agreement that governs the functioning of the World Bank, International Monetary Fund, and the World Trade Organization is no longer valid. The conditions which prevailed almost a century ago, soon after World War II, have very little to do with the conditions of today. It is time to move from growth and development to sustainable development and beyond; from competitiveness and exclusion to equity and inclusion; from market-dominated societies to human and nature rights-based societies; from countries-dominated international governance and institutions to citizens' empowered national and international democracies and decision-making; etc. The challenge will be to move from material reconstruction to spiritual human consciousness.[9]

New Treaty of Westphalia

Such a treaty became instrumental in establishing geopolitics of peace based on the notion of the "Nation-State." The four principal agreements (e.g., the basis for a new world order) were: national self-determination; ending wars through diplomatic means; peaceful coexistence among sovereign states as the norm; and acceptance of the principle of non-interference in the internal affairs of other sovereign states. A treaty whose mandala puts all its functioning energies at the "border."[10] It emphasized the power of exclusion and the insistence of pushing individual country interests. Today, we know this form of governance is not only impracticable, but it is destroying any possibility of constructing a shared future. It is imperative to move from nation-states to one planetary vision and livelihood. We are too interdependent to claim independence at any cost.[11] A new form of democracy is to emerge now.

World Environmental Organization

The United Nations Environmental Program (UNEP) has to embody a new status, i.e., it must become the World Environment and Sustainable Development Organization (ESDO). ESDO has to have all the ingredients and instruments to be an organization of the highest stature. The main constraints are not any longer technological but ecological in nature and impacts. A new set of bylaws must emerge in the immediate future and a Director-General be elected.

Reforms of the United Nations System

The UN must also be reformed. The first step must be the inclusion of citizens and their organizations in the decision-making processes. We live in the era of citizenry, and this must be reflected at the highest levels of governance. The UN Trusteeship Council must be transformed into The Citizens Council.

Changing the Narratives and Social Grammar

We are in the era of communications, and it behooves us to have the best communication strategy to raise awareness, attention and consciousness about the challenges facing a new civilization.[12]

New narratives and social grammar have to emerge, reflecting the true meaning and attributes of our shared future. Several ideas have to be transmitted, including those around Eco-Morality (e.g., all forms of life matter equally), Eco-Security (e.g., the issues emerging as a result of progressive deterioration of ecology and environment, including the social dimensions), and Eco Migration (e.g., where the engine is the depletion of natural resources like water, climate change and desertification).[13]

Avoiding a Planetary Collapse

The probability of planetary ecological collapse is not zero. In my view, we are not prepared to deal with such eventual collapse. Let us be aware that when something like that happens it is almost impossible to avoid the immense quantity of negative impacts everywhere on the planet. Just consider the recent experience with the COVID-19 pandemic. It is better to prevent than to cure, once it has happened.

We Have a Choice!

The moment is now. Tomorrow will be too late. Humanity must make a choice right now if we are to construct a new future together. Yes, together. Otherwise, to do more of the same will yield more of the same.

I am fully aware of the difficulties that addressing human development and institutional transformation entail. It would have been simpler and, perhaps, simplistic, to end this message with a list of material actions which, most probably than not, will fail to be implemented properly. Sometimes, listing a large number of actions gives the impression of completeness and concreteness; but development experience shows that it is not, particularly when there is no agreement on a planetary vision. When action is not preceded by a vision, proposed solutions are short lived.

Vision is a Mandatory Precondition for Action

In this case, a vision not only of our individual future, but, of our planetary future as well. Many of those actions are known by almost everyone. Certainly, they are known by most decision-makers around the world (e.g., to address the pollution of the oceans and rivers, the melting of glaciers, and the demise of biodiversity). What is lacking now is a higher level of consciousness and awareness for new collective solutions to emerge. The consciousness that created the problems does not have the attributes to identify, select, and implement new solutions.

When the emphasis is on human and institutional attributes of our collective future, we ought to rise to a state of inner acknowledgement that transcends today's vision, political frontiers, and economic paradigm. Real and lasting solutions must emerge from within ourselves. A sustainable transformation must begin first in the human mind; paradoxically, the same mind that originated the problems we witness today. This demands a solid bridge, which would enable us, together, to cross into a new future.

It Seems Evident That We Are at a Crossroads

We are on the top of an inflection point, calling for a definite choice regarding a better collective future. This is a moral quest, as it affects not only us but all future generations.

Let us not become the victims of our own mistakes and indifference with regards to our shared responsibilities.

History has progressively brought us together. History has progressively demised our artificial borders. History has progressively made us One.

Now Is the Time to Self-Realize and Act Accordingly

A new future is waiting for our choice about a mutually shared livelihood on this beautiful planet, for the betterment of all manifestations of life.

I am ready to meet you on the bridge and cross it together into a world of hope, harmony, and happiness.

Notes

1 Sfeir-Younis, A. (2007, January 19). Violation of Human Rights is a Threat to Human Security. *Conflict, Security and Development*, 4(3), 383–396.
2 Blaikie, P., & Jeanrenaud, S. (1996, February). Biodiversity and Human Welfare. *UNRISD Discussion Papers*. UN Research Institute for Social Development, DP 72.
3 Duncan, D., & Phillips, M. (2019). Cultivating the Right Livelihood. *Kosmos Journal*, Spring.
4 Earth Overshoot Day (n.d.). *How Many Earths? How Many Countries?* https://www.overshootday.org
5 Sfeir-Younis, A. & Tavanti, M. (2020). *Conscious Sustainability Leadership: A New Paradigm for Next Generation Leaders*. Planet Healing Press.
6 University of Stockholm (n.d.). *The Nine Planetary Boundaries*. Stockholm Resilience Center. https://www.stockholmresilience.org/research/planetary-boundaries/the-nine-planetary-boundaries.html
7 Wallimann, I. (2013). *Environmental Policy is Social Policy—Social Policy is Environmental Policy: Toward Sustainability Policy*. Springer.
8 Sfeir-Younis, A. (2020, March 30). El Ciudadanismo Global, Educacion y Consciencia Planetaria (Global Citizenry, Education, and Planetary Consciousness). *VIDASANA Newslette*.
9 Sfeir-Younis, A., & Tavanti, M. (2021, October 10). *Preventing the Collapse of Multilateralism: Towards Planetary Governance*. https://medium.com/@planethealingpress
10 Steffan, W. et al. (2015, January 15). Planetary Boundaries: Guiding Human Development on a Changing Planet. *Science*, 347(6223).
11 UN Department of Economic and Social Affairs (2013). *Report of the Secretary General on Globalization and Interdependence*. New York.
12 Sfeir-Younis, A., & Escobar, U. (2021). *Hacia la Construcción de Una Humanidad Planetaria* (Towards the Construction of a Planetary Society). Editorial Alma. Colombia.
13 Sfeir-Younis, A. (2004). Reconciliar la Economía Materialista con la Espiritualidad: EL Gran Desafío del Nuevo Milenio (Reconciling Materialistic Economics with Spirituality: The Great Challenge of This New Millennium). *POLIS: Revista Latinoamericana*, (8).

Index

Milton Keynes UK
Ingram Content Group UK Ltd.
UKHW031501071224
451979UK00015B/154

9 781032 779287